HENRY WILLIAM RAVENEL, 1814–1887

History of American Science and Technology Series

General Editor, Lester D. Stephens

The Eagle's Nest: Natural History and American Ideas, 1812–1842, by Charlotte M. Porter

Nathaniel Southgate Shaler and the Culture of American Science, by David N. Livingstone

Henry William Ravenel, 1814–1887: South Carolina Scientist in the Civil War Era, by Tamara Miner Haygood

Henry William Ravenel, 1869 (Courtesy of South Caroliniana Library,
Columbia, South Carolina)

HENRY WILLIAM RAVENEL, 1814–1887

South Carolina
Scientist in the
Civil War Era

TAMARA MINER HAYGOOD

The University of Alabama Press

Tuscaloosa and London

Publication of this book was made possible, in part,
by financial assistance from the Andrew W. Mellon
Foundation and the American Council of
Learned Societies.

Library of Congress Cataloging-in-Publication Data
Haygood, Tamara Miner, 1956–
  Henry William Ravenel, 1814–1887: South Carolina
scientist in the Civil War era.

  Bibliography: p.
  Includes index.
  1. Ravenel, Henry William, 1814–1887.   2. South
Carolina—History—Civil War, 1861–1865.   3. Botanists—
South Carolina—Biography.   I. Title.
QK31.R3H39   1987   580.92′4 [B]   85–28961
ISBN 0-8173-0297-2

British Library Cataloguing-in-Publication Data is available.

With love and gratitude to
my father
W. A. Miner
and
to the memory of my mother
Mimi Louise Miner

Contents

Illustrations

Acknowledgments

During the course of work on Henry Ravenel, it has been my pleasure to meet many kind people who paved my road with their knowledge and enthusiasm. I am glad to have this chance to thank them for their help. Personnel at all the archives I consulted were, without exception, patient and encouraging and often went to much trouble on my account. I should mention in particular Allen Stokes of the South Caroliniana Library, Donald Pfister of the Farlow Herbarium, and Betsy Shaw of the Gray Herbarium. In addition, staff at the Academy of Science of Philadelphia and the Hunt Institute in Pittsburgh took time to look for Ravenel material in their collections. The Herbarium and the Humanities Research Center at the University of Texas in Austin on several occasions provided access to some of the rarer published works. Larry Davenport of the Mohr Herbarium at the University of Alabama helped me with Ravenel's Alabama correspondent Thomas Minott Peters, as did Alexander Sartwell of the Alabama Geological Survey. Among librarians, special mention must be made of Fondren Library's Ferne Hyman, Kay Flowers, and Janet Pollens.

For food, shelter, and companionship as I toured the archives I must thank Maureen Burke, Mary Spencer, Sharon Price, Phoebe Tussey, Susan Schweitzer, and Dr. and Mrs. Michael McVaugh. Joseph and Nesta Ewan gave me their hospitality on two trips to New Orleans.

They opened their magnificent botanical library to me and both times sent me back to Houston loaded with information and ideas. Their friendship and guidance were invaluable. I am indebted as well to many others for information, encouragement, or guidance. At the risk of neglecting some, let me note Edmund Berkeley, John Boles, William Culberson, A. Hunter Dupree, Thomas Haskell, S. W. Higginbotham, Evelyn Nolen, Ronald Numbers, Ronald Petersen, Nancy Reid, David Rembert, Harry Shealy, Lester Stephens, Roger Storck, and most of all, Albert Van Helden. For insights into the history of South Carolina, I particularly want to thank Albert Cannon, James J. Ravenel, Albert E. Sanders, Mrs. Roy E. Daniell, and Mrs. Hugh C. Minton, Jr.

Special thanks to University of Alabama horticulturist Mary Jo Modica for picture research that led to the jacket illustration.

For financial assistance I thank the Department of History of Rice University and Vinson & Elkins, a Houston law firm that employed me as a legal assistant, and particularly partner Jack R. Sowell who patiently accepted the sometimes conflicting needs of my graduate student existence. My parents helped me financially, and their emotional support was even more important to me. I regret that my mother did not live to see the book. My husband Mike cheerfully helped with financing the work.

For quick, competent word processing I am grateful to Gen Riettie. Thanks also to Carolyn Cope for use of a fine typewriter while I was doing my last revisions.

Houston, Texas

HENRY WILLIAM RAVENEL, 1814–1887

Introduction

Thomas Cary Johnson opened discussion of the nature of science in the antebellum American South in 1936.[1] His *Scientific Interests in the Old South* showed that there was widespread interest in science among southerners throughout the entire antebellum period. Contradicting Samuel Eliot Morison's belittlement of antebellum southern scientific inclinations, Johnson argued that many southerners enjoyed attending scientific lectures, viewing natural history exhibits, or collecting plants and animals. In the colleges, courses in science were overtaking the classics in popularity. Furthermore, as the nineteenth century neared the halfway mark, southerners became more interested in science.

Johnson's positive outlook on southern science had less effect on historical opinion than he might have liked. Only four years after the publication of *Scientific Interests in the Old South,* Clement Eaton published *Freedom of Thought in the Old South,* which claimed that the South's refusal after the mid-1830s to tolerate heterodoxy on religion and slavery stifled creative thought in all other aspects of southern intellectual life. Eaton made a bow in Johnson's direction by listing a few southern science teachers, but he ignored the larger implications of Johnson's thesis. He stated blandly that the classics reigned supreme in southern colleges while science languished, and he emphasized "the suppression of academic freedom" under which southern professors labored. To discuss slavery unfavorably or free-soil favorably was to

I

risk being fired or harassed into resignation. Many professors, annoyed by this state of affairs, left the South to teach in the North. Presumably, suppression of academic freedom and subsequent loss of personnel could affect any branch of learning or any department in a college. Eaton, however, by combining this discussion with remarks on the neglect of science by southern schools and by using the chemist Benjamin Sherwood Hedrick as his prime example, implied that his thesis was most readily applicable to science.[2]

In the 1960s he made this connection explicit. In *The Mind of the Old South,* Eaton conceded that Johnson was correct about the high level of scientific interest in southern colleges and among the general populace. He maintained, though, that the efforts of serious scientific workers were limited by "a special influence that militated against the development of the scientific attitude, namely, the subtle and pervasive effect of slavery." The South's need to defend slavery from northern criticism closed the southern mind to new and liberal ideas, creating an atmosphere unfavorable to the pursuit of science. Another factor contributing to this unfavorable climate, according to Eaton, was the South's rural environment. Furthermore, said Eaton, the predominant romanticism of the South made her people disinclined to do the close, painstaking observation necessary in serious science.[3]

Eaton's views on science in the Old South represented only one facet of a larger thesis. This "Cotton Curtain" version of antebellum southern history has found wide acceptance in its entirety among historians of the South and has commonly been presented in under-graduate texts on the subject.[4] His ideas have also found favor with some historians of science. They have expanded his list of the South's inadequacies in the pursuit of science to include her hot climate.[5]

Now, however, discriminating scholars are subjecting Eaton's con-clusions about science, as well as his approach to his subject, to closer examination and revision. Todd Savitt has argued that slavery may have had some stimulating effect upon medical science because slaves were used as subjects of medical experiments. Similarly, Ronald and Janet Numbers have presented evidence that the antebellum South supported a significant amount of scientific activity. If the growth of southern science failed to keep up with that of northern science, demographic and environmental factors were more at fault than was proslavery orthodoxy. A new consensus of opinion seems to be developing that finds both Eaton and Johnson guilty of exaggeration. Eaton overestimated whatever negative impact southern views on slavery and religion may have had on science, and Johnson's error, in the Numbers' words, "lay in implicitly trying to prove equality with the North."[6]

Johnson and Eaton's use of scientific development in the South to argue politico-historical positions also caused them to distort somewhat their portrayal of southern scientists. Though neither applied statistical methods to his information or attempted to define an "average" southern scientist, each allowed a composite picture to emerge from the many examples with which he illustrated his point of view. Johnson wished to show that the southern people, as a group, had a vague, diffuse interest in science, but he was less concerned with the contributions of the South's capable, serious scientists. He provided the names of some of these scientists with brief descriptions of their work but did not clearly distinguish between the varying levels of commitment existing among southerners interested in science. In contrast, Eaton, especially in *Freedom of Thought,* was concerned with the plight of college teachers. His *Mind of the Old South* echoes the earlier work, repeating some of its conclusions and its frequent use of college professors for illustration. Eaton's model southern scientist was a Yankee professor of the physical sciences striving manfully to resist the South's social pressures for conformity, especially with regard to slavery. Of course such individuals would feel alienated from their environment and would be subject to some psychological stress. Ironically, it was southern-born scientists and those who shared southern views whom Eaton treated as oddities.

In addition, Eaton paid scant attention to the South's numerous naturalists. From the time of the Revolution onward there was actually more interest in natural history south of the Mason-Dixon Line than north of it, and many competent botanists and zoologists lived and worked in the South.[7] Indeed, the typical scientist in America, and particularly in the South, was the natural historian, not the physicist or chemist.

Because naturalists were so typical of southern scientists, they are the ideal group to study in order to characterize southern science. A prime exemplar of southern naturalists was the botanist Henry William Ravenel. Although his fame cannot be compared with that of many other southerners of the period, he has never sunk into obscurity. Often, on mentioning his name to a group of botanists, I have elicited pleased smiles and exclamations of recognition. Southern historians have from time to time spiced their books with quotations from his manuscript diary, and many may be familiar with a good, one-volume edition by Arney Robinson Childs that concentrates on his political views.[8] Historians of science may recall an article on his work that appeared in *Isis* many years ago.[9] More important than his familiarity is his rank among the premier American botanists and his membership in the southern planter or professional class. Ravenel's scientific credentials will become apparent in later chapters, but with regard to his position as the quintessential upper-class southerner, it is interesting to note that his societal and political outlook was so characteristic of that group that historians Francis Butler Simkins, Kenneth Stampp, Steven Channing, and even Clement Eaton himself have on different occasions used him as a spokesman for the planters' view of the world. Making similar use of quotations from Ravenel's diary, South Carolina historian Herbert Ravenel Sass explicitly characterized him as "by birth and position as completely a member of the Lowcountry planter 'oligarchy' as any man could be." Indeed, wrote Sass, "One could find no truer representative of that society than Henry William Ravenel."[10]

Slaveholder, planter, South Carolina aristocrat, Ravenel was also a scientist. This book will address Ravenel's interaction with his society and how the changing fortunes of the South, including its growing conservatism in the late antebellum period, the frustrating defeat of its bid for independence, and its reacceptance of the Union, affected him personally and as a scientist.

Growing Up in the Low Country, 1814–1829

Henry William Ravenel began life among the wealthy planter families of Saint John's Parish in South Carolina's swamp-ridden tidewater plain. The family into which he was born in 1814 was typical of the time and place. His mother's people were French Huguenot and British, and his father was of pure French Huguenot descent, the fifth generation in America. The Ravenels, like other Huguenots who settled in South Carolina and along the American coast, were driven from France by a mounting tide of political and religious persecution. René Ravenel fled France as a young man in 1685. He went first to Holland, then to England, and finally to South Carolina, where he joined a large number of French Protestants settled between Charles Town and the Santee River, north of the city.[1] There he and his sons and grandsons prospered.

Second- and third-generation Huguenots mixed easily with their British neighbors, adopting their language and giving up Calvinism for the Episcopal church. René Ravenel, great-grandson of the immigrant, and his wife Charlotte Jacque Mazyck Ravenel were evidently Episcopalian. They had their children baptized as infants, carrying the eldest, Henry, born May 23, 1790, to Charleston when he was only four months old to be baptized by the Reverend Robert Smith.[2] Like their neighbors, the couple also educated their children, often sending them to take lessons at one or another nearby plantation. When the number of school-aged Ravenels reached four, their father hired a private tutor who gave them lessons for about two years.[3]

Henry aspired to become a doctor, and his father sent him at the age of eighteen to Charleston to study medicine with Dr. Samuel Wilson. After a little less than a year with Dr. Wilson, Henry sailed to Philadelphia, where he spent the winters of 1809–1810 and 1810–1811 and earned the M.D. degree. Following the completion of his education, Henry returned to South Carolina to begin his medical career.[4]

On June 17, 1813, Dr. Henry Ravenel married twenty-one-year-old Catherine Stevens, daughter of Oneil Gough Stevens and Catherine Richbourgh Stevens. The newlyweds moved to Woodville plantation, where their son, Henry William Ravenel, was born on May 19, 1814.[5] That September Henry William was baptized at Trinity Chapel-of-Ease, just outside the gates of grandfather René's plantation, by the Episcopal minister Charles Snowden. He was sponsored by his father and by his father's brother John and sister Susan.[6] In April 1816 the young family moved to Pineville, one of the many little towns where planters took refuge from malaria each summer, evidently to take up permanent residence, but on June 12, 1816, Catherine died.[7] Two-year-old Henry William was sent to live with his grandparents, René and Charlotte Ravenel.[8]

Dr. Henry Ravenel soon remarried. The bride was twenty-one-year-old Mary Esther Dwight, but Mary Esther was dead within a year, and again on May 21, 1821, Ravenel remarried. Henry William remembered clearly the wedding of his father and Elizabeth Catherine Porcher, daughter of Thomas and Charlotte Mazyck Porcher of Ophir Plantation in Saint Stephen's Parish. The little boy had stayed with his grandparents through both of his father's courtships, and he remained with them now. René Ravenel died in 1822, and Henry William continued to live with his grandmother until her death in November 1826. His father then inherited the family plantation, Pooshee, and turned entirely to planting as a career. He moved out to the plantation with his wife and Henry's small stepbrothers and sisters.[9]

There is no evidence that Dr. Ravenel's decision to leave Henry with his grandparents indicated any lack of affection for his little son. Indeed, his material generosity with Henry William and his obvious desire in his old age for frequent visits from this eldest son indicate the opposite. He could feel sure the boy would receive good treatment from his grandparents and unmarried aunts and uncles, one of whom, Susan Mazyck, continued to feel quite motherly towards Henry William all her life, though she married his maternal uncle Charles Stevens on October 31, 1816, and soon started a family of her own in Pineville.[10] If Henry William resented the separation from his father, he gave no indication of it later in his diary or letters.

A favorite childhood activity of Henry's was to go to the Pooshee slave quarters and beg stories from the old men and women. Some were native Africans who gave him fantastic accounts of giant snakes, elephants, and fierce lions. They told grimmer stories, too, of their capture and march to the sea and of the middle passage. Of all their tales, though, the ones that had the greatest effect on him were of the American Revolution. The area around Charleston had been overrun by British troops, and men of fighting age, including young Ravenel's grandfather, had gone into the surrounding swamps to join Francis Marion. The slaves' tales often highlighted their own efforts on behalf of the colonials. The hours Henry William spent listening to their stories permanently impressed upon him a feeling that the old men and women were worthy of, in his words, "respect and veneration." The tales of the American Revolution also inculcated in the young boy a great, patriotic love for his native land. By manhood that feeling had been enlarged to include the United States, but it was always associated first and foremost with the very swamps and plantations where Marion and the British once skulked.[11]

Home to young Ravenel was a twelve-hundred-acre rice and sea island cotton plantation. The house, though easily visible from Black Oak Road, was located nearly a mile from the gate down a broad sand and gravel drive. Its appearance was fairly typical of the simple colonial-style architecture of Saint John's plantation houses. The first floor was high enough off the ground to allow a man to walk under it. Rooms at ground level, under the living quarters, served as storehouse, meat room, dairy, and woodbin. A strip of lawn, dotted with old water oaks, sycamores, and elms, separated the drive from the first cultivated fields and surrounded the house. Each tree was provided with a hitching ring for visitors' horses. Stables stood to one side and carriage houses to the other side of the house, presenting a symmetrical appearance but imposing an inconvenient distance between the two. One or two hundred yards from the plantation house stood the slave quarters—rows of wooden houses, each about eighteen by thirty feet and divided down the middle to accommodate one large family or two small ones.[12]

One unusual and nearly tragic incident stood out during Henry William Ravenel's childhood years at Pooshee. On June 23, 1818, when the little boy had just turned four, he was thrown from a horse and severely injured. The scalp, torn back from his forehead, had to be replaced and held securely by stitches and adhesive straps until it healed. The serious nature of the injury was obvious to all, and it was recorded in tones of concern by both his father and grandfather. The wound apparently healed without complications, though it left a scar, but his family long remembered the frightening incident and linked it with his much later attacks of deafness. The accident's dramatic effect was also apparent from the impression it made upon the Ravenels' slaves, who told the story so often that, according to legend, they eventually convinced themselves that Henry William had a silver plate in his head.[13]

When the time came for the boy to begin school, his grandfather sent him to Pineville Academy, where his aunts Maria and Catherine had received instruction only a few years before.[14] Private schools such as Pineville Academy were common in antebellum South Carolina, for there was only a very limited system of free public education. South Carolinians generally recognized the importance of education to the public interest but considered its provision a parental responsibility.[15] The state's private academies varied considerably in quality. Some were poor, but others achieved a great reputation and attracted students from throughout South Carolina and neighboring states.[16]

Pineville Academy, where Henry William began lessons on June 25, 1820,[17] was operated by a board of trustees who functioned also as the town council of Pineville. It was equipped with a schoolhouse and a house for the teacher. New teachers came fairly frequently and varied greatly in ability. Frederick Porcher, a near neighbor of Ravenel's, five years his senior, fondly recalled John Service, an assistant teacher, who had charge of the youngest children and whose patient instruction inspired him in reading. Service was also Henry William's first teacher. The schoolmaster during the same period was Jacob Gillett, a graduate of Dartmouth. Gillett's major asset was an amiable wife who won the affection of his students. His major liability was his inability to teach Greek. For a time he simply restricted his subject matter to English and Latin, but when he finally embarked with his older pupils upon the study of Greek, his deficiency soon became apparent, and the trustees refused to reelect him at the end of the 1823 term.[18] Ravenel, only nine years of age and too young to have begun Greek when Gillett was dismissed, probably suffered no serious setback from his faulty instruction.

Most of the male students at coeducational Pineville Academy were college bound, and the curriculum reflected their needs. The youngest children were schooled in English grammar, reading, and arithmetic. Latin was soon added to their studies, and then Greek. Both were necessary to enter college and were taught at Pineville through endless drills and oral recitation.[19] Some geography, history, algebra, and geometry were probably also part of the curriculum, but science does not seem to have been taught at Pineville. By the late 1820s a few academies or high schools in the United States had begun teaching some science, but it was ordinarily considered too difficult for children. Even colleges usually confined it to the junior and senior curriculum.

Though science may not have been formally taught to Ravenel during his childhood, the atmosphere in which he grew up was conducive to the development of any innate interest a child might have in natural history. Low country South Carolina had a rich native flora and fauna. In many places, including the swamps and pine forests, this wilderness remained in its natural state. Outdoor childhood games, as well as the adults' outdoor agricultural work, brought people into frequent contact with nature. In addition, the Charleston area had at the time a scientific tradition, particularly in natural history, going back a century.[20] Thomas Walter (1740–1789) of Saint John's Parish had contributed greatly to this tradition. Many years of collecting and observing plants culminated in 1788 in the publication of his *Flora Caroliniana,* a Latin catalogue of the plants of the locale, arranged according to the Linnaean system. René Ravenel, Henry William's grandfather, was in his twenties when Walter died and might have had stories to tell of his botanist neighbor. Walter's grave and the barely discernible remnants of his botanical garden were only a few miles from Pooshee, an easy trip for a curious boy on a pony, had Ravenel been so inclined.[21]

Many things more interesting than a grave and a tangled garden could be seen on occasional trips to Charleston. America's oldest museum collection, begun in the 1770s, was on display in Chalmers Street. Fossils, seashells, an Egyptian mummy, a polar bear, a duck-billed platypus, and bright minerals and birds—things many children saw only in picture books—were parts of a growing collection.[22]

Ravenel's childhood in low country South Carolina was not very different from those of other children in his place and time, yet many advantageous circumstances combined at his birth to produce a situation favorable to the full development of his inborn abilities. He was male and white in a society rigidly dominated by white men; his family was wealthy in a society where even the rudimentary education of poor children was uncertain. To be male, white, and wealthy was a distinct advantage anywhere in nineteenth-century America, but the intellectual implications of these advantages could easily have been lost on Ravenel had he not lived in an old, settled part of the country where schools were available and where the concentrated labor of establishing profitable agriculture had been done years before, freeing the minds and hands of Ravenel's generation for other tasks. In addition, he was born into a social class that considered an education based on the Greek and Roman classics and mathematics as almost a birthright to their children. The Episcopal church into which he was baptized insisted, as well, on a learned ministry and recognized the value of universal acquisition of at least the rudiments of education. To live within fifty miles of Charleston was in itself a special advantage for anyone with an inclination to study natural history, for the Charleston scientific community exuded an atmosphere of sympathy unmatched in any American city, with the exceptions of Boston and Philadelphia. Because of this happy combination of circumstances, Ravenel could look forward to a life whose limits would be set, to an enviable degree, by his own talents and desires.

College and Young Manhood, 1829–1839 **2**

Ravenel left Pineville Academy at the end of the 1828 term, and in January 1829 his father escorted him, in company with his neighbors Isaac and Edward Porcher, to Columbia, South Carolina, where they continued their studies under the private tutorship of James M. Daniels, who had taught the year before at Pineville.[1] The boys' study with Daniels was evidently directed at polishing their lower-school education to prepare them to enter South Carolina College (later the University of South Carolina) soon after they turned fifteen, the minimum age for enrollment.

South Carolina College, where Ravenel was to spend the years from December 1829 until his graduation in December 1832, was founded by low country planters, who controlled a disproportionate number of seats in the legislature, to resolve sectional disputes between the coastal region and the piedmont. Governor John Drayton suggested to the Assembly of South Carolina on November 23, 1801, that the state should establish a college at the piedmont town and state capitol of Columbia, in the hope that "the friendships of young men would thence be promoted and strengthened throughout the State, and our political union be much advanced." Acting with amazing rapidity on the advice of the governor, both houses of the assembly read and approved a bill to establish the college. Final legislative approval came on December 19, less than a month after the governor's address.[2]

South Carolina was not the first state to found a college, for by 1801 both North Carolina and Georgia had state universities. The degree of control exercised by the state over the college at Columbia, however, as well as the splendid financial support given by the legislature, placed South Carolina College on a firmer initial footing than the other two. With fifty thousand dollars in hand, the trustees of the new institution, all members of the government or elected by the legislature, proceeded to establish the new college. They chose a site, received bids from architects and contractors, and by January 1805 had constructed a substantial building, Rutledge College. South Carolina College opened on January 10, 1805, with a faculty of two and a student body of nine.[3] From this small beginning, the college grew, and by 1829 the student body numbered nearly a hundred, and the faculty had increased to six.

Before these six men, on December 1, 1829, Ravenel appeared with several other prospective students to be examined for entrance into the sophomore class. The faculty's examination took two days, and at the end, Ravenel was among the successful candidates and a sophomore at South Carolina College.[4] To enter the sophomore class directly, as Ravenel did, was not the accomplishment it might seem in these days when four-year college courses are the norm. Improved preparation of students by South Carolina's academies had so reduced the enrollment in the freshman class that in 1831 the class was dispensed with entirely.[5]

Ravenel's entry at the age of fifteen into the sophomore class indicates that his years at Pineville had given him a strong, though by no means outstanding, background in English, Greek, and Latin. Thomas Cooper (1783–1839), elected a professor in 1819 and president of the college from 1821 through 1833, had in 1820 persuaded the Board of Trustees to make fifteen the minimum age for enrollment and to establish rigorous entrance requirements including extensive translation from Latin and Greek. Admission to the freshman class required legible handwriting, correct spelling, and an acquaintance with mathematics, including common and decimal fractions and the extraction of roots. Accurate knowledge of English, Latin, and Greek grammar was a necessity, and the prospective freshman had to demonstrate an ability to translate from Latin Virgil's *Aeneid* and from

Greek the four Evangelists and the Acts of the Apostles.[6] Requirements for admission into the sophomore class were not specifically established by the trustees, but the minutes of faculty meetings during these years give indications of what was considered an acceptable level of ability beyond the freshman requirements. Familiarity with more of the ancient authors was a necessity. A candidate for the sophomore class might be required to translate from the odes of Horace, or his *Art of Poetry,* from Cicero's orations, Lucian's dialogues, or Xenophon. A somewhat more thorough knowledge of mathematics was also in order. One aspiring sophomore was disappointed in his ambitions because he was deficient not only in Cicero's orations but also in quadratic equations.[7]

South Carolina College's physical plant, like its student body and faculty, had expanded dramatically between 1805 and 1829. De Saussure College, whose construction was begun in 1806, mirrored Rutledge College across the grassy mall known, then as now, as the Horseshoe. These two large structures were flanked by smaller ones—Steward's Hall, houses for the president and faculty, and the Library and Science Building—arranged to preserve the harmonious symmetry of the Horseshoe. An astronomical observatory huddled behind two of the other new buildings.[8]

That this still-small campus possessed an observatory and a separate building housing library and science facilities hints that South Carolina College was a remarkably scientifically oriented institution for its time. The composition of the faculty, the administration of the library, and the subjects studied by the students also point to this scientific orientation, but perhaps the single most revealing clue was the professorial pay scale. South Carolina College was one of the few colleges in the United States that, as early as 1812, made it a policy to pay all professors equally, without discrimination against those teaching science. Despite this policy, however, some adverse discrimination may have existed, for the only science teacher other than the president during the early 1830s was not accorded the title of professor and was paid only half the salary of a professor. Even so, his earnings compared well with salaries offered at other colleges of the period. At South Carolina College, the president received $3,000 annually, professors $2,000, and tutors $1,000. By comparison, Harvard paid professors

$600 to $1,500, Yale $1,100, and Brown $800 to $1,000, while the president of Brown University was paid $1,400 to $1,500, plus graduation fees and the use of a house.[9]

South Carolina's hundred students were taught by a capable faculty, headed by the English chemist Thomas Cooper, who served as president and taught chemistry, belles lettres, and political economy. Professors included Thomas Park, professor of ancient languages; Robert Henry, a young, ambitious professor of mathematics; and Henry Junius Nott, teacher of the "Elements of Criticism, Logic, and Philosophy." Robert W. Gibbes, considered Cooper's assistant, taught chemistry, geology, and mineralogy. During 1829 and 1830 Edward Michaelowitz, styled "Teacher of Oriental Literature and Modern Languages," offered instruction in German, French, and Hebrew. In addition, there were always one or two tutors who lived among the students and taught mathematics or classics to the two lower classes.[10] Two graduates of this period, James Henry Hammond, later governor of South Carolina, and James H. Thornwell, both found the Cooper-era faculty highly stimulating. Ravenel's own classmate J. Marion Sims, later a famous pioneer in the field of gynecology, was favorably impressed only by Cooper and Henry.[11]

Library resources, aided by a substantial grant from the legislature in 1823, included modern authors of physical science and mathematics, the most widely respected critical editions of ancient works, and current literature. Particularly in the physical sciences the college attempted to establish a research library sufficient for the professors as well as the students. Library hours, which allowed teachers much greater access than students, also reflected the attempt to meet professors' research needs. Unfortunately, poor administration during the 1820s threatened the continued usefulness of the library. The books were in disarray, and no one had maintained accurate records of those taken out and those returned. In December 1829 the trustees ordered that a librarian be hired to call in and arrange the collection. This work was successfully accomplished, and in November 1830 the trustees received the report that "The management of the Library . . . during the last session fully answered all the reasonable expectations of the faculty."[12]

Despite liberal support for the physical sciences, natural history was underrepresented in the library of the South Carolina College in the late 1820s. The 1823 appropriation was partly used to enhance the collection of scientific works, particularly in astronomy and mathematics, but studies of animals, plants, and minerals were neglected. The Committee of Trustees who selected the books mourned: "In the important and daily increasing department of Natural History a few of the most valuable elementary works have been inserted. It is greatly to be regretted that in this department in which the most important treatises are too costly for the acquisition of private individuals, some public Collection could not be made."[13] These remarks, addressed to the legislature, were perhaps designed to bring forth additional money with which to buy works in natural history. They recognize the importance of that subject but, at the same time, clearly subordinate it to the physical sciences.

Faculty members certainly had a hand in recommending books for the library, so it is scarcely surprising that South Carolina College's faculty also reflected a preference for the physical sciences. There was, in fact, no member specializing in life sciences, nor was this state of affairs unusual. America's first colleges—Harvard, Yale, William and Mary—and those relative newcomers of the eighteenth century— Princeton, the College of Philadelphia, Columbia, Brown, Rutgers, and Dartmouth—concerned themselves much more with physical science than with natural history, and the tradition they established was carried into the nineteenth century. This was hardly surprising, for biology did not emerge as a discrete science until the nineteenth century,[14] and comparative anatomy and botany were considered mainly the province of the medical curriculum. Only in 1816 did the College of Philadelphia, for example, begin to offer instruction in natural history outside the medical school.[15] In the South, as in the North, devotion to the physical sciences often came at the expense of botany and zoology. Early southern teachers of natural history were often polymaths who taught several subjects in addition to natural history and whose specialty might actually lie outside the area. Constantine Samuel Rafinesque, for example, taught botany in addition to modern languages at Transylvania University in Lexington, Kentucky, from 1819 through 1825; Gerard Troost, though best known as a geologist, lectured on natural history, particularly zoology, at the

University of Nashville from about 1828 through 1849.[16] Not until 1846 when Richard Owen Currey began teaching at East Tennessee University was laboratory-based botanical instruction available anywhere in Tennessee, though laboratory classes in chemistry were offered twenty years earlier by George Thomas Bowen of the University of Nashville.[17] When the University of Mississippi opened its doors in the late 1840s, three of its five professors taught some aspect of physical science or mathematics, but there was no teacher of natural history.[18]

Obviously whatever botany or other natural history Ravenel may have learned at college, he picked up informally. He may have had the chance to work with Lewis Reeves Gibbes, the young kinsman of faculty member Robert W. Gibbes, who was on the faculty between 1831 and 1835, first as tutor of mathematics and then, for a year, as acting professor of mathematics. Lewis Gibbes's dominant interest was astronomy, but from boyhood botany had also claimed his attention, and his plant studies were continued in Columbia. In October 1835 Gibbes published a pamphlet entitled *A Catalogue of the Phoenagamous* [sic] *Plants of Columbia, S.C. and Its Vicinity,* and from time to time, Gibbes published other papers on botanical subjects. He and Ravenel later corresponded regularly on natural history topics, but it is not known whether they worked together during the year that their stays at South Carolina College overlapped. Ravenel was not among the few individuals whom Gibbes credited with having helped him on the *Catalogue,* but since he was there for only one of the four years during which Gibbes worked on the botanical study, this is scarcely evidence that he was not involved. The two very likely did know each other, for Ravenel later confided to Gibbes that his laboratory at the College of Charleston brought back pleasant memories of college days.[19]

Robert Gibbes's scientific interests also extended beyond the physical sciences. During the early 1830s, when he was still a young man, he found time in the midst of his teaching and a growing medical practice to keep up with a broad range of scientific literature. Later, he developed a wide reputation in paleontology for his article on a mysterious fossil animal discovered in 1845 on the Santee Canal plantation of Robert W. Mazyck. The animal combined the dental characteristics of mammals and reptiles, and the naming of the beast threw Gibbes into an argument with the great British comparative anatomist Richard Owen, a battle that seems to have been settled by the combatants' successors in favor of Gibbes.[20]

Ravenel applied himself fairly diligently to those studies formally offered at South Carolina College. His habit of hard work was well known to his family. In 1829 while he was studying with Daniels, his uncle Charles Stevens devoted most of a four-page letter to advice that Henry not study too hard. "No person can be always engaged in elevated pursuits. Periods of relaxation are absolutely necessary, not only to the health of the animal system; but to the healthful operations of the mind itself," suggested Uncle Charles.[21] Ravenel apparently had some trouble adjusting to the relative freedom of college, however, for after his first semester, which he later admitted had been spent slothfully, he failed the faculty's examination in mathematics, though he passed in Greek, Latin, and modern geography. He made up this deficiency over the summer and never failed another college exam. Ravenel later worked especially hard in chemistry, mineralogy, natural philosophy, and metaphysics, which were reserved for the senior curriculum.[22]

Following old tradition, college students in the early nineteenth century were raucous and disruptive. Open rebellion, physical threats against professors, assaults upon townspeople, and drunkenness were common.[23] South Carolina College had its share of disorder. Even in 1816 when first president Jonathan Maxcy effusively praised the students, saying that after thirty years as an educator he had never known "an instance in which a College was conducted with such order, peace, and industry, as this has been during the past year," he had still to deplore "the resort of certain individuals to taverns and other places of entertainment."[24] In 1827 an organized boycott of the dining hall led to the expulsion of so many students that only thirteen graduated that year, compared with twenty-eight in 1826 and thirty-two in 1825.[25]

While Ravenel walked its hallways, however, South Carolina College was remarkably peaceful. In 1828, the year before he entered, the trustees finally defused the discontent that had sparked rebellion in 1827 and lesser disturbances in prior years by eliminating compulsory attendance at the Steward's Hall. Students who preferred could thence-forth take their meals at licensed boardinghouses.[26] Discipline problems facing the faculty during Ravenel's years at the college were relatively minor. Students were frequently called up and admonished for late returns from home, riding about campus at night, neglect of their studies, or absence from chapel or recitations.[27] Nothing more serious was mentioned in the faculty minutes, but the students of these years did love to remove (often by burning) the wooden staircase leading to the door to Rutledge College so they could enjoy watching the unathletic professors, particularly stout Thomas Cooper, struggle up a makeshift ladder to teach classes or attend assemblies.[28]

When not burning down staircases, the college boys upheld a long and honored South Carolina College tradition by retiring to Isaac Lyons's "oyster saloon" for oysters and wine. The well-heeled young man who invited his friends would treat them, and if, upon having done so, he found his pocket unequal to the occasion, he need have no worries. Lyons was never so crass as to ask for money and would even make loans when needed. The students' concept of honor allowed them to destroy both private and public property, but reportedly none ever failed to repay their host and benefactor Lyons.[29]

The sociable yet quiet tenor of Ravenel's later life would suggest that he took a moderate part in these student frolics and was probably well known at the oyster saloon. Surely, however, he was not a burner of staircases, and if he did cause any mischief, it escaped the censorious attention of the faculty, which never once singled him out for admonishment.[30]

Like many nineteenth-century colleges, South Carolina College had two active debating societies, the Clariosophic Society and the Euphradian Society, and all the students took part in one or the other of them. On November 28, 1829, several days before his acceptance as a student at the college, "H. Ravenel of Pineville" was unanimously elected an honorary member of the Clariosophic Society and had an introduction to college debating. His fellow society members considered the issues of whether Napoleon had been justified in repudiating Josephine and whether it would be beneficial to South Carolina to secede from the Union. Both questions were decided in the negative. At the meeting of December 5, Ravenel, again by unanimous vote, was made a regular member of the society.[31]

Ravenel remained an active member in the Clariosophic Society throughout his college years, serving the society as a critic, treasurer, and then as a recorder.[32] In his turn, he participated in the debates, the subject matter of which testified to the students' wide-ranging concerns. National and international politics, moral issues, and the promotion of human progress were frequent themes. Hopefulness and idealism were readily apparent, as when the society decided that free religious discussion, as well as an unlicensed freedom of the press, should be allowed and that it was probable that the whole world would become civilized and enlightened.[33]

Although not particularly successful in debate, losing more than he won the first year, Ravenel evidently enjoyed the meetings. Minute books of the society, available for Ravenel's sophomore year, but not for the later two, record that he attended more often than many of the other members, being present about two-thirds of the time.[34]

Ravenel's enjoyment of debate is hardly unexpected, for he was accustomed from childhood to the planters' gregarious society, particularly the constant summertime socializing in Pineville. During his college years, he returned home to pass the summer vacations in Pineville with his family. There he fell one summer into the pleasant habit of gathering with four or five other young men to make late-evening rounds of the neighborhood, serenading the eligible young ladies. Frederick Porcher and Ravenel played the flute to accompany the others, who sang. Out of politeness they gave their musical attentions to all the young ladies, though the more beautiful or charming received the best songs and longer serenades. When Ravenel went back to college, the group dispersed.[35]

Although the students of 1829–1832 were comparatively peaceable, Thomas Cooper, president of the university, was not. He chose that very time to recommence, after several years of forbearance, a vitriolic and apparently unprovoked attack upon the clergy. Cooper singled out Presbyterians for special criticism but touched all religions with his acid pen. This bitter parading of his unusual anticlerical views aroused public outcry, and he was forced to resign from the presidency of South Carolina College in 1833. He maintained a position teaching chemistry for another year, then dropped all connection with the college.[36]

Cooper claimed that he never tried to influence the religious feelings of his students, but his position of authority over them made his denials ring hollow, the more so since his unorthodox views, both religious and political, were known to all. His anticlericalism was no secret even at the time he was invited to South Carolina College. By 1824 he had publicly declared his extremist view of states' rights, and in 1827, long before it was fashionable to do so, he had urged the citizens of his adopted state to "calculate the value of the Union." During the Nullification crisis of 1830 he naturally sided with the nullifiers. Cooper's racial views were also more extreme than those of many of his contemporaries. He believed the black race innately inferior to the white and defended slavery on the grounds of economic necessity and by the claim that the lives of American slaves were better than those of their ancestors in Africa or of European laborers. These views, put forth in 1826, influenced the proslavery arguments of later writers including Thomas R. Dew, William Harper, and Cooper's student James Henry Hammond.[37] Many South Carolina College students, like Hammond, adopted Cooper's opinions on states' rights and slavery and were later to be found in the ranks of the most ardent secessionists.[38] Henry Ravenel, however, found Cooper's religious views abhorrent[39] and rejected along with them his political and racial ideas. During the Nullification crisis, while he was yet a student, Ravenel, like many of his family and neighbors in Saint John's, favored continuation of the Union. By 1860 his patience had worn thin, but even then he stood among the more moderate of South Carolinians. With regard to slavery and race, Ravenel maintained an older southern opinion that blacks were at a less civilized stage of development than whites but could show progress both as individuals and as a race.

Ravenel graduated from South Carolina College in December 1832, placing seventh in his class.[40] He returned home from Columbia hoping to study medicine and actually made a beginning that winter reading a physiology textbook. His father, however, feared that his son's health was too delicate to withstand the rigors of a country medical practice, with the midnight calls, traveling, and exposure to disease that it entailed. He advised him to turn instead to planting and offered to set him up on a plantation, where slave labor would largely free him from physical work.[41]

It is curious that delicate health was the reason cited by Ravenel's father for dissuading him from medicine. No record has survived of childhood illness, and certainly there was none so serious as to impede the normal progress of Ravenel's schooling. College debates and flute playing indicate, too, that he did not yet suffer any inconvenience from the deafness that would plague him in later years. To the nineteenth-century mind, however, health seemed a delicate balance, easily upset, and it is likely that Ravenel's father had many reasons to worry about his son's health, reasons born, however, more of his own fears than of any actual weakness in Ravenel's constitution. The father had already lost two wives in childbirth and their infants with them. In addition, two little daughters had died within days of each other in the fall of 1827.[42] These losses, combined with the memory of Ravenel's serious injury at the age of four, may have made him overly concerned about his son's safety. At the same time, having himself retired from medical practice at least partly because of the toll it took upon his own strength, the father was in a good position to judge the effect such a career might have upon his son. Certainly he had no other reason to discourage Ravenel from medicine; the career was both remunerative and respected, physicians being acknowledged as members of the same class as the planters they served.[43] René Ravenel, one of his younger sons, did follow his father's medical career.[44] For his namesake, however, the elder Ravenel obviously wanted an easier life.

From the standpoint of the botanist that Ravenel later became, medical school might have been a very desirable finish to his education. In the 1820s nearly all medical schools included at least a semester of botany and *materia medica* in the curriculum. Many of Ravenel's colleagues in science received preliminary training in medical study. Asa Gray, for example, graduated from a small country medical school in 1831, and Francis Peyre Porcher took his degree from the Medical College of South Carolina in 1847.[45] When he graduated from college Ravenel was not yet a botanist, however, and probably had no idea of the turn his life would shortly take. Though the botanist would later regret a missed opportunity, the youth of eighteen was happy to settle down at Northampton, begin farming, and take up an adult's role in Saint John's society, which meant, in part, becoming involved in some of the area's many clubs and associations.[46]

The second Thursday of every month, for example, was dedicated to the meetings of the Saint John's Hunting Club. Ravenel, his father, and his brothers were members of this all-male organization. For men of the Ravenels' social stratum, membership conveyed no great distinction, for ordinarily every planter within ten miles was a member. The club was formed in 1800, modeled on a similar organization in Saint Stephen's Parish.[47] Despite its name, by the 1830s the club was a social organization quite unrelated to hunting. The central event of each meeting was the dinner provided by individual members in rotation according to precise directions laid out in the rules of the club.[48]

Ravenel's father seldom missed a club day and served for some time as secretary. His son apparently also enjoyed the occasions, for even after he moved to Aiken and was no longer a member, he attended the meetings whenever he was in Saint John's and not otherwise occupied.[49]

Simple enjoyment was only one reason to attend. Membership in the Saint John's Hunting Club, because it was available only to planters and their sons, provided a valuable public recognition of one's station in life. In addition, on club days neighborhood men could relax and converse, the talk settling on agriculture or politics. To attend the meetings was to have a say in many matters of community life not directly related to the club. Conclusions reached there could be as binding as if reached formally at meetings of other organizations, for the membership of all Saint John's leadership groups was nearly identical. Moreover, the influence exerted by the hunting club was enhanced by the tradition that the Saint John's, Saint Stephen's, and Saint Thomas's clubs met at different times, so members of each club could attend the meetings of the others. The custom ensured that a larger group of men, representing a broader geographical area, could meet together more frequently than would have been the case had each club held its meetings entirely privately.[50]

Two other formal associations claimed some of Ravenel's time in the years following his return from college, though neither was as influential or as time-consuming as the hunting club. The Saint Stephen's Jockey Club was a purely social organization that met once a year, in October, for the sole purpose of planning two days of horse races and dancing in Pineville. Ravenel was drafted as a member in

1834 and promptly elected a manager of the ball. After 1834 he took no more active part in the club and in 1840 resigned his membership. Ravenel also joined the Pineville Police Association. Formed in 1823 in the wave of fear following the Denmark Vesey slave uprising of 1822, the organization set ambitiously to its task of protecting the local population against similar rebellions. It acquired a thick book in which to record the details of anticipated meetings, duly noted its own formation, and then fell silent for seventeen years. In 1839 some zealous member drafted an association constitution and lists of officers and members, Ravenel among the latter. Silence again descended. The very few written pages in the very big book say much about the activities of the association.[51]

For a young bachelor, other social events held more promise than the meetings of all-male clubs and associations. Dancing, carriage drives, and horseback riding were favorite activities among young people and provided excuses for young men and women to spend time together in less formal surroundings than the ladies' parlor.[52] Dances and serenading produced results for Ravenel not long after college. In March 1835 he became engaged to Elizabeth Gaillard Snowden. Elizabeth, like Ravenel, was from a wealthy South Carolina family. She was the middle child of five, the daughter of William and Lydia Gaillard Snowden.[53] The location of the Snowdens' principal home is uncertain, but the family spent at least part of the year in Charleston, where Elizabeth and her two younger brothers, Charles and Peter, were born.[54] It was there that Elizabeth and Henry Ravenel were married December 1, 1835. The Episcopal ceremony took place in Elizabeth's father's house and was performed by the Reverend, soon to be Bishop, Christopher Gadsden.[55]

As is often the case in marriages between two members of a wealthy class, there were business considerations to be thought of. As trustee, Ravenel received substantial property under the marriage settlement with the Snowdens, including eighteen slaves and seventy-eight shares in various banks.[56] Ravenel also brought considerable property to the marriage. His principal material asset was his plantation, Northampton, which his father had given him along with the equipment and field hands necessary to run it.[57] A tract of quite respectable size, six hundred acres or more, Northampton had the potential to be profitable. When Ravenel acquired it, however, its reputation was poor. It had been the scene of William Moultrie's dismally unsuccessful experiment with sea island cotton in 1793, seven years before Peter Gaillard's remarkable success with the same crop at the nearby Rocks Plantation. A bad growing season and unskillful management were two reasons cited for Moultrie's failure, but local stories hinted that the land itself was to blame. Of course, the Rocks had the advantage over Northampton in being planted among the outcroppings of limestone that gave the plantation its name. A fairly rapid succession of several owners between Moultrie and Ravenel also boded ill.[58]

In the 1830s ancient knowledge of fertilizers was just being rediscovered in America. Virgin land had been so readily available that it had not paid farmers to protect their soil too actively. Yet land in many old, settled regions of the South had been under constant cultivation for four or five generations. When cotton and rice became established as staple crops, even proper regimens of crop rotation were skimped. Thus treated, farmland throughout the older regions of the South, particularly Virginia and South Carolina, was wearing out. Northampton was apparently a victim of poor, transient management and depleted soil. It would be a challenge, but not an insurmountable one, to make Northampton productive.

Ravenel and his bride spent the winters of 1835–1836 and 1836–1837, and perhaps the following one or two as well, with his father's large family at Pooshee.[59] Ravenel's father and stepmother had six children—Thomas, René, William Francis, Elizabeth Charlotte, Maria Catherine, and John Charles—ranging in age from eleven to one at the time of Henry William's marriage. This was not an unusually big family for the time or for the Ravenel clan, nor had it stopped growing. On December 20, 1835, Ravenel's stepmother Elizabeth gave birth to Henrietta Mary. The family soon lost the youngest boy, John Charles, who died March 29, 1836, and Elizabeth Charlotte, who died soon after her brother, but another daughter was added to the family by the birth of Rowena Elizabeth on November 22, 1837.[60]

During these years Ravenel and Elizabeth started their own family. Catherine Stevens was born January 10, 1837, followed by Lydia Snowden, July 14, 1839. Catherine died at the age of five, the only child Ravenel ever lost at a tender age.[61]

By 1839 the young couple were living a much more settled existence. Ravenel built a summer home at Pinopolis, Pineville having fallen into disfavor because of an outbreak of malaria in 1834. A smaller settlement than Pineville, Pinopolis had only about a dozen houses, but the Ravenels returned to spend every summer there from 1839 until their move to Aiken in 1853. The winters they began to spend in their own house at Northampton, a two-story wooden structure on a stone foundation.[62]

Marriage and participation in Saint John's social activities did not prevent Ravenel from developing, apparently very soon after he left college, a casual interest in natural history. As he put it, "I lived in the country & took up a fondness for Botany making a few collections— plants & fossils."[63] In this pursuit he was not alone. A short walk took Ravenel between Cedar Spring and Brunswick plantations to Sarazen, the home of William and Isabella Porcher. William, about fourteen years older than Ravenel, a physician and a graduate of South Carolina College, had a local reputation as a zealous botanist.[64] His enthusiasm was shared by his wife, Isabella, a granddaughter of the botanist Thomas Walter. She had picked up from her grandfather a great liking for botany, and with her husband spent many hours in the woods studying the wild plants.[65]

Frederick Porcher also had an interest in the science. A distant but fond cousin of William's, Frederick grew up on Cedar Spring Plantation and caught some of his cousin's devotion to botany. Frederick found that botany could make a favorable impression upon young ladies. During the summer he courted his wife, he always brought her a bouquet of wild flowers when he returned to Pineville after a ride to the plantation. She, in turn, occasionally sent over a flower with the request that he identify it for her.[66]

William Porcher died June 4, 1833, while on a trip to Charleston. Without his continued encouragement, Frederick Porcher gradually lost interest in botany, but how much ill effect, if any, William's death had upon Ravenel's botanical career is hard to calculate. William Porcher's local reputation as a botanist was not supported by publication, nor did he correspond with any of the nationally famous botanists of his time.[67] Therefore, the depth, accuracy, and timeliness of his information are questionable, and all that is certain is his enthusiasm. This alone, however, could have been a valuable spur to Ravenel's interest.

Even after William's death and Frederick's defection, Ravenel was not totally without sympathetic botanical friends. Isabella communicated some of her own interest to her second son, Francis Peyre, called Frank, who was only eight when his father died. When he was about ten, Frank began attending Mount Zion Academy, but during holidays at home he and Ravenel fell into the habit of taking walks together. In this way they embarked upon a botanical comradeship that lasted until Ravenel's death.[68]

During the years between late 1832 and 1839, Ravenel found his place as an adult member of the Saint John's planter aristocracy. Taking advantage of the numerous social opportunities available, he entered into the complex net of friendship and mutual obligation that bound the low country planters into a cohesive group. He planted rice and sea island cotton and learned firsthand how to manage a large plantation. He married a young woman of similar background, and they had two baby girls. At the same time he cast about for an activity that would fill his leisure time and exercise his intelligence. Natural history presented itself, and he recognized in it a study well suited to his tastes and abilities. It remained for the time a hobby, an expression of his individuality, submerged beneath the more important work of establishing himself within a social group, shouldering the responsibilities and assuming the privileges that were withheld from schoolboys and reserved for mature members of the society. By the end of 1839 Ravenel, at the age of twenty-five, had a wife and family; land, slaves, and the equipment and knowledge necessary to raise rice; a winter house at the plantation and a summer house in Pinopolis. He was established, settled, as secure as any man could be, and he could easily have stagnated in that situation and done nothing more than grow rice all his life.

American Scientist, 1839–1849   3

Growing rice was not an occupation to be taken lightly. Careful planters did not leave cultivation to the unsupervised attentions of slaves and overseers. They inspected growing crops almost daily, and many kept meticulous records on the care of plants and animals and the health of their slaves.[1] Ravenel's efforts at Northampton apparently were rewarded, and he made a comfortable living. In April 1840 he had sufficient funds accumulated to buy eight additional hands from William Jervey for $6,800. He paid half in cash and signed a bond for the remainder. After paying interest each year, he paid off the note in 1849.[2]

Ravenel's purchase of slaves indicated prosperity for him, but the early 1840s were not auspicious years for planters of rice and sea island cotton. Market prices on cotton were remarkably low during the first half of the decade, and rice prices were still in a slump that had begun in 1830. Difficulties were compounded for growers in Saint John's. That parish, which marked the northern boundary of the sea island cotton region, was unable to produce as fine a fiber as the more southerly islands of South Carolina and Georgia. Factors in Charleston differentiated the Saint John's product from the better-quality island cotton, calling it Santee cotton. Planters in Ravenel's area brought in new seed from the Sea Islands every year or two to prevent degeneration of their crop.[3]

In 1842 planters in Ravenel's neighborhood decided to take positive action to improve the agriculture of their region. They formed an association to serve as a rallying point for their efforts. On February 10 the planters gathered to listen to a committee's report on the advantages of forming an association and to the committee's proposed constitution. The Saint John's planters accepted both the report and the constitution, and they elected officers to serve the new association, which they named the Black Oak Agricultural Society.[4]

Samuel Dubose, elected president at this first meeting, was forty-two. As a young man, with only six field hands and much ambition, he had doubled his worth in two years. Later he had acquired a large plantation, Harbin, a gift to his first wife, Eliza, from her father. Dubose was universally respected and a popular companion to young and old alike. His election as president was a tribute to his success in planting, his position as a leader and servant of the community, and the affection of his neighbors. Dubose did not play a very active role in the society, though he did present a paper, more interesting from the standpoint of local history than of agriculture, on the introduction of cotton planting.[5] Ravenel's classmate, Isaac Porcher, was elected vice-president and Ravenel himself, at the age of twenty-seven, was elected secretary and treasurer.[6]

Dubose, Porcher, and Ravenel were reelected to their offices annually until 1848, when James Ferguson replaced Porcher as vice-president, and 1849, when the offices of secretary and treasurer were divided. Ravenel retained the secretary's office, while Thomas Walter Peyre became treasurer.[7] Frederick Porcher was another particularly active member.

At the first meeting of the society, March 7, 1842, Ravenel focused the members' attention on the need to produce and disseminate knowledge. He introduced a resolution encouraging experimentation by individual members, and the resolution carried. Ravenel also accepted appointment to committees to inspect growing crops and to study the problem of crop rotation. The latter committee had a chemical analysis made of cotton, corn, and sweet potatoes to determine the best means of rotating the three crops. According to the then-recent work of Justus Liebig, minerals were crucial to the development of plants. Even soils rich in organic matter could be infertile if deficient in particular minerals. Fertility could be preserved by crop rotation arranged so that plants that excreted certain minerals were followed by plants that needed those minerals for healthy growth. Soil analyst Charles Upham Shepard, a New Englander who taught chemistry part time at the South Carolina Medical College, carried out the investigations and reported to the Black Oak Society in 1846.[8]

As secretary, Ravenel in December 1842 read a paper before the State Agricultural Society in Columbia. It described the work of the Black Oak planters and encouraged other local societies to take up similar experiments. Ravenel began with a description of the soils of Saint John's, using the type of native forest growth to characterize the quality of the soil and its location with respect to rivers or ridges. Apparent in his discussion was a naturalist's knowledge of wild plants and awareness of ecological succession. Already capable of using occasional Latin binomials, Ravenel also demonstrated the good judgment to use English names in ordinary prose, as when he spoke of forest succession. "Whenever the pine has had possession for any length of time, and fires are excluded, a young growth of oak, hickory, gum, or of some other plant, which indicates good land, invariably springs up; and at the time the pines are disappearing from old age, this second growth is ready to take possession of the soil." Replacement of pines by hardwoods, Ravenel noted, was consistent with Liebig's theories concerning the exhaustion of particular nutrients from soil by long-continued growth of one plant. His discussion of the action of quicklime, slaked lime, and marl as fertilizers also indicated knowledge of Humphrey Davy's *Elements of Agricultural Chemistry in a Course of Lectures for the Board of Agriculture* (London, 1813) and of the work of some of Davy's American disciples, including Charles T. Jackson, Edmund Ruffin, and C. U. Shepard. In reading their contributions, Ravenel reaped the benefits of his college acquaintance with chemistry.

As intended, Ravenel's *Memoir* also described crops grown in Saint John's, especially the Santee cotton. In addition, Ravenel touched on a theme that in the following two decades would become common in southern agricultural and states' rights literature. The soil of Saint John's, he asserted, was quite capable of producing crops other than the three or four usual staples. He urged diversification for South

Carolina agriculture, suggesting a return to indigo culture and mentioning silk, tobacco, wheat, and castor beans as valuable additional
crops. Ravenel suggested, as well, that rice production could be expanded by planting in the inland swamps, a habitat abundantly available in Saint John's.[9]

Diversification and renewal of southern agriculture was a rallying
cry for men anticipating secession, who saw agricultural reform as
the key to establishing within the borders of the slave states an economy capable of serving an independent country. James Henry Hammond, already noted in the early 1840s as a hotheaded secessionist,
organized the State Agricultural Society in 1839 to rouse interest in
the revitalization of South Carolina agriculture. When he was elected
governor in 1842, he turned for help with his pet project to Edmund
Ruffin, Virginia's prophet of marl, whose advice had aided Hammond
in restoring fertility to his own worn-out plantation. Ruffin was
invited to come to South Carolina to conduct a survey of marl beds
and to instruct planters and farmers in the use of the valuable calcareous
earth. The invitation reached him when he was sunk in self-pity over
Virginia's lack of appreciation of his efforts on her behalf, and he
accepted with alacrity. Armed with five hundred copies of his *Essay
on Calcareous Manures* (Petersburg, 1832) to distribute along with his
words of wisdom, the new state agricultural surveyor of South Carolina took up his task.[10]

Ruffin's duties as agricultural surveyor of South Carolina occupied
him for the greater part of 1843 and brought him into direct contact
with many of the state's planters. He needed to persuade them of the
value of his work, for he realized that the success of the survey
depended on help from others. By himself Ruffin could never perform
the extensive and detailed observation necessary to bring the survey
to completion. Through Whitemarsh Seabrook, president of the State
Agricultural Society, he appealed to local societies for aid. Their response was gratifying, and several submitted reports on the marl beds
of their area in time for inclusion in Ruffin's report to Hammond.

Gentlemen of the Black Oak Agricultural Society were among
those who offered help, and most prominent among them was Ravenel. Already well enough impressed with Ruffin's *Essay* to cite it in
his 1842 memoir to the State Agricultural Society, Ravenel naturally

was interested in the Virginian's survey work. He provided marl samples from Northampton and apparently tested them and other samples for carbonate of lime. In addition, he kept his eyes open for any signs of marl and passed his observations on to Ruffin. If Ravenel appreciated Ruffin's work, it is equally clear that Ruffin appreciated Ravenel. He credited Ravenel in his report on the agricultural survey, and he also expressed his regard for Ravenel privately. In May 1843 he wrote to Ravenel of his desire to organize a group of South Carolina planters to travel to Virginia to see Ruffin's results with marl. "I should be particularly gratified," Ruffin pleaded, "if you would join in the visit—& I know no one whom it would more benefit, or who could by it do more public good to S. Ca." If Ravenel could finance his own transportation to Coggins Point, Ruffin and his son would pay his expenses in Virginia.[11]

Ruffin's visit to the Saint John's area stimulated the interest of local planters in marl and other fertilizers. Frederick Porcher had begun a successful trial of marl on seventeen acres in 1840, but the other Saint John's planters did not follow his example until Ruffin spread the gospel in 1843, whereupon Philip Porcher commenced an experiment with the new fertilizer. Keeping one acre of a seven-acre field unmarled for comparison, he applied marl to the remaining six acres at the rate of 250 or 130 bushels per acre and obtained encouraging results. On another six-acre field, he applied 120 bushels of marl per acre, together with stable manure and ground cottonseed, and reaped twenty bushels of corn per acre. Application of an additional 100 bushels of marl per acre the following year resulted in a yield of forty-four bushels of corn per acre. Two other planters also began experiments but kept less accurate records of their efforts. S. G. Darant achieved an apparent four- or fivefold increase in cotton production on a fifteen-acre tract, and Robert Mazyck approximately doubled his cotton crop on his experimental field. In a letter dated November 22, 1844, Ravenel communicated to the State Agricultural Society the results of these experiments by Black Oak planters and told the society that about twelve hundred acres of land had been marled in his locality during the past year. By the following spring, he expected the acreage to double. Ravenel evinced great enthusiasm for marl, writing, "A vast mine of agricultural wealth has been unfolded, which only requires the energy and industry of the planter to be made available." If he undertook any such experiments, and it is hard to think why he would not, he did not describe them.[12]

Popular though marl became, it did not replace other, more traditional fertilizers. In a series of complicated trials carried on in 1844 and 1845, Thomas Peyre used various combinations of marl from a number of different plantations, stable manure, cottonseed, gypsum, bone dust, urine, and oak ashes. Frederick Porcher, in a report read to the Black Oak Agricultural Society November 19, 1844, particularly recommended horse manure, gypsum, cottonseed, and oak ashes as fertilizer for cotton.[13]

Ruffin's agricultural survey temporarily focused an unusual amount of geological attention on Saint John's. Marl is composed of clay combined with fossil shells, some microscopically small, others much larger. Excavation of a number of marl beds in the area yielded fossils interesting from the point of view of their taxonomy and useful as an indication of the age of various deposits. Ruffin realized that the study of such fossils would be a useful tool in categorizing groups of marl beds varying in their value as fertilizer. He began a private collection of fossil shells in Virginia, and his report to the governor of South Carolina indicated a fairly detailed knowledge of marl bed geology, including acquaintance with the work of Charles Lyell (1797–1875) and of South Carolina geologists Edmund Ravenel (1797–1871) and Michael Tuomey (1805–1857).[14]

Scientists, like agriculturists, found the marl bed excavations interesting. Robert Gibbes's controversy with Richard Owen was sparked by an odd fossil animal discovered in the marl pits of Robert Mazyck's plantation. Edmund Ravenel also found specimens to interest him in marling operations on his own plantation, the Grove, located only a few miles outside of Charleston, and he made several trips to Saint John's, where he inspected the local marl beds. Henry Ravenel took advantage of Edmund's visits to renew his acquaintance with this elder, distant cousin and onetime hunting companion whose medical practice had removed him from his home in Saint John's to Charleston and the Grove. They shared fossil-hunting expeditions and discussions on marl geology, and when Edmund returned to his practice, he wrote back to Henry with a list of recommended works on geology. The older cousin strongly recommended Charles Lyell's *Elements of Geology* (London, 1838) and the works of Samuel Morton, including his papers in the *Journal* of the Academy of Natural Sciences of Philadelphia. Edmund also recommended that his cousin peruse *Silliman's Journal* for its many valuable papers on American geology and William Buckland's Bridgewater Treatise reconciling geological discoveries and Christian theology, which he thought "quite a remarkable work." In the hope of setting up an exchange, Edmund also sent a box of shells to "assist you in your Studies of one of the most dilightful [*sic*] branches of Natural History."[15]

Edmund Ravenel's apparent desire to turn Henry into a geologist was doomed to frustration. Instead, a chance meeting in 1842 or 1843 transformed Henry's recreational interest in plants into a self-appointed task which, in the intensity of its demands, prevented him from developing more than a mild interest in any other science. The transformation was begun by a visit from a traveling naturalist named Olmstead who initiated Ravenel "in the mode of making collections, & so interested me in the subject that I commenced then to collect & study."[16]

Neil Stevens has tentatively identified the visitor as Charles Hyde Olmstead of East Hartford, Connecticut, who, Stevens wrote, was known to have made a botanizing trip to the South about this time. His exact identity is relatively unimportant, however. There was in the 1840s no botanist of importance named Olmstead, and there is no indication of continued correspondence between Ravenel and Olmstead, so any mutual influence was exerted during a very short period of time.[17] Within those few days Olmstead stirred Ravenel's interest to new proportions by teaching the planter proper methods for the drying, mounting, and preserving of plant specimens.

If a flowering plant is to be useful year after year as an object of scientific study, it must be dried flat, with a minimum of wrinkling, bending, or twisting. A small branch, or a few leaves, should be turned so that the underside is exposed to view. If the plant is not prohibitively large, the entire specimen should be preserved, roots and all, and several individuals, showing all stages of development, should be collected. After the plant is thoroughly dry, it must be mounted on heavy paper and kept safe from the depredations of rodents and insects.

These procedures, though simple, were not obvious to the uninitiated, and in the nineteenth century they were often the subject of correspondence as older botanists coached the younger ones who sent them specimens for naming. Exchange of specimens was an immensely valuable form of nonverbal communication, for a specimen could tell another scientist things that its collector had not even noticed. Both because of the importance of such specimens and because of the hazards encountered in sending them to other scientists, proper collecting technique was crucial. Shipment of specimens from Ravenel to colleagues in the North or Europe could take two months or more, and plants improperly mounted or packed were liable to be damaged during the long trip.[18] Specimens arriving broken, detached from their labels, or chewed by mice would be next to useless to their recipient, and those retained by the collector would have no more value if they were allowed to deteriorate. Olmstead's lessons in collecting technique were thus invaluable, but he had more to teach than technique. He also conveyed the idea that Ravenel's botany was valuable and interesting to others and worth cultivating as more than a hobby.

When Olmstead left, Ravenel's newly strengthened interest was sustained by neighbors who had also become involved in collecting plants, some, perhaps, through the influence of the same Mr. Olmstead. Francis Peyre Porcher, Ravenel's younger friend from Sarazens Plantation, was attending South Carolina College at the time of Olmstead's visit. He graduated from that institution in 1844 and went on to take the M.D. from the Medical College of South Carolina in Charleston in 1847. Summer vacations gave him time to go on collecting excursions with his neighbor Ravenel. Isabella Porcher, Francis's mother, may also have been an inspiring presence, but it was her brother, Walter Peyre, a friend of Ravenel's for many years, who accompanied him on many collecting trips. Ravenel's much younger sister, Rowena, remembered later how the two men would go off botanizing together and happily bear home specimens that she, at least, thought quite uninteresting. Peyre even lived with Ravenel in Pinopolis through the summer of 1844.[19]

Of more long-term significance to Ravenel was the assistance and encouragement of the Reverend Cranmore Wallace. Born in Atworth, New Hampshire, in 1802, Wallace came to South Carolina as a young man to take charge of a school at Cheraw. Ordained a minister of the Protestant Episcopal church in 1836, Wallace held various teaching and ministerial positions until 1842, when he was appointed rector of Saint Stephen's Parish, the Episcopal parish to which people of Upper and Middle Saint John's then belonged.[20] He played no more than a small part in the history of botany, for his parish duties were so demanding that he actually had less time to devote to the science in the three or so years immediately following his move to Saint Stephen's than he had earlier. Yet, during his years in the parish, especially during 1846 and 1847, he maintained an herbarium, did some collecting, and entered into a botanical correspondence with another young Episcopal minister named Moses Ashley Curtis.

Wallace and Ravenel traded specimens and conferred on matters of identification and useful literature. Ravenel's herbarium of this period, now preserved at the Charleston Museum, contains a few of Wallace's specimens, and Wallace's herbarium, or the portion of it that has survived, contains many examples from Ravenel's collections.[21] In addition to Francis Peyre Porcher, Isabella Porcher, Walter Peyre, and Cranmore Wallace, there was an unnamed young lady botanist, one of Wallace's parishioners.[22] With Ravenel included, this group was large enough to provide effective encouragement of each other's interest, and of the six, two went on to become significant botanists.

Encouragement from others was vital to the dramatic deepening of Ravenel's interest in botany that occurred in the early 1840s. Little less important to any botanist are the tools of his trade. Collecting equipment—a knife, a trowel, blotting paper, a basket or some other container—was cheap and readily available, but books were much harder to come by. Most were expensive and few were suited to a novice student. Amos Eaton's *Manual of Botany* (Albany, 1829, many later editions) had fallen into disfavor among botanists for its simplistic presentation of Linnaean sexual taxonomy and its neglect both of plant physiology and of the natural taxonomy of Bernard and Antoine de Jussieu. In 1836 a young Harvard University botanist, Asa Gray, published *Elements of Botany* (New York), which replaced Eaton's *Manual* in his classroom, but it, too, had flaws. Gray's treatise included information on plant physiology, but it was inadequate as a field guide. Moreover, both Gray and Eaton were northerners, and neither treated knowingly or fully the characteristic flora of the South. The best southern flora was Stephen Elliott's *Sketch of the Botany of South Carolina and Georgia* (Charleston, 1821–1824), but this two-volume work, written in both Latin and English, would not have been an easy book for a beginner. Nevertheless, until 1860 it remained the standard source on the botany of the South. Although Elliott's *Sketch* followed the Linnaean system, it was accepted by his botanical contemporaries, escaping the disrepute heaped upon Eaton for that offense, perhaps because when Elliott died in 1830 he had the good grace to be working on an appendix utilizing the natural system.[23]

With Elliott's *Sketch* as his surest field companion, Ravenel entered a very exciting period of his career. Every new plant was an adventure, and its identification a triumph. Frederick Porcher later wrote admiringly of Ravenel's "patient industry and habits of observation" during this early period. "He never left home without a satchel or convenient paste-board box in which he collected whatsoever struck his eye. He would take it home and there diligently examine and study it, and record it, if it had not already been noticed by his predecessors."[24]

Plants collected and studied in this manner were stored away to create an herbarium, which, like books and the simple tools of collecting, was an indispensable aid to a botanist and a resource that would become more valuable with each passing season of collecting. Unfortunately, Ravenel lost plants, books, and other personal belongings in the first winter after he began his serious botanical work. Fire broke out in the middle of the night and burned Northampton to its foundation. The family, including on that night Ravenel's stepmother and her younger children, all escaped the house safely, but the whole plant collection and most of Ravenel's books went up in flames. The Ravenels moved to Pooshee, where they lived for the next few winters until Northampton was rebuilt.[25]

Ravenel's calm, sensible personality did not let him remain long discouraged over his loss. He began collecting with renewed vigor the following spring and by 1846 had achieved familiarity with the *phanerogams,* a term used by contemporary botanists to describe plants with sexual organs visible to the naked eye, in other words, the flowering or seed-bearing plants. These relatively large and showy plants, including herbs, trees, and shrubs, were the usual first objects of study for young botanists. They were distinguished as a group from plants such as the mosses, lichens, ferns, and fungi, which reproduce by spores readily observable only with a microscope. To these, the cryptogams, Ravenel began to turn some of his attention in 1846. When he did so he, like all interested in this area, ventured into a little-studied field. Where was he to begin, and where could he turn for help?

If Ravenel had not yet discovered the value of correspondence with other scientists and of exchanging small favors with them, he soon did. A box of shells dutifully sent to his kinsman Edmund along with a letter mentioning his new interest in mosses produced an enthusiastic reply. Two pages on geology were followed by a rambling paragraph on botany:

I am gratified that you are attending to the Mosses—I have always looked at them with much interest, & once hoped that our own Species would have been illustrated by Mr. S. Elliott, he was long in correspondence with Schweinitz upon the Subject, & received from him quite an extensive collection of European Speceis [sic], & must have written much upon our own, as he habitually thought upon paper—but what has become of his Notes upon this branch I have never heard.[26]

What a tempting possibility! If Edmund did not know what had become of Elliott's material, Henry apparently was pretty sure. Edmund's letter was written on the fourteenth of December and hand-carried to Henry. On the fifteenth Henry fired off a letter to John Bachman, Lutheran minister and noted mammologist in Charleston, who also replied with speed: "The Herbarium of Elliott is still in my possession & it will afford me great pleasure to assist you in comparing your plants with it. My own Herbarium is rather more full than that of Elliott & has been compared with the other. Both are in one room & both very freely at your service. . . . Come in the mornings—take pot luck with me & work all day." This generous offer had but one small string attached. Could Ravenel perhaps obtain some pregnant opossums during the coming spring?[27]

Another South Carolinian who encouraged Ravenel during this period was State Geological Surveyor Michael Tuomey. Ravenel may have met the Irish-born geologist on the edge of a marl pit, introduced by their mutual friend Edmund Ruffin. Each recognized the other as a potential source of help, though their major interests lay in separate fields. Ravenel helped Tuomey collect fossils from the Pooshee marl beds and apparently sent him botanical specimens occasionally. For his part, Tuomey wrote friendly letters to Ravenel describing unusual plants he had seen.[28]

Ravenel also began to write to Harvard's Asa Gray, sending his first letter through Benjamin Silliman, whose *Journal* featured many articles and short notices from Gray's pen. Gray soon responded. As usual for the Cambridge botanist, he was willing to help. If Ravenel would send as full a set of his duplicate plants as possible, Gray would name them, select some for his own herbarium, and pass the others on to two other northeastern botanists. He also asked Ravenel for lichens, probably thinking of his fellow Massachusetts botanist Edward Tuckerman. For mosses, Gray suggested that Ravenel try Ohio's William Starling Sullivant, who would likely be glad to correspond, and as though proof were needed of his sincerity, he sent to Ravenel a copy of the text of Sullivant's *Musci Alleghanienses* (Columbus, Ohio, 1846) which he had just reviewed favorably in *Silliman's Journal*.[29]

Bringing American botanists into contact with others of similar interest in their own country and in Europe, as Gray had begun to do for Ravenel, was one of the Harvard botanist's most important contributions to botany. By the 1840s the science had already become so multifaceted that no one individual could contribute personally to more than a few of its branches. Yet Gray, a specialist in American, particularly northeastern, phanerogamic botany, served other branches ably through his extensive network of personal contacts and his constant willingness to aid others who shared his commitment to botanical science.

Gray, Tuomey, and Cranmore Wallace were all in touch with an Episcopal clergyman and botanist in Hillsboro, North Carolina. Moses Ashley Curtis, like Ravenel, had begun his botanical study with the phanerogams. Two early publications, "Enumeration of Plants Growing Spontaneously around Wilmington, North Carolina," (1835) and "Account of Some New and Rare Plants of North Carolina," (1843) both dealt almost exclusively with the flowering plants. By 1845, however, he had become interested in the cryptogams, appar-

Moses Ashley Curtis, 1858 (Courtesy of South Caroliniana Library,
Columbia, South Carolina)

ently at the urging of Edward Tuckerman, who wrote to him in October to propose an exchange of lichens from North Carolina for named species from New England. Curtis accepted Tuckerman's proposal and became a willing collector of lichens, joking with Gray in December, "I am not sure but I have deranged my head somewhat (I am sure I have my fingers) in getting Lichens off my firewood for Tuckerman. I am getting interested in these things, which I have long wanted the means of understanding."[30]

By 1846 Curtis was so interested in the cryptogams that he began casting about for another cryptogamic correspondent. Tuckerman, Curtis was certain, could help him out of any difficulties he encountered with the lichens, but he asked Gray, "can I get the like help on the Fungi? Can you introduce me to any botanist, American or foreign, who understands these things & will exchange with me, or will name my specimens for the gift of them?"[31] Gray recommended the British mycologist Miles Joseph Berkeley and the Swede Elias Magnus Fries.

When Ravenel wrote to Gray the following August, he, knowing of Curtis's interest in the fungi, recommended Curtis as a correspondent for Ravenel. This reinforced Tuomey's suggestion of a year earlier that Ravenel write to Curtis, and Wallace had apparently been saying the same thing. So on September 8, 1846, Ravenel wrote the first letter of what would be a long correspondence with the North Carolina botanist. He desired, Ravenel wrote, to exchange and compare all their plants, of which he had some eight or nine hundred, including lichens, ferns, and fungi. He would begin by sending Curtis the duplicates left after he made up packages for Tuomey and Gray.[32]

Ravenel's letter could not have been entirely unexpected. Curtis had heard of him from Tuomey, and Wallace had written of him in glowing terms only days before, calling him "a young gentleman of great industry & sagacity, who has nearly exhausted the phaenogamous plants of this Parish. If he lives, I see not why he should not equal Macbride or Elliott in acquirements. He is at the same time an excellent planter & a devout communicant of the Church." Wallace then mentioned that Ravenel had some plants that he wished Curtis to determine.[33] At about the same time that Ravenel wrote to Curtis, days before he received the letter, Curtis sent a message through Wallace indicating his own willingness to begin a correspondence.[34]

Ravenel's letter to Curtis suggested exchange and comparison, Ravenel apparently anticipating a trade in which he and Curtis would participate as equals. Curtis hardly possessed the sort of reputation that made Ravenel somewhat deferential towards Gray, nor did he, so far as Ravenel knew, have the resources to make a collector-authority relationship worth Ravenel's while. In his response, Curtis hastened to lay his cards on the table. He confessed himself a beginner and admitted that he expected it to take some years before he was an accomplished mycologist. He had, however, secured the assistance of Berkeley, "the finest Mycologist in Great Britain," and hoped also to enlist the aid of Fries. Sullivant and Tuckerman were among his correspondents, and with the help of these worthies, he expected to accomplish something of value. "If I am successful," he continued, "I may elaborate all the known American species, & furnish a Mycologia Americana, which is a great desideratum." Ravenel's role, as Curtis then saw it, was to contribute specimens from South Carolina and wait patiently while Curtis or his correspondents examined and identified them. Unlike Gray who freely suggested correspondence with others, Curtis wanted to act as a go-between, reserving to himself a direct relationship with the main authorities in the field.[35]

At the same time, Curtis was quite deferential to those authorities and seemed, perhaps because of his own position as a New Englander transplanted to the South, to be convinced that foreigners and northerners could do a better job on the fungi than he could, with or without Ravenel's help. In November 1846 he asked Gray to try to persuade William Oakes to devote himself to the fungi, even suggesting that Oakes produce the desired Mycologia Americana. "He shall have all my aid, if he will fairly give himself to the work. I am accumulating material & knowledge pretty well, & am in fine humor with the subject. I only want a little more sympathy from some one or two good fellows. Berkeley is too far off for frequent conference."[36] The hierarchical scheme that Curtis envisioned could work, with considerable softening of the corners, for a correspondent like Wallace, whose botanical interest was little more than a hobby. For a serious student like Ravenel, however, it was doomed to failure. From Ravenel's other correspondents, especially Gray, would come suggestions and invitations to enter into exchange with an ever-widening circle of other botanists, including the very men whose correspondence Curtis so cherished. In fact, only a month after Curtis appealed to Gray to enlist Oakes as a mycologist, Gray wrote to Ravenel. Both Oakes and Stephen Thayer Olney would gladly exchange with Ravenel, Gray believed. Oakes, he said, had a large collection but was slow; Olney was prompt "and a truly good fellow."[37]

Curtis's attempts to dominate Ravenel eventually led to a sometimes unpleasant, low-key rivalry between them. At first, however, it was reasonably justifiable. Though Curtis's lead was not large, he was the more experienced man, and Ravenel undoubtedly realized that he had much to gain by accepting the role assigned him, for Curtis was by no means miserly with his help. His first letter contained advice on literature. If Ravenel could find it, the "Synopsis fungorum Carolinae superioris" of Lewis David von Schweinitz, published in Leipzig in 1822, was valuable, as was his more accessible "Synopsis fungorum in America boreali media degentium," in the *Transactions* of the American Philosophical Society for 1832. Also essential to the study of fungi were Fries's *Systema Mycologicum* (3 vols.; Lund and Gryphiswald, 1821–1832) and *Elenchis Fungorum* (Gryphiswald, 1828). "If you are willing to go to *any* expense for books, Greville's Illustrations of the Cryptogamiae of Scotland with finely drawn figures & analyses would be a great assistance. I never saw it. It costs some $50!" Curtis dismissed Eaton as "a quack. His Botany has been only valuable because we have had no other Manual." As an afterthought Curtis recommended Kurt Sprengel's *Botany* as a cheaper and therefore perhaps preferable alternative to Fries's *Systema*.[38]

Curtis also commented on the preservation of fungi. Drier species could best be saved in alcohol, though this method was objectionably expensive and required too much room. Fleshy fungi, the mushrooms, could best be preserved by pressing between sheets of blotting paper. Good results could not be guaranteed, for the specimens lost shape, faded, and had to be coated with poison to protect against insects. To make determination of such preserved specimens easier, Ravenel should be sure to note the color and dryness or moistness of the various parts, the color of the spores, whether or not the gills attached to the stipe, and whether the stipe were solid or hollow. A note on the habitat was also desirable.[39]

A flurry of correspondence ensued between Curtis and Ravenel, and the latter did his best to provide a large number of specimens for study and to be sent on to Curtis's correspondents. In June 1847 Curtis assured Gray that "Ravenel is constantly sending, & is collecting vigarously [*sic*]."[40]

Many of the letters touched on the same two problems on which Curtis had advised Ravenel in his first, that is, the preservation of fungi and botanical literature. Fleshy agarics, the gilled fungi such as common table mushrooms, presented the worst problems for preservation. They disfigured too badly on drying, Ravenel complained. Ignoring Curtis's considerate counsel that alcohol was too expensive, Ravenel experimented with whiskey as a preservative. To stop the rapid and seemingly inevitable degeneration of the inky cap mushrooms, he tried very rapid drying of younger specimens, but without success. He also had trouble with insects eating his fungi but found that a concoction of the roots and berries of pride-of-India would discourage them. A shelved cabinet made especially for fungi storage helped with organization. Ravenel took his correspondent's advice and ordered Fries's works. When they had not arrived in time for the spring collecting in 1847, he complained that he felt "as if my hands were tied & I was groping in the dark." That fall he ordered Greville's beautifully illustrated volumes.[41]

It soon became ob·vious that the study of fungi would require a microscope as well. The many small details to be observed and the need to determine spore coloration in order to fit the gilled fungi into the proper group according to Fries's organization made some kind of magnification imperative. "Without good glasses how do you find specific differences between these little items of organized matter?" Ravenel mused. Even without a microscope, he demonstrated a good eye for detail, however. "Well what do you make of those Sphaenoidal dots on the upper surface [of *Aecidium pynatum*]?" he asked Curtis, for example. Still, he would like to own a microscope, if not too costly. When, after trying for months, Russell's bookstore in Charleston was unable to find a doublet, a then-popular type of simple microscope consisting of one double lens, Ravenel asked Curtis to try to get him one through Berkeley. Berkeley apparently also had some trouble finding one and sent back a recommendation for a microscope by Chevalier, a French manufacturer, but the cost was more than Ravenel could afford in the fall of 1848. He repeated his desire for a doublet exactly like that sent by Berkeley to Curtis. Only if it couldn't be had, would he try to get a Chevalier.[42]

Identification and technical details concerning the specimens each collected, and particularly those sent by Ravenel to Curtis, were the most common topics of their discussions. For one who confessed a former horror even of touching fungi, which had reminded him of toads and lizards, Ravenel quickly developed an appreciation of their beauty. The variety of their colors amazed him ("I believe the most fanciful calico printer would be at fault in imitating their changeful hues"), and the growth of the tiny plants was reason for praising God. Close observation of the variations among them developed his understanding of the different degrees of similarity that might place two individuals in the same species, the same genus, or entirely different genera. Curtis's help in identifying plants and correcting errors was especially valuable in this early period, and in Ravenel he had an apt pupil. By July 1847 the pupil even ventured to question the teacher. Curtis had identified one of Ravenel's plants as *Cantharellus cornucopioides.* "But can it be a Cantharellus?" Ravenel asked. "It has no lammellae or pores & the outer, which I take for the fruit bearing surface, is merely roughened as in Tremella—See my 'C. cibarius' (No. 171). There is no generic character by which these two plants can be assimilated."[43]

Ravenel's doubts may have indicated that he had studied a publication either not owned or slighted by Curtis. After receiving in October 1847 a copy of Gray's 1835 monograph on *Rhynchospora,* a genus of Cyperaceae, the sedge family, Ravenel in December questioned Curtis's determination of some plants of that genus. At the same time, a look at Augustin Pyramus and Alphonse de Candolle's *Prodromus* made him wonder about four species, all referred to one species by de Candolle. Worried that Curtis might not be receptive to his thoughts, he hastened to assure him that he freely expressed his doubts and questions only in the interests of "eliciting information & establishing truth." The arrival of his European mycological books in February 1848 helped considerably. Greville's plates he thought were "splendidly executed," and by May they had already proved useful. Ravenel found an inky cap mushroom of unusually large size and identified it with the help of one of the Scottish illustrations as a probable variety of *Coprinus comatus.*[44]

Increasing ability and familiarity with botanical literature brought a similar increase in self-confidence and a desire to enter directly into correspondence with Curtis's own contacts. Evidently through the agency of Gray, Ravenel had been in direct contact with William S. Sullivant in early 1847 and had passed along to Curtis some of Sullivant's knowledge on mosses.[45] Ravenel wished, in addition, to establish contact with a European mycologist and may have brought the subject up while visiting at Curtis's new home in Society Hill, South Carolina, in March 1848. Curtis still wanted to act as Berkeley's sole American agent, but he brought Ravenel's request to Berkeley's attention and suggested the French botanist Camille Montagne as a possible correspondent. Berkeley preferred to suggest his own new co-worker, Christopher Broome. Curtis was agreeable and arranged with Berkeley that Ravenel and Broome should exchange specimens with each other. Ravenel, Curtis said, would send only determined specimens. "All his *unknown* species come to me, & thence to yourself. At my suggestion he will send abroad no unnamed species." While arranging for the exchange between Ravenel and Broome, Curtis tried to squelch whatever desire Berkeley may have had for direct communication with Ravenel, but his words may inadvertently have made the idea sound tempting. "I will say again, in reference to Ravenel," he wrote, "it will be no advantage to *you* to concern yourself at all about his proposal, because all his species of any interest to you will go to you through my hands. He has lately made me a visit of some days, bringing several hundred species, some of them very fine, & new to me."[46]

Ravenel assured Curtis that he would be pleased to have Broome's address. In July he asked Curtis about the possibility of direct communication with Berkeley, but Curtis put him off. A seven-week collecting trip through northern Georgia found Ravenel back in Pineville in late October and ready to begin his exchange with Broome. He also expected to assume a more equal role with Curtis in the description of new species. Apparently unaware of Curtis's agreement with Berkeley that he should send only determined species to Broome, Ravenel explained to Curtis his intention to send to Broome only such plants as had not already been sent to Berkeley so that the two Englishmen would not separately describe the same plant. With regard to any sent to Berkeley in the future, Ravenel desired to put in a joint claim with the English mycologist, though Ravenel and Curtis should share credit for species they discovered together. He also wrote that he was sending Broome's first package to Curtis to be forwarded to England, but would Curtis please send Broome's address.[47]

Curtis's reply to Ravenel's stated intentions has not survived, but it was evidently scathing. Ravenel wrote back in tones of injured innocence. He acknowledged the debt he owed Curtis for his assistance and encouragement and assured him of his satisfaction with the disposition that had been made of his specimens. He expressed appreciation for the compliment Curtis had paid him by acknowledging his contribution in a November article in *Silliman's Journal*. As for the joint claim he had hoped to have on new species, had Curtis not mentioned laying down a claim to some sent in his last package to Berkeley? Was such a claim entirely without foundation when he or Curtis might find a plant, examine and describe it fully in its fresh state, search for it diligently in literature at their disposal, and only then send it, along with a description and provisional name, to a European mycologist for his opinion, which could, in such a new science, prove wrong in any case? Should providing an opinion transfer all credit away from the discoverer and first describer, especially when the very characteristics upon which the new species would be founded might be unclear in the preserved specimen and have to be taken from the description of the fresh plant? If this was common usage, Ravenel was ignorant of it, but he was willing to adhere to the rules. He closed with a curt remark that he would make up a package for Broome containing only ascertained species.[48]

Curtis wrote to soothe Ravenel, and relations were soon cordial again. Ravenel was willing to settle back into the role of faithful collector, at least temporarily: "Your last letter has made me feel quite easy again & I shall continue to send you my collections, perfectly satisfied with whatever disposition Berkeley & yourself may make of them. . . . As long as I continue to send, it will be with this understanding, that they are wholly at your disposal."[49] Yet, although Ravenel agreed to resume his old relationship with Curtis, he was not cowed by his somewhat authoritarian colleague. Less than a month after the unpleasant incident, he expressed disagreement with Berkeley's identifications of two species.[50]

Seven years later Ravenel had come to see the wisdom in the rules laid down by Curtis, and he passed them on to another young botanist whom he was helping: "It is customary among Botanists, that those who receive & name plants for beginners, describe also any new species that may occur—this is only just & proper. As you have been sending a large number of things to me, should you also send the same things to Fries or any other Botanists, there will undoubtedly be confusion in the matter for the same thing may be described under different names." Once the plants were named, the beginner could make up sets for distribution to as many scientists as he desired, without fear of causing confusion. Of course, any botanist capable of determining and naming new species by himself would also have the privilege of publishing them, but that was not possible on a large scale, Ravenel believed, for American mycologists. "Our means in this country," he noted, "are too limited for that full comparison which should precede the publication of a species as new. We are compelled to obtain aid from the older European Mycologists who have been making these things their study for half a century & who have large collections from all parts of the world."[51]

Despite the resistance he experienced in trying to establish communication with Berkeley, the number of Ravenel's botanical correspondents grew dramatically during the late 1840s. Edward Tuckerman was one of the most valuable of them. Though two years younger than Ravenel, he had begun serious botanical work at a much earlier age and thus was ahead of Ravenel in developing expertise among his favorite plants, the lichens. By 1845, when he persuaded Curtis to begin collecting lichens for him, the young resident graduate of Harvard, as he styled himself, had decided that these small plants were to be his life's work and that he could not afford to devote time or attention to any others. The interest, however, was even then not a new one. Tuckerman had begun to make his reputation in lichenology as early as 1839 and 1840 with the publication of a short series of articles in the *Boston Journal of Natural History.*[52]

Tuckerman had received a share of the lichens sent by Ravenel to

Ravenel's home at Northampton, sketched in pencil by Lewis R. Gibbes, 1852 (Courtesy of Charleston Museum; original enhanced with ink and watercolor by Albert E. Sanders, 1986)

Edward Tuckerman, ca. 1867–1869 (Courtesy of South Caroliniana Library, Columbia, South Carolina)

Gray with other plants in 1846, and it would have been very strange indeed had he not desired to open a direct tap to a new source of lichens. Tuckerman, in fact, had special reasons to desire communication with Ravenel. He was openly curious about the lichens of the South and had evident ambitions to be recognized as an authority of national proportions. In addition, his correspondence with Curtis had proven less than satisfactory. When preparing a package for Tuckerman, Curtis would rifle through his large box of recently collected specimens, often selecting things quite at random and sending them off without examination and in excessively large quantities. This careless approach meant that he often sent the same species on several occasions without recognizing the fact. In August 1848 he received embarrassing complaints from Tuckerman for having sent in his last package as many fungi as lichens. In July 1848 the exasperated Tuckerman began a correspondence with Ravenel, whose collections had already won praise and a promise of European plants from Asa Gray.[53]

Correspondence with Tuckerman gave Ravenel an alternative to Curtis as a connection with European cryptogamic botany. When the Massachusetts botanist wrote that he was preparing for a lengthy trip to Europe and offered to take some of Ravenel's plants, the South Carolinian jumped at the chance. He sent off another bundle of plants and particularly urged Tuckerman to take one strange specimen, which he had thought a fungus but which Curtis had opined was a lichen. He also asked Tuckerman to record the title and place of publication of European works on fungi and to give out his name and address to anyone mentioning a desire to trade specimens, especially Fries. "If M. Fries would accept a full sett of my Fungi & give me his opinion upon them, it would be only a partial return to him for the great profit I have derived from his works on this order."[54]

In phanerogamic botany, also, Ravenel's correspondence and expertise increased. As early as 1846 Ravenel had had in mind the compilation of a catalogue of the plants of Saint John's. Impetus in this direction came from his friend and botanizing companion Frank Porcher, who had chosen the medical botany of South Carolina as his thesis topic at the Medical College of South Carolina. He graduated in 1847, taking top honors in his class, and his thesis was chosen by the faculty for publication. Ravenel helped on the project, allowing

Porcher access to his own herbarium and catalogue so as to include a number of grasses and other plants that his friend had not seen. He also arranged for Gray to examine and send an opinion on Ravenel's plants, and when the opinion was slow in coming wrote to the Harvard botanist to urge haste. The "Medico-Botanical Catalogue of the Plants and Ferns of St. John's, Berkeley, South Carolina," appeared in the May and July numbers of the *Charleston Medical Journal and Review* and included Gray's determinations, which arrived just barely in time. Porcher included a warm acknowledgment of Ravenel's help in determining species and adapting Elliott's species to the nomenclature used by Eaton and, more especially, by John Torrey and Asa Gray. Ravenel's pleasure at his friend's success and the kind words was marred, however, by disappointment at the large number of typesetting errors that, he feared, made the catalogue nearly worthless.[55]

Ravenel's own first botanical publication (with the exception of a short letter in the *Southern Journal of Medicine and Pharmacy* of 1846) appeared in the *Charleston Medical Journal and Review* in 1849. The brief article, of the type known as a "state record," noted his discovery in South Carolina of a number of phanerogamic plants not previously known in the state. In several cases, the species were only newly established, split off from older species by taxonomic revision. The article, though otherwise unremarkable, does demonstrate the depth of Ravenel's acquaintance with the literature. Walter and Elliott, of course, were the standard references for South Carolina. Ravenel mentioned pioneer botanist André Michaux, but he seemed to be familiar with him only through Elliott. In his introduction Ravenel politely credited both Gray and Curtis for help in determining doubtful species, but the text made clear that John Torrey (1796–1873) and Asa Gray were the systematists to be followed when considering the flowering plants. Gray's revision of the Rhynchosporae, his recent *Manual of the Botany of the Northern States* (Boston, 1848), Torrey's revision of the Cyperaceae (1836), his report on the botany of New York (Albany, 1840), and the *Flora of North America* (New York, 1838–1843), for which Gray and Torrey shared authorship, were all cited as authority for newly established species. Other notations indicated Ravenel's familiarity with the work of two other botanists whose careers and reputations would grow alongside Ravenel's own, George

Engelmann, a German transplanted to St. Louis, and Alvan Wentworth Chapman, a physician in Apalachicola, Florida. Ravenel did
not mention the much-maligned Constantine Samuel Rafinesque in
his article.[56]

John Torrey, whose work on the Cyperaceae had so impressed the
South Carolina botanist, was drafted into the ranks of Ravenel's correspondents in late 1848, when Ravenel took the liberty of shipping
off to him a number of southern members of that family for his
opinion. Torrey was happy to cooperate, and offered rare northern
plants in return, but his responses did not arrive in time to be included
in Ravenel's article. Two little-known botanists, S. B. Mead of Illinois
and Edward Tatnell of Delaware, exchanged plants with Ravenel, and
Olney was quite generous in sending him specimens.[57]

Even as Ravenel's contacts with other botanists increased, the small
group of local collectors, whose companionship had sustained him in
the early 1840s, dwindled away. Following his graduation from medical school, Frank Porcher went to Europe to study for two years.
Cranmore Wallace resigned his ministry in Saint Stephen's Parish
November 1, 1848, and took charge of another Saint Stephen's Church
in Charleston.[58] Walter Peyre's interest apparently faded, and the two
ladies were scarcely suitable companions for a young married man's
strolls through the woods. Ravenel was beginning to see that there
could be advantages to collecting by himself. As he wrote to Curtis
in May 1849, "I sighed once for company in my rambles, but I believe
it is better to be alone—No one would have stood patiently with me
for 5 hours Last Saturday, in a Pineland branch among the Snakes &
red bugs—& all that for only some bits of bark & rotten wood!" At
the same time, however, he was cheered by the affectionate interest of
his three little daughters Lydia, Charlotte, and Henrietta, who, as he
wrote to Curtis, were "large enough to run about & say Agaricus &
Boletus" and who were fond of hunting fungi in hopes of finding
something that their father had not seen before. He could anticipate
similar help soon from little Emily and a son, Henry St. Julien, who
was then only a baby.[59]

His neighbors and other Carolinians received Ravenel's interest in
botany with friendly sympathy. Frederick Porcher's admiration was
plain, while another planter donated specimens of one of the plants

Ravenel treated in his 1849 state record. When Ravenel began to think of publishing the article, he received a very encouraging letter from P. C. Gaillard of the *Charleston Medical Journal and Review,* who declared the *Journal's* willingness to publish the article and praised Ravenel for the example he had set by his interest in science and particularly for the aid he had given Porcher in his well-received thesis.[60]

Members of the Black Oak Agricultural Society also appreciated Ravenel's efforts in science and realized their potential value to agriculture. In 1845, for example, they appointed him, with Morton Waring and Frederick Porcher, to form a committee to study the problem of cotton rust, a destructive disease of then unknown cause. Many people had speculated about possible causes. The Black Oak planters looked to the soil, while Edmund Ruffin blamed "the depredations of myriads of very minute insects." After studying the problem, however, Ravenel became convinced that the agent was a fungus, and he turned some of his attention to the investigation of this and other fungi affecting crops. He also kept tables recording rainfall and temperature, which were published by the Black Oak Agricultural Society, and in 1849 the society published a paper in which he explained in simple terms some of the principles and techniques of meteorology and urged others to collect similar data:

It may be said that, as we have no control over the seasons and weather, such information is useless. We contend that every kind of positive information is useful. If we cannot prevent these causes which affect us injuriously, we can, at any rate, know what they are and how they affect us. It is a notorious fact, that when statistical information is collected and preserved, it is never useless. It sets men to thinking—it opens new lights to them—it gives them often a hint which may be improved to some valuable purpose.[61]

Sympathetic friends and family; contact with Edmund Ravenel, John Bachman, Michael Tuomey, and others of South Carolina's intelligentsia; and correspondence with many of America's prominent botanists brought Ravenel in the 1840s into America's scientific community.

Watershed Years, 1850–1853   **4**

Henry Ravenel's circle of American scientific contacts grew to significant proportions in the 1840s as he became acquainted with established botanists. Valuable though these contacts were, Ravenel coveted direct correspondence with a European authority, but though he began to write to Christopher Broome, the leaders of mycology, Miles Joseph Berkeley, Elias Fries, and Camille Montagne, eluded him.

Efforts to use Curtis or Tuckerman as a go-between largely failed, but when Ravenel acceded to Curtis's wishes and began to send material to Broome, his plants spoke more loudly for him than had either of his friends. By the end of 1849 Berkeley wanted to correspond with Ravenel as badly as Ravenel wanted to correspond with him. "I wish . . . [Ravenel] would send me duplicates of many of his new species," Berkeley wrote to Curtis in December 1849, complaining that he had "mere scraps" of the specimens Broome had received from Ravenel.[1] Curtis could no longer stand in the way, and the elusive contact was soon made. In March 1850 Ravenel took full advantage of the new situation, sending Berkeley the greater part of his undetermined collection and additional samples of a few species that he thought Berkeley might have pronounced on incorrectly.[2]

Also in 1850 Ravenel received public confirmation of his position in the American scientific community. Robert Gibbes wrote to him in January of that year to say he had nominated Ravenel for member-

Miles Joseph Berkeley, 1867 (Courtesy of South Caroliniana Library, Columbia, South Carolina)

ship in two prestigious scientific societies, the Academy of Natural Sciences of Philadelphia, and the American Association for the Advancement of Science. Membership in the AAAS was especially interesting to residents of South Carolina in 1850, for the young association had voted to hold its third meeting in Charleston. For Ravenel it was a rare opportunity to meet other scientists who would come from afar to attend the meeting. Of course, there was some feeling that attendance was a duty as much as a pleasure. Hospitality demanded that South Carolina scientists welcome their colleagues with a fitting demonstration of the scientific glory of the city. "I hope you are preparing some papers for the Scientific meeting in Charleston in March," Robert Gibbes prodded his former student. "We must all bestir ourselves."[3]

Although Ravenel intended to take an active part in the upcoming meeting, his attention in January 1850 was drawn to another, much smaller, scientific conference he hoped to arrange. The Episcopal diocese of South Carolina was meeting in convention at Saint Michael's Parish, Charleston, in February. Hearing that his friend Curtis, an Episcopal priest, planned to attend, Ravenel urged him to stop for a visit on his way. Though living in the same state, the two had met only twice before, once when Ravenel visited Curtis in Society Hill in 1848, and briefly at the Episcopal convention of 1849. Ravenel was now eager to play the host and introduce Curtis to his family, friends, and favorite botanical haunts.[4]

Curtis arrived in Saint John's early enough to preach the Sunday sermon at Black Oak Chapel-of-Ease on February 17. Monday Ravenel sent his family over to Pooshee to spend the week, and he and Curtis went to Charleston. The Episcopal convention was not scheduled to begin until Wednesday, February 20, so the two had at least one full day to tour Charleston and visit other scientists. Curtis had met John Bachman briefly when, as a young man living in Wilmington, he had made a trip to Charleston. Now that the two found themselves allied, for reasons both religious and scientific, as supporters of the traditional idea of a single creation of mankind, over the rival theory of multiple creations put forth by the American school of ethnologists, Curtis was probably hoping for a second meeting with Bachman. When the three-day convention was over, Ravenel and Curtis returned to Saint John's in time for another Sunday sermon by Curtis.[5]

In Saint John's, Ravenel had at least two things to show off to Curtis. One was a new microscope. The doublet that Ravenel so desired in December 1848 had arrived by the following May. Its ability to sharpen detail and allow a more sophisticated comparison of similar plants pleased him, at the same time that it demanded he sharpen his own analytical ability. Months before its arrival, however, he had already decided he would need a more powerful instrument. At Berkeley's recommendation, he had had a simple microscope made to order by the best of French instrument makers, Vincent and Charles Chevalier of Paris. Good quality French microscopes by such makers as Chevalier, Oberhauser, and Nichat were among the best available in the world at the time and had the advantage over their British counterparts, which were of equally high quality but more decorative and therefore more expensive. Ravenel's new Chevalier was fitted with five doublet lenses that could be exchanged to give magnification of five different powers, the highest being about three hundred diameters. Ravenel fretted impatiently until it came, complaining that he was working to disadvantage with his smaller glass. Russell's bookstore in Charleston finally sent the microscope through its Paris branch. Ravenel was so well pleased with its clarity and power that he kept it even though at forty-five dollars it exceeded by five dollars the price limit he had set. Again, as when he had acquired the doublet, he was impressed by the minute details he was able to discover and by the instrument's value in aiding identification. He tried it out on the spore-bearing sacs, or sporidia, of the mushroom he and Curtis had been calling *Agaricus mimosus* and became convinced that it was not, in fact, the same species as that described under the name by Greville in his Scottish cryptogamic flora.[6]

Acquisition of a well-made, powerful microscope was an important step in bringing Ravenel's mycological work closer to the standards set in the mid–nineteenth century by European workers. The most influential taxonomic scheme of that period was the system of Elias Fries, who made extensive use of the color and shape of the extremely tiny spores to classify cryptogams. Although Fries's system demanded a good microscope, it was elaborated before the perfection in the 1830s of techniques to correct spherical and chromatic aberration, so by the early 1850s, the classification system most commonly used in Sweden, England, and the United States lagged behind state-of-the-art microscope technology. Descriptions of new species were, however, already beginning to make use of observations of the spore sacs, the tiny features of which were impossible to discern without a high-power microscope with good definition. Ravenel's enthusiasm for his new instrument was, unfortunately, not enough to convince Curtis of its desirability, and neither Ravenel nor Berkeley was ever able to persuade him to acquire one.[7]

Ravenel received a much more satisfying response when he showed Curtis a particular pine tree that had been the subject of much recent discussion between them. During 1849, partly out of his own interest and partly to oblige a request from Asa Gray, Ravenel had studied the trees of his region. Coming upon a new pine, he had recognized immediately from its form of growth that it was different from the relatively common *Pinus mitis* described by Michaux. He identified it as *Pinus glabra* of Thomas Walter, a species missing since Walter's description of it in the eighteenth century. Ravenel sent cuttings to both Curtis and Gray, but they were skeptical about his discovery of Walter's pine and believed he had found Michaux's instead. Not wanting to contradict them both at once, Ravenel allowed himself to be silenced but not convinced. He took advantage of Curtis's visit to reopen the case. He showed him the pine, and to his everlasting pleasure, Curtis conceded at once. His friend even wrote to Gray to tell him that Ravenel had, indeed, rediscovered the rare tree.[8]

That Ravenel could tell *Pinus glabra* from *Pinus mitis* should not have astounded anyone. He had already developed enough proficiency with trees to spot a new oak when he saw it, despite its marked resemblance to two other species. The able botanist had discovered the rare dwarf oak *Quercus georgiana* growing on Stone Mountain, Georgia, during his collecting trip in 1848. A year later Curtis published it as a new species.[9]

The *Pinus glabra* incident helped Ravenel put into perspective the roles of field observation and analytical diagnosis in the proper identification of specimens. Ravenel's extensive experience in collecting had given him an eye for the differences in color, shape, texture, or size that could indicate separate species but were not readily reducible to terse botanical description. Such characteristics can all vary markedly between individuals unquestionably of the same species, however, as Ravenel was aware. Just months earlier he had discovered the shortcomings of too heavy a reliance upon intuition in identification. Two specimens of cryptogam appeared to be distinct species. Size, color, and texture were all different, and Ravenel's magnifying glass showed just the outlines of detailed anatomies that also seemed quite different. Yet when he applied his microscope to the task, it became plain that the two specimens were much more closely related than he had at first thought. Ravenel's successful identification of *Pinus glabra,* based on the same variable and relatively intangible evidence that had failed earlier, helped in future years to bolster his faith in the value of observing plants in their natural state. He did not allow field observation to eclipse more rigorous examination and comparison with herbarium specimens and published descriptions, but at first impression or when close study yielded ambiguous results, the intangibles could be important.[10]

Less than a month after Curtis's visit, the AAAS descended on Charleston for its third meeting. The city's scientists turned out in force to greet the visitors. Ravenel apparently took no active part in the organization of the meeting, but he led off with the first paper. He presented a list of families of plants he had discovered within about a twenty-mile radius of his home. He also named the genera within each family and gave the number of species he had found belonging to each genus. For the phanerogams, the Saint John's botanist believed the search had been sufficiently diligent that few species were missed. The cryptogams presented rather a different case. Ravenel numbered more cryptogams than phanerogams—1,338 to 1,075—but even so felt himself on the verge of many more discoveries. Even after three years of collecting fungi, he could easily find new types for his herbarium, and he suspected that half the species in his neighborhood were still awaiting discovery.[11]

To make the paper interesting to as wide a spectrum of scientists as possible and to provide an introduction to the Charleston area, Ravenel placed his work on the flora of the Saint John's area within the context of larger scientific goals. Through the 1840s the practical thrust of his work had been to familiarize himself with the contributions of his predecessors in taxonomy. He believed that taxonomy, just as it formed the groundwork for his own career, was also a necessary foundation to the whole science of botany. At least for phanerogamic botany the foundation was now well enough set that botanists could build upon it to study the geographical distribution of plants over the surface of the earth. Ravenel hoped that his paper, as a part of a detailed study of one geographical area, would be a contribution to the development of an understanding of plant distribution.

Few in attendance at the AAAS meeting could have argued with Ravenel, for long-standing concerns with paleontology had already made botanists aware of the significance of plant geography. Ravenel, however, brought to the question a different perspective. His agricultural orientation was clear as he urged the importance of collecting data on the meteorological and topographical factors that could influence the growth and distribution of plants. Rainfall, humidity, average temperature at different seasons, temperature range, and the direction of the prevailing winds could all determine the types of plants able to grow in a locality. Depth of the surface soil, its chemical composition, and proximity to bodies of water were physical features of the land that could also affect the flora. Ravenel, in his work with the Black Oak Agricultural Society, had already discussed the connection between meteorology and agriculture, and now he extended the principle to the growth of plants in nature.[12]

Absent, however, from the coordinates of measurement that he proposed, was the element of time, a key parameter of investigation to many nineteenth-century scientists.[13] He was, of course, aware of contemporary theories extending the antiquity of the earth and of the changes in fossil life forms that had occurred over the eons. Modern geology caused him no religious qualms, and like many pious scientists of his time, he did not doubt that geology could, indeed must, accord with the biblical creation story. Apparent discrepancies were due to error in interpretation of either nature or scripture, and with time and further research by both scientists and theologians, differences would be ironed out.[14] It would appear, therefore, that the dimension of time was not left out of his scheme through either ignorance or misplaced piety. The reason, we may suppose, lay instead in the way in which, throughout his career, he linked his interest in botany with an equally lively interest in agriculture. Promotion of agricultural improvement was an essentially ahistorical concern. Ravenel did not make science the slave of agriculture. His own botanical efforts were not directed at providing information immediately useful to agriculture, nor did he feel that his research was any less meaningful for his inability to turn much of it to practical good. He did suppose, however, that botany and agriculture were kindred subjects and that inquiries and methods of study applicable to one might easily be applicable to the other.

Although Ravenel's AAAS paper hints that his approach to natural history was a little outside the mainstream, the meeting increased his contacts with fellow scientists and, in that sense, moved him closer to the international scientific community. There he met the oceanographer Matthew Fontaine Maury, with whom he had been corresponding on meteorology.[15] A new acquaintance was William Henry Harvey, keeper of the University Herbarium of Dublin University. A friend of William Jackson Hooker and a noted specialist on algae, Harvey was a competent botanist, though his influence was not so great as Hooker's, Robert Brown's, or Berkeley's. Since 1849 he had been in the United States giving a series of lectures in Boston and New York; he had traveled to Charleston where he attended the AAAS meeting and was enrolled as a member. Ravenel's knowledge of the plants of his neighborhood made a favorable impression on the Irish botanist. Soon after his return to Ireland, he wrote to Hooker to tell the English botanist about the state of botany in the American South. He singled out Ravenel as a good botanist with a fine knowledge of the southern flora but mourned Ravenel's abandonment of the phanerogams in favor of the fungi.[16] Soon after the Charleston meeting broke up, Ravenel wrote to Harvey, sending along a box of plants. Harvey reciprocated and asked Ravenel to procure some dried specimens of *Dionaea muscipula,* the Venus flytrap. Ravenel and Harvey's interaction was short-lived, perhaps limited to one exchange, for in 1853 Harvey set sail for an extended trip to the Indian Ocean and Australasia.[17]

Ravenel also widened his contacts with Charleston's intellectual elite at the AAAS meeting. Of course, he already knew Edmund Ravenel, Michael Tuomey, and John Bachman. St. Julien Ravenel, a nephew of Edmund's then on his way to a notable career in agricultural chemistry, was by 1849 also an acquaintance.[18] Frank Porcher's attendance at medical school in Charleston and his medical practice in that city probably also provided Ravenel with a chance to meet other scientists. Nonetheless, though Ravenel lived less than a day's journey away from Charleston, his trips to the city were apparently infrequent, and before the 1850 meeting there probably were still a number of Charleston scientists whom Ravenel did not know. The meeting brought together the whole of the city's scientific community. In particular, Ravenel's long correspondence with Lewis R. Gibbes began soon after the AAAS meeting, when Gibbes sent Ravenel a number of printed copies of his paper.[19]

In the late 1840s and early 1850s Curtis and Ravenel's mycological efforts began to bear fruit in publication. With the concurrence of Berkeley, Curtis in November 1848 brought out in *Silliman's Journal* the first of a short series of papers on North American mycology. It listed twenty species not previously published as inhabiting North America and described ten new species. Unfortunately, the article contained several errors, and Berkeley took steps to ensure that in the future he would have control of publication of material that he and Curtis had worked on together. The English mycologist decided that he and Curtis would publish jointly. Their articles would appear first in the *London Journal of Botany* and afterwards would be reprinted in *Silliman's Journal,* also called the *American Journal of Science and Arts.* In accordance with Berkeley's plan, the mycological team of Berkeley and Curtis brought out three more articles, one in 1842 and the last two in 1850, bringing the total number of species so treated to 130.[20]

Specimens examined in preparation of the articles came mostly from Curtis's own collections, but Ravenel's contribution was by no means small. In nineteen cases, including eight new species, the material came from the herbaria of both men, and in twenty-one other instances, including four new species, Ravenel alone gathered the specimens. Curtis and Berkeley acknowledged Ravenel's help, and not for the first time, he was paid the standard compliment given by one botanist to another. Not just one, but two of the new species published in this series bore his name. *Helminthosporium ravenelii* Curt. was christened in November 1848 and *Lentinus ravenelii* B&C in March 1850.

Meanwhile, though Ravenel continued to turn new species of fungi over to Curtis and Berkeley, as he had promised to do in 1848, he persevered alone on the flora of the Saint John's region. At this time he published a few more articles in a series of preliminary studies that he hoped would lead eventually to a complete Saint John's flora. Ravenel's state record, published in January 1849, which dealt with newly encountered phanerogamic plants of the Santee Canal, was the first article of the series. Three more articles, published in July 1849, May 1850, and March 1851 and appearing, like the first, in the *Charleston Medical Journal and Review*, dealt with the cryptogamic plants. In the first of these three Ravenel took up the mosses and liverworts, most of his species of which had been examined by William S. Sullivant of Ohio. The topic of the second paper was the lichens, determined with the aid of Edward Tuckerman, and in the third Ravenel turned finally to the fungi.[21]

In all these articles, Ravenel wrote very much in the style of the collector. Latin he eschewed, aside from obligatory binomials. Except where he found a few specimens particularly interesting and worthy of an aside, he also avoided giving descriptions of species that had already been published and described elsewhere when they were first determined. Always, though, he noted when and where or on what substrate the species could be found. The fungus *Hydnum gelatinosum* Schw., for example, would be found in winter "on putrid logs of pine," while *H. erinaceus* Fr. must be sought in autumn "on dead standing trunks of oak."[22] Obviously Ravenel enjoyed searching for his plants, for as he told Tuckerman, "My labors are . . . more in the woods than in the closet—I love to follow them in their haunts, in the deep forrests watch their development, & there to study their 'ways.' "[23]

Ravenel intended to complement his article of March 1851 on fungi with additional studies that would eventually provide a complete flora of the Santee Canal. It was not to be. Ravenel never finished his study of the flora of Saint John's, for by the close of 1851 another project had forced this one aside. First proposed by Moses Ashley Curtis, the new project was the issuance of a set of dried plants illustrating the fungal flora of South Carolina.

Such sets, called *exsiccati*, were a common and useful form of publication popular among botanists in the nineteenth century. Simple in concept, they were nothing more than bound volumes containing labeled specimens of dried plants. Little writing was involved in their preparation. The work came, instead, in identifying a selection of species to be included, collecting a large number of specimens of each species, preparing labels, and assembling the bound volumes. An exsiccati's value to researchers lay in the distribution to a select group of individuals and institutions of uniform sets of identified specimens that could be used as standards. This value was greatly increased when the exsiccati included specimens of new species collected or approved by their original describers. Botanists could acquire an exsiccati and have an instant miniature herbarium including a number of authorized cotypes of new species.

Curtis and Ravenel's proposed *Fungi Caroliniani Exsiccati* would not be the first set issued in the United States. William S. Sullivant had issued his exsiccati of mosses, the *Musci Alleghanienses* in 1846, and Edward Tuckerman was then working on publication of sets of lichens, his first volume having appeared in early 1851. It would, however, be the first fungal exsiccati to be issued and appear in America.[24]

Ravenel and Curtis intended to work together on their exsiccati. They planned to share the job of collecting and identifying the specimens, and Curtis was to have the additional task of comparing the specimens with species of America's first major mycological collector, Lewis David von Schweinitz (1780–1834). Schweinitz had collected widely in North Carolina but had published a relatively small proportion of his collections and then with often inadequate descriptions. Schweinitz's microscope lacked the spherical and chromatic corrections available in well-made microscopes of Ravenel and Curtis's day, and therefore, its definition was poor.[25] The limitations imposed by his microscope had resulted in distortions that ultimately rendered his descriptions inadequate. The inaccuracies that had crept into Schweinitz's descriptions made determination of his species difficult for later workers, and there was every reason to believe that some of his species had been published again under new names.

In the fall of 1851 Curtis had taken a trip to Philadelphia where Schweinitz's herbarium was preserved in the collections of the Academy of Natural Sciences. There he had spent more than two weeks

studying Schweinitz's material and had cajoled the curators into allowing him to bear off duplicate Schweinitzian specimens whenever there
were more than two examples of a single species.[26] It was not long,
however, before Curtis was writing to Ravenel begging to be let off
the hook: "What say you to taking Fung. Carol. off my hands, &
issuing it by yourself, I giving you what stock I have myself gathered,
say 25–30 species? The more I think of the business, the more averse
I become to it. The amount of labor & time requisite is, more than I
wish to expend in that direction. It is only lately, that I began to make
some estimate of it."[27]

Time was, indeed, a problem for Curtis. His ministerial duties kept
him quite busy, and he worried that people would think he was
devoting too much time to botany and neglecting his flock. In any
case, the exsiccati was not the only botanical project he had on hand,
for he and Berkeley were anticipating a critical study of the Schweinitz
material. To make matters worse, the Schweinitz specimens, so necessary to both studies, were still lying about his house in confusion.
Although it was about four months since he had acquired them, he
had not yet put them in order. Several months, he thought, would be
necessary to complete that job.[28]

Curtis did not leave Ravenel entirely without aid. He did contribute
some specimens and helped with determination of synonymy with
Schweinitz. Ravenel's major help in species determination, of course,
was Berkeley. He had been regularly sending his specimens across the
Atlantic for Berkeley's opinion, first through Curtis and then, from
1850 on, directly. Curtis also offered some advice on selection of
specimens, cautioning that they should be mature plants, neither too
old nor too young. It would also be as well, he thought, to leave out
new or uncertain specimens, though he sent along three specimens
from outside South Carolina and suggested Ravenel might at times
want to include examples from outside the state. They could be useful
for filling in gaps in a volume or for illustrating particularly interesting
fungi not found within the state.[29]

In the matters of selecting the species to be included in the volume
and collecting sufficient numbers of each species, Ravenel worked
pretty much alone. He was concerned that Curtis's abandonment of
the project might undermine the authority of the exsiccati in cases of

species first described by Berkeley and Curtis. Curtis, however, reassured him on this point. Ravenel himself, having personally inspected, if not collected, all the type specimens upon which the Berkeley and Curtis species were founded, would be able to authenticate his own specimens quite satisfactorily.[30]

Ravenel made rapid progress on his *Fungi Caroliniani Exsiccati*. The first volume, which had just barely been started in January 1852, was nearing completion by April. Ravenel made arrangements with Russell's of Charleston to print the labels, title pages, introduction, and index, and he wrote to Asa Gray to see about having a notice of the work printed in *Silliman's Journal*.[31] By July, Ravenel was nearly done, and from Curtis, who had provided encouragement throughout the whole course of the job, he received congratulations. "I must confess," said a relieved Curtis, "that I am heartily glad to be free from the task in which you are engaged. I could not have finished my share before next Spring. I am much gratified that you have undertaken it alone, & have got on so expeditiously." Ten days later, he was congratulating his friend on the completion of the first fascicle. "I hope however that you do not now regret the labor, as it is one of those things that tell *in perpetuum*. It is not labor lost."[32]

A final detail remained, for Ravenel had not yet fixed the price or made arrangements for distribution. Exsiccati were not usually profit-making ventures. Like journal articles, they were simply a way to share information and material with others. Ravenel finally settled on a price of four dollars per volume, an amount that might repay his out-of-pocket expenses but would never compensate him for his time and effort. For recompense he would have to look to other benefits. As Curtis wrote, Ravenel could expect to gain "a name & authority by it, which will be better than lucre."[33]

Ravenel gave nearly half the copies away to other botanists or to scientific institutions. He sent complimentary copies to European botanists Miles Berkeley, Elias Fries, and William Harvey, as well as to Americans Moses Ashley Curtis; Francis Porcher; Elias Horlbeck, a Charleston physician and amateur botanist; and Thomas Minott Peters of Alabama, one of Curtis's more recent correspondents. In addition, free copies went to the Smithsonian Institution, the Academy of Natural Sciences, and the Boston Society of Natural History. Asa

Gray turned down Ravenel's offer of a copy, saying that the difficulties involved in preserving fungi were too great for him to feel free to accept, but that he hoped to make one of his wealthy Lowell patrons a subscriber.[34]

Curtis looked at his copy as soon as it arrived and wrote off a short critique that, though mild and mixed with praise, sparked some bickering between the two. "The Volume is very neatly got up," Curtis wrote, "& is in all respects creditable, except in numerous typographical errors. Pray take care about that in future. I may have some small criticisms to make hereafter; but just now I only remember to say that the Latin for Louisiana is Ludoviciana, & instead of '*misit* c! Hale', it should have been *legit* Hale."[35] Ravenel evidently did not take Curtis's comments in very good spirit. The latter complained to Asa Gray, "Ravenel is no scholar, & does not always know the right when he is told.—He justifies 'Louisiana' in Fasc. I, because 'there is no such place as Ludoviciana.'—He sees no important difference between 'Hale misit', & Hale legit, although there is the difference between a truth & a falsehood, since *I* sent him the plant, which Hale collected."[36]

That Curtis would so emphasize form and style over content was the probable reason Ravenel was irked; yet the emphasis is understandable. Curtis had been in close communication with Ravenel in the months preceding the issuance of the first fascicle. He had a good idea what specimens were to be included, indeed had reviewed most of them and had supplied some of them. When the volume arrived at his home, its form and style were the unknowns to be explored, and so on them he focused his remarks. Some of the remarks were, of course, justified. Typographical accuracy is a proper goal for any publication, and there is a difference between collector and supplier. On the other hand, to insist on the use of Ludoviciana for Louisiana was pompous even by nineteenth-century standards. It was not unusual to break into English to describe the place of collection.

Fascicle I of the *Fungi Caroliniani Exsiccati* was, then, launched into the botanical world on the little rippling waves of a small controversy, and Ravenel awaited the opinions of others.

He had completed the first volume of the *Fungi Caroliniani Exsiccati* in the face of deteriorating health. Signs of trouble first appeared during the late summer or fall of 1851. Ravenel's usually robust constitution gave way before nagging, painful dyspepsia. Chronic stomachache and indigestion, perhaps induced by stress associated with the exsiccati, robbed Ravenel of his vigor. To combat his disorder, Ravenel left South Carolina's summer heat to journey to the cool hills of North Carolina. There, in the beautiful Smoky Mountains, he hoped to rest, regain his strength, and take advantage of the unusual North Carolina flora, a mix of northern and southern species. Ravenel's illness was too persistent, however, to allow him much opportunity to collect. Though he spent a summer in the mountains, he only regained his health during the last three or four weeks of the trip and, even then, was unable to accomplish much.[37]

Ravenel returned to Saint John's in October 1851 and began work on the exsiccati in reasonably good health, but about eight months later the dyspepsia reappeared. Ravenel began complaining of the trouble in his letters in late June or early July and received sympathy and advice in equal doses from his acquaintances. "I am sorry that you are again troubled with your 'dyspeptic feelings,' " wrote Curtis. "I have never been a great sufferer in this way, but I have had experience enough to know what the intensity of the disease *might* be, & I cannot but sympathize with one who is steadily subject to it."[38]

Curtis suggested that Ravenel give up tobacco, coffee, and tea, and by experiment try to isolate other, seemingly innocuous substances that might be exacerbating the problem. Curtis also recommended "the tonic influence of Porter, good Ale, or Brandy, or good Cider."[39] William Gilmore Simms recommended Ravenel try cold water as a potential cure. The South Carolina author and editor of the *Southern Quarterly Review,* for which Ravenel had prepared a couple of articles early in the 1850s, had himself suffered for years with dyspepsia until he came upon his novel remedy. Now each morning he drank a glass of cold water and took a cold bath as well. He, too, had found it beneficial to refrain from coffee and tea, but, unlike Curtis, he was inclined to include wine in the forbidden list.[40] When Ravenel's exsiccati was ready to be issued in July, his health was no better. Curtis urged him to seek another change of climate but hesitated to recommend any particular place, suggesting Ravenel might do better to consult a physician.[41]

Ravenel gave up his cigars and tried a change of air. He spent June with his father in Pineville and in July went with his family to Charleston. While there, he decided to go with Francis Simmons Holmes and Francis Turquand Miles to explore upper Georgia and Aiken, South Carolina. Ravenel could anticipate compatible company from these two men. Holmes, like Ravenel, was enthusiastic about scientific agriculture, and both Holmes and Miles had wide-ranging interests in natural history. Curtis wrote approvingly of the expedition, saying he had "frequently heard of the air of Aiken being serviceable to persons with *diseased lungs*" and that he hoped Ravenel would find it as beneficial to his stomach complaints.[42]

Ravenel did find Aiken's climate to be an improvement over Saint John's, and he began thinking about selling Northampton and moving to Aiken. Situated at about the same latitude as Charleston, the town lies approximately 120 miles farther west in a region of gently rolling hills. Its higher altitude and greater distance from the ocean make it drier, and in the nineteenth century it was not so prone to malaria or yellow fever as was the coast. Aiken's relatively dry air and the fact that it had a direct rail connection with Charleston combined to make it a popular resort for ailing Charlestonians. It developed a reputation as a healthful place for people suffering from pulmonary or other chronic, debilitating illnesses.[43] In fact, people close to death were sometimes whisked away to Aiken in the hope of their recovery.[44]

By the end of October 1852 Ravenel began to inform his correspondents that he had decided to move to Aiken.[45] Once resolved to relocate, Ravenel quickly put his affairs in order. An herbarium for the Charleston Museum, which he had been working on since the previous spring, received high priority. Devoting all his leisure time to finishing it before the move, he put aside the second volume of *Fungi Caroliniani Exsiccati* and the task of overhauling his duplicate specimens. When Lewis R. Gibbes requested some plants characteristic of Saint John's, Ravenel offered his hospitality and suggested Gibbes come pay a visit and go through the herbarium himself.[46] Curtis's botanical demands were not so easy to take care of. He had earlier sent Ravenel a list of some mosses and fungi he needed, and when November came and many of the specimens did not, he wrote to jog his friend's memory.[47] Ravenel successfully put Curtis off until after he was settled in his new town, but Curtis did not let him forget the promised plants again. In playful indignation he wrote, "Now listen to the revenge I have contrived.—On the next page is a specimen, a small specimen of what I can do for you, whenever I *can get time:* & I am always so busy, that I do not think I shall find time to send you another parcel, until *you* have found time to furnish what I want of you."[48]

Ravenel devoted much of his time to relocating his family. Selling the plantation was a major step in the preparations. Northampton was estimated by Ravenel in 1850 to consist of six hundred acres, of which two hundred were improved and four hundred unimproved. Its fields that year yielded a main crop of three thousand bushels of rice, the plantation having a history of good rice production. Ravenel had produced little cotton, only eight bales in 1850, but he had also raised other southern staples, including corn, field peas, and sweet potatoes. He grew some oats and hay, as well as the less common crops wheat, rye, and Irish potatoes, and he produced some wool. Ravenel gave the census taker an estimated value of six thousand dollars for his diversified and, by the 1850s, relatively fertile land. Unless the estimate was deliberately low, however, he was to receive a pleasant surprise. Henry L. Stevens, a family friend, bought Northampton on November 25, 1852, for ten thousand dollars.[49] After Ravenel purchased another farm, he invested the remaining money, together with an apparent gift from his father of ten thousand dollars, in stocks, bonds, and private, income-producing loans.[50]

For the moment, the sudden abundance of cash was a good excuse for generosity at Christmas, a time of special merriment on plantations throughout the South. At Pooshee during the prosperous 1850s, the holidays stretched to several days of celebration. Ravenel's father presided as host over large gatherings of family and friends. Christmas dinner for fifty was not unusual. He was assisted by one or another of his unmarried daughters, his wife Catherine having died in 1846, and he and the hostess alone were exempt from practical jokes and tricks.[51] Gifts were hung from the branches of a large tree erected in the hall. "We had a Christmass *Tree* which was very briliant with presents & some very handsome & valuable," recorded Ravenel's younger brother Thomas on Christmas Day 1852. "I received from Brother Henry on the tree 1 doz. Silver forks." It was the only Christmas present Thomas ever mentioned in his diary.[52]

After the sale of Northampton, Ravenel and his family lived there until the seventeenth of January when they moved to Pooshee to stay for a while before going on to Aiken. While there, Ravenel sold some unneeded horses, furniture, provisions, and a wagon. Extra slaves he kept together in families, selling a group to each of his brothers William and Thomas and three families and one single man to his father. Leaving Pooshee on February 3, Ravenel and his family went on to Aiken. He returned to fetch his remaining slaves, arriving with them in Aiken on February 16.[53]

Settled into rented quarters in Aiken, the Ravenels were quite comfortable. Pleasant surroundings and friendly neighbors created a good first impression of the town.[54] They had carried with them a letter of introduction from the Reverend William Dehon of Saint Stephen's Church to give to the Reverend John Cornish of Saint Thaddeus, Aiken. "I feel assured," Dehon wrote, "that my loss will prove your gain, & that your hands may be strengthened & your heart cheered by this addition to your flock of two devoted Christians, with their children, the lambs of his fold." With their way thus smoothed, the Ravenels joined the Episcopal church of Saint Thaddeus, and Ravenel began to sing in the choir. About twenty-five other families already gathered at Saint Thaddeus to worship, among them the families of future friends Amory Coffin, a physician, and Octavius Dawson, a former resident of Saint John's.[55]

By April 1853 Ravenel was sending good reports on Aiken to Edward Tuckerman and had decided to make it a permanent residence if his health improved, which it did.[56] That summer he purchased a farm from the heirs of Richard Hampton and began building a house at Hampton Hill.[57] Frequent visits between Aiken and Saint John's in the first years away indicate that Aiken seemed more like a pleasant exile than a home. Yet the exile was eminently worthwhile. Whether from coincidence or from the real value of Aiken's dry air and bracing climate, Ravenel experienced several years of good health after his move.

International Mycology, 1853–1859

5

Soon after settling in Aiken, Ravenel was busy again with botany. He wanted to explore Aiken's flora, and from a collector's point of view, he had arrived at just the right time, the beginning of a new spring season. He noted with interest a number of species that were uncommon in Saint John's, offering to send specimens to his Charleston correspondent, Lewis R. Gibbes. He also sent examples of his collections, hoping to lure Gibbes to Aiken for a visit.[1]

Not all his labors were in the field. Ravenel spent part of March attending to the necessary but disagreeable task of sorting through his cryptogamic herbarium and arranging bundles of duplicates for distribution.[2] Curtis gave him some urging in this direction, reminding him of the long-promised set of mosses and fungi:

I have no notion of missing any new thing that I can possibly get hold of. Pray do not be careless with me again. *Carelessness is catching. . . .* How would you like a couple of species of Trichomanes from the Mts of Alabama? I have two such things; one of them undescribed, detected last month by a correspondent of mine; the other T. radicans, discovered a few weeks before. I say I have got such things, but—*a he-m-m!*[3]

If a promise of two ferns, *Trichomanes radicans* and one that Asa Gray would soon name *T. petersii* for its discoverer, Thomas Minott

71

Peters, were not motive enough for sorting duplicates, Ravenel had another reason. Late in 1852 Curtis had received an unsolicited box of plants from a Swiss botanist, Edmund Boissier. The Swiss was interested only in phanerogams, and so, while he reciprocated with one set of American plants, Curtis preferred not to become involved in a long exchange. He suggested Ravenel take his place in the correspondence. Boissier promised plants from Spain and Algeria and had already sent Curtis specimens from Syria, Arabia, and Egypt. Curtis wrote that Boissier had "the reputation of being a fine fellow" but that he himself had "no time for foreign Phaenogams," and Ravenel agreed to the proposal.[4] He learned in February that Boissier had accepted the substitution, too, and in August a letter arrived from the Swiss, promising that a package of plants would follow. The letter was written, as Curtis had predicted, "in French, & in the most unreadable hand I have ever dealt with, a little worse than Fries."[5]

Ravenel was also preparing to recommence work on the exsiccati. In considering his previous volume he had two favorable reviews to balance against Curtis's critique. Fries sent through Gray a flattering comment upon the value of the exsiccati for accurate determination of fungi. He hoped the exsiccati would be continued and promised to send specimens in return. That promise in itself was a compliment and an indication that Fries was willing to consider Ravenel his equal in science. In addition, an anonymous, praise-filled review appeared in the *Charleston Medical Journal and Review* late in 1852.[6]

Curtis, however, was still displeased about the typographical errors that marred the first fascicle. He evidently persuaded Gray to give the volume a less favorable notice than Ravenel might have liked. "I have your note of March 26th," he wrote Gray, "& reply instanter, hoping I may be in season for next N° of Sill. Journ. The Fung. Carol. does not want much notice. In the material on the other leaf, you will find more than text enough for a Bibliographical touch." Later, he wrote, "I will explain to Ravenel about the notice. I have however prepared him already for the disappointment, by advising him of our late action."[7]

Gray's notice of the *Fungi Caroliniani Exsiccati* did not appear until July 1853. It was not a long report, but it was much more than just a bibliographical note. Gray followed many of Curtis's suggestions. He praised the neatness of the volume's binding and said the specimens were good and sound and generally supplied in sufficient quantity. They were particularly interesting for illustrating species established by Schweinitz and by Berkeley and Curtis. Gray then took much of the credit for this merit away from Ravenel, however, attributing it, as Curtis had not, "to the careful revision of the specimens by our leading and best instructed mycologist, the Rev. Dr. Curtis." The typographical errors he ignored.[8]

Ravenel did not hold any lingering resentment against Curtis for his remarks on the typographical errors. Never, in letters or diary, did he evidence grudges, and he counted the forgiving aspect of his nature as one of his greatest blessings. In April, when Curtis planned a trip to Charleston, Ravenel welcomed him to Aiken for a week's visit. Ravenel spent so much time and trouble showing Curtis around that soon after the visit Curtis wrote to Gray, saying, "If you have need of Elliottia, I dare say you can put Ravenel up to getting roots. . . . Try him. He has nothing in the world to do but herborize."[9]

Even while Curtis visited him, Ravenel was planning a trip of his own as far north as New York and Boston. The plans were well formed by the first week of July, when, at Tuckerman's request, Ravenel gave him the itinerary so the two could meet in Boston.[10] He did stop to see Tuckerman and various scientific attractions along the route, but the main purpose of the trip apparently was rest and recreation. He hoped to secure further improvement in his health, which had already strengthened considerably after his move to Aiken, but he set such a grueling pace for himself that whatever benefits he may have attained were cancelled by exhaustion. Leaving home on July 11, he rode the train to Charleston where he caught a steamer to Wilmington, North Carolina. There he boarded a train for Richmond, whence another train carried him to meet a steamer on the Potomac. The steamer carried him up the river to Washington, D.C., where he stayed a day. Ravenel then went on by train to Philadelphia and New York, and by boat from New York to Boston, arriving there on the morning of July 26. After only two or three days in Boston, he turned south again, repeating his northbound itinerary in reverse, adding Saratoga Springs between Boston and New York. Aiken was never such a welcome sight as when he finally returned home on August 9.

He had not much enjoyed the large cities he visited, as he had complained to his family in a letter:

I dont like the climate of the cities, & never feel as well as when I am up in the country & at a distance from the humid, sultry air of the seaports.—I find Pha quite warm, oppressive & debilitating—Whilst travelling through the country from Boston to Saratoga & whilst at Saratoga I felt invigorated & strong, but since reaching New York & Pha, I have not felt well—I hope our dry salubrious Aiken with the comforts of home, will be a beneficial change for me.[11]

On the whole, he had a miserable time. Traveling alone, he missed his wife and children during the whole trip. He wrote them at least once a day, often keeping a letter a few days and adding to it during every available moment, sometimes two or three times in the course of one day. At every city he checked the post office to see if a letter had come from his wife. If one was waiting for him, his happiness and relief were obvious, and if there was none, he could not hide his disappointment.[12]

His letters home related all the interesting features of his journey. In Washington for a day, he visited the Capitol building; the Washington Monument, then under construction; and the Patent Office. At the Patent Office he particularly enjoyed the exhibits from Charles Wilkes's exploring expedition; he strolled through the hothouses to view the expedition's live plants.[13]

Boston and Philadelphia, where Ravenel was able to attend to botany, were the bright spots on his trip, though his stay in Boston began gloomily with a rainstorm and a crowded hotel. Ravenel was assigned to share a room with a stranger and made plans to change his quarters before nightfall. He confided to his family his intention of going to visit Tuckerman as soon as the rain stopped to give his correspondent an opportunity to invite him to stay the night. The invitation never materialized ("perhaps he is not prepared to have company," thought Ravenel), but Tuckerman seemed very glad to see him. He took Ravenel up to his study, showed him his herbarium, and invited him to come again the next day to look over his extra specimens and help himself to whatever he wanted. Tuckerman was conscious that he had somewhat missed the mark in hospitality. In reply to Ravenel's letter thanking him for his attentions and for the lichens, he explained that health and an ongoing courtship had prevented him from paying as much attention to his visitor as he would have liked. Tuckerman hoped on Ravenel's next visit to give him a tour of the northern mountains, where he collected many of his own botanical specimens.[14]

Ravenel apparently did not visit Asa Gray in Cambridge. His relations with Gray, while cordial, were not as close as those with Tuckerman. He did, however, schedule an evening's visit with the Reverend Jared Curtis, Moses Ashley Curtis's father. The elder Curtis took him on a tour of the navy yard, including the *Vermont,* a man-of-war of 110 guns; the dry dock machine shop; and the rope manufactory. He offered to take his visitor to see anything he would find of interest around Boston and finally allowed Ravenel to leave with an invitation to come back for a cup of tea.[15]

In Philadelphia, Ravenel saw the herbarium of Lewis David von Schweinitz, preserved in the cabinets of the Academy of Natural Sciences of Philadelphia. His status as a corresponding member of the Academy, elected in 1849 on the nomination of Robert Gibbes, assured him a welcome from the curators. He spent only one morning among the Schweinitz specimens but was allowed, as Curtis had been a few years earlier, to carry away nearly 150 duplicate specimens.[16] While in Philadelphia, he also made the acquaintance of another botanist, Thomas Potts James.

Tired though Ravenel was on his return to Aiken, his travels were not over. About two weeks after his return, Ravenel's father came to Aiken for a visit. He was joined on September 7 by Ravenel's brother William, and the three men trooped off together to Tennessee for a week or two at Chattanooga and Lookout Mountain.[17]

Once more at home, Ravenel found a letter from Francis S. Holmes, seeking to lure him to Charleston. "The heat of Summer has passed, and the weather is now cool & pleasant, and I think a trip to Charleston would do you good," he opened. If Ravenel would come spend a week, he could share Holmes's garret room and have a chance to overhaul two new cartloads of Stephen Elliott's herbarium material, just presented to the College of Charleston by Elliott's daughter. In addition,

two cases had been constructed to hold the herbarium recently presented by Ravenel to the Charleston Museum, and Ravenel could
arrange his specimens in them according to his own taste. These ideas
sound suspiciously like hard work, though they were meant to be
tempting, and only after detailing them did Holmes get around to his
real reason for wanting Ravenel in Charleston at that particular time.
He and Dr. Miles were about to launch a natural history society, the
first to grace Charleston since the decline of the Literary and Philosophical Society following Stephen Elliott's death. "We have prepared
every thing," he wrote, "and wish you to be numbered among its
founders— . . . and we wish you to be present at a meeting which
we propose having at my house as soon as you come down."[18] None
of Holmes's blandishments or entreaties could coax Ravenel away from
home and family just then. He remained in Aiken and had to be
informed by mail that the Elliott Society of Natural History had been
successfully placed on its feet and that he had been unanimously elected
one of its curators.[19]

　　Ravenel's old friend John Bachman was elected president of the
Elliott Society, and among the six vice-presidents were Lewis Gibbes
and Edmund Ravenel. The others were James Moultrie, William
Hume, E. Geddings, and S. H. Dickson. The organizers, Holmes and
Miles, became secretary and treasurer, respectively. Henry Ravenel
was one of thirteen curators, as was his younger friend Francis Peyre
Porcher. With twenty-two offices available, it seems the founding
members were eager to attract the fealty of Charleston's scientific men
by bestowing honors freely. Appointment as a curator was probably
calculated, in addition, to give Ravenel and the others a proprietary
interest in the society's collections and to encourage them to donate
specimens. The cabinets of the Elliott Society and the Charleston
Museum were both at this time watched over by the College of
Charleston, which employed Francis Holmes as a curator and teacher.
The collections of the Elliott Society and the museum, which had
reopened January 24, 1852, after being closed for a number of years,
received substantial support and encouragement from Charleston's
scientists. Ravenel had already donated to the Charleston Museum an
extensive collection of plants, and soon after his election as a curator
by the Elliott Society, he made another gesture of support, donating

to the society a collection of viviparous fish from Barnwell District, South Carolina. When Boissier's plants arrived, some of them also went to the society.[20]

Holmes and Miles's evident eagerness to secure Ravenel's participation, contrasted with the small part he actually played in the formation and early activities of the Elliott Society, is symbolic of Ravenel's somewhat ambiguous position vis-à-vis the Charleston scientific community. There was evident mutual respect, but two factors limited the depth of Ravenel's involvement with them. The first was his residence at a distance from Charleston and his dislike of cities. When business called, or occasionally just for amusement, he would go down to spend a few days or a week in Charleston and would drop in to visit Holmes or Gibbes or Bachman, but these visits were infrequent, and he could not count on attending a very high proportion of Elliott Society meetings. Even less frequent were visits paid by these men to Ravenel. Gibbes, who was often invited in the course of their steady correspondence, visited only once or twice, the others apparently not at all, though Holmes and Miles had been Ravenel's companions on the trip to Aiken when Ravenel first decided to settle there. A second factor was the rather narrow specialization of Ravenel's work. He had only the most casual interest in sciences other than botany, and in the 1850s he had turned his attention almost exclusively to the cryptogams. In botany there was little beyond friendship and moral support that the Charleston scientists could offer Ravenel, for he was by far the best botanist among them and was already in touch with the leading men of his field.

While his Charleston friends were busy with the formation of the Elliott Society, Ravenel was occupied with the second fascicle of his *Fungi Caroliniani Exsiccati*. Even at the time the first issue appeared, he already had accumulated some of the specimens needed for the second. He had made considerable progress before his move to Aiken, and now he was prepared to finish up his collections and issue a second set. By early December 1853 he had the labels back from Russell's print shop and showed them to Curtis. Curtis complained to Gray that the labels were "sadly corrupt with typographical mistakes & bad Latinity." He tried to persuade Ravenel to have the labels reprinted but apparently without detailing the errors. Ravenel refused to redo the labels, saying he had already taken pains to ensure accuracy and would now hope for a charitable interpretation. Finally Curtis wrote up a bland, brief notice and sent it along to Gray for publication in *Silliman's Journal* under Curtis's own name.[21]

Issuance of the second fascicle of the exsiccati largely depleted Ravenel's stock of suitable material, but he was soon gathering material for a third. In the case of the first fascicle, Curtis had collected about one-fourth of the specimens and had donated the three extra-Carolinian species collected by others. The second fascicle had, by contrast, been Ravenel's almost entirely. Curtis had collected a few things for him but was too much occupied during late 1852 and 1853 with overhauling his own collection to do much new collecting.[22] As Ravenel began collecting for the third volume, several recreational botanists volunteered to help collect specimens. Ezra Michener of Pennsylvania wrote in July at the suggestion of Thomas P. James. He admitted that he had little time to spare for collecting, but he was "anxious to contribute . . . [his] humble mite to the advancement of science," as well as to enlarge his own herbarium. He would do whatever he could to help, on the basis of an equitable exchange of specimens.[23]

Curtis had for some time been receiving help from Thomas Minott Peters, a lawyer in Moulton, Alabama, whose special interest was the cryptogams. By the early 1850s Peters had made considerable progress in studying them. He soon began corresponding with Ravenel and Tuckerman, and when he met John F. Beaumont, another Alabama resident with an interest in botany, he drew Beaumont into the circle.[24] Beaumont's first letters to Ravenel showed him to be a generous and knowledgeable helper. He enclosed specimens of fungi and offered to procure any number of additional specimens should Ravenel desire them. Nothing was asked in return, not even identification of specimens.[25]

With three new correspondents willing to help collect for the exsiccati, Ravenel should have been in a good position to put together his third fascicle. By the fall of 1854, however, he had developed a strong dislike for microscopy, and though he struggled against it, his perseverance only increased his antipathy. He thought he was simply getting tired and frustrated with devoting too much attention to the fungi to the exclusion of other things. To overcome his aversion, he decided to lay the fungi aside for a while.[26] At the end of November, just days after that decision was reached, he took his family to Pooshee to spend the winter. A flurry of visits earlier that fall from his father, sisters, and brothers had not damped his enthusiasm for family togetherness, and he was looking forward to a long, leisurely Christmas holiday.[27]

Christmas Day and its festivities were slightly marred by worry over his wife's health. Elizabeth had suffered a mild attack of paralysis, but there seemed no immediate cause to fear for her recovery. In early January, Henry made a few days' trip back to Aiken to check on the farm, leaving Elizabeth and the children at Pooshee, and a week or two later there seemed no reason why sixteen-year-old Lydia should not be allowed a visit to friends in Charleston.[28]

A second stroke of paralysis abruptly changed Elizabeth's condition. Lydia's uncle William went to town January 28 to bring her back, and all the family gathered together to help nurse her mother. Their devoted attentions could do nothing to save Elizabeth, however, and on February 5 she died.[29] Ravenel and his children remained in the comforting presence of the Pooshee family for several more weeks, finally returning to Aiken in the middle of March. Alone with his children, Ravenel felt his grief descend in full force, and he poured it out in a letter to his sister-in-law Liz. "We have got back to our home which we all left a few months ago, but what a change that short time can make! It is home now without the light which always made my home so sweet to me," he wrote. As heavy as were his own sorrows, Ravenel grieved also for his children, too young to realize fully what they had lost.[30]

Quiet, steady Christian faith helped greatly to make Ravenel's burden bearable. He was certain that his beloved wife had gone on to a perfect existence. He would not wish to call her back from the presence of her God to live with him once more. It was, therefore, not for Elizabeth that he mourned, but for his own loneliness and his children's. Yet even that misery was ameliorated by his faith. Ravenel was sure that in the course of time he would receive the grace and strength necessary to overcome his grief and go on with life. It was comforting, too, to think that his wife's death had a purpose and was a part of God's plan. Perhaps someday he would know the purpose, and with understanding would come further comfort.[31]

Sympathy came freely from family, friends, and his botanical correspondents. Asa Gray, told by Curtis about Elizabeth's death, wrote in July to express his own sense of grief over Ravenel's bereavement. He also paid Ravenel a professional compliment, writing: "To show that you were not 'out of mind' tho' it may be long since I wrote to you, . . . only yesterday I was describing a remarkable new Compositae found among the *debris* of Berlandier's collection . . . and casting in my mind what Botanist ought to be commemorated by it, I concluded that it was most proper to call it *Ravenelia*—under which name it accordingly went into my herb^m & my MS."[32] Both the compliment and the sympathy were well appreciated, though Berkeley and Curtis had already given the name *Ravenelia* to a genus of fungi.[33]

Even more comforting than the condolences of his friends was the companionship of his plants and books. Ravenel had, as planned, given little attention to botany during his stay in Saint John's. Coming back to Aiken in the spring, he was physically rested and quite recovered from his temporary distaste for the microscope. He plunged back into his botanical studies and found them a cool salve for his wounds. He worked with the enthusiasm of his early days in botany, yet also with the maturity of a seasoned naturalist. In terms of botanical accomplishments, the year or two following his wife's death were among the most productive periods of his entire career.

As he resumed botany, Ravenel accepted a new responsibility. A letter came to him the second week of March from a beginning botanist in Alexander, Georgia. Ravenel wrote back within days promising to identify plants for the new collector in exchange for specimens to be used in *Fungi Caroliniani Exsiccati*. "I have correspondents in different states," he wrote, "who are aiding me in the collection of specimens for my work, & I will be glad to have your services enlisted in the same good cause."[34]

Ravenel's new correspondent was Job Bicknell Ellis, a native of Potsdam, New York, who had studied some botany at Union College in Schenectady, where he graduated A.B. in 1851. After teaching at a number of northeastern academies he traveled to Charleston in February 1855. He obtained a position at an academy in Alexander, not far from Aiken. During his travels he had maintained his interest in botany, collecting and studying on weekends. Ellis had noticed the fungi but ignored them, not knowing where he could look for competent instruction, until at some point, probably during his short stay in Charleston, he happened upon a notice of Ravenel's exsiccati.[35] The letter he directed to Ravenel from Alexander in March was the opening of a long and profitable exchange. In Ellis, Ravenel had for the first time a student, someone to whom he could pass on his expertise in collecting and who, in turn, would aid him with the exsiccati. In Ravenel, Ellis had a patient and interested teacher, a man who knew the plants, literature, and other scientists and who would willingly give him much guidance.

Ellis's enthusiasm for mycology was as great as Ravenel's own had been when he first took up the science. Ellis sent new sets of specimens every week or two, and Ravenel kept up with him, sending identifications of each new batch of plants along with advice on collecting techniques. Look for the little plants in undisturbed woods and low, swampy areas, he suggested, and when possible collect large quantities for later exchanges.[36] Ravenel early suggested Ellis get a copy of Greville's five-volume *Scottish Cryptogamic Flora,* which had been so useful to him, and he particularly recommended Fries's *Systema,* the *Elenchus,* and a new work, the *Epicrisis* (Upsala, 1838). In his reliance upon and admiration for Fries, Ravenel was typical of mycologists of his time. "Fries," he explained to Ellis later, "is quite an old man now, but as adroit a Botanist as ever—He is the highest authority living, in the orders Fungi & Lichenes, & has done much in other departments of Botany."[37]

Besides giving much attention to Ellis's needs, Ravenel was hard at work gathering the final specimens necessary for the third fascicle of his exsiccati and then gumming them down in the volumes. They were ready to be distributed by the end of May.[38] Although printed, as the others had been, by Russell's, this volume was more neatly done and had very few typographical errors. Again Ravenel had provided good specimens in sufficient quantity for the illustration of each species. The volume contained contributions from Peters and Beaumont in Alabama and one species each from the Texas collector Charles Wright, from Ezra Michener in Pennsylvania, and from Henry Parker Sartwell in New Jersey. Over 60 percent of the species represented distinctly American forms, and about a quarter of them were undescribed; so the fascicle was sure to be of interest to Ravenel's European correspondents.[39]

No sooner had he issued the third fascicle than Ravenel began organizing a fourth. The manuscript for this one was ready by the beginning of August 1855, and this time Ravenel took extra precautions to see to its accuracy. He sent the manuscript to Lewis Gibbes, who was something of a Latin scholar as well as a scientist. He asked that his friend proof the manuscript and take it to Russell's and that Russell's send the proof sheets back to Ravenel for a final review before printing.[40] As he sent off the manuscript of the fourth volume, he was already looking ahead to a fifth. "I would be glad to have Peziza scutellata in quantity for my work," he petitioned Ellis near the end of August, "as I have not yet collected it in sufficient numbers. Wherever you can get Fungi which can go between the leaves of the book, & suitable for my purpose, & which are not contained in any previous issue, they will be very acceptable for the future vols of my work."[41]

Ravenel's fourth fascicle was ready to be sent out by the middle of November. As he prepared to mail copies to his various correspondents, he found he had unwittingly added another European botanist to the list of those to be sent presentation copies. In 1854 he had used the services of a traveling fellow South Carolinian to send a gift of lichens, mosses, and liverworts to French botanist Camille Montagne. Montagne thanked him profusely, and a few months later Ravenel wrote back offering to make him up a package of fungi and saying he would appreciate receiving copies of papers or other publications in return. He casually mentioned his work on the exsiccati, which was, it turned out, exactly what Montagne wanted. Nothing, the French botanist said, could give him greater pleasure than to take up Ravenel's generous offer to trade his beautiful collection of exsiccati for Montagne's publications.[42] Ravenel had no graceful way out of the misunderstanding and quite possibly did not desire one anyway. Accordingly, he packed up a set of all four fascicles and shipped them off to Montagne.

Montagne's response was gratifying. The French botanist thanked Ravenel warmly for the gift. No other collection of exotic cryptogams could have given him such pleasure. In every volume of one hundred species, he had found one or two identifications with which he had to disagree, but in every case, the difference was small or somewhat in dispute. *Sphaeria verrucosa* Schw. number 50, Fascicle I, for example, he declared to be a *Nectria* but admitted that name had not yet been generally adopted.[43]

John A. Stevenson, a modern expert on fungi exsiccati, has agreed with Montagne's favorable opinion of Ravenel's work. The species included were "an excellent representation" of southern fungi, "including all groups which were adaptable to use in an exsiccati." The individual specimens "were well selected" and "carefully prepared." Because the volumes were well made, most sets had survived the approximately 120 years between their issuance and Stevenson's examination in fair condition. Stevenson did have one complaint. Following custom established by Fries, Berkeley, and others, Ravenel had carefully glued each specimen in place on its sheet. This was labor lost, so far as Stevenson was concerned, for specimens so mounted were quite susceptible to damage. It would have been better to place them in small packets.[44]

After issuing his fourth fascicle of exsiccati, Ravenel did not immediately begin work on the fifth, although he had some of the materials available. His usual winter trip to Pooshee interrupted the flow of his work, and he spent some time catching up with the needs of some of his correspondents.

Ellis, who had abandoned Georgia in August 1855 and moved back to Potsdam, continued to send bulky packages of plants through the mail for identification. They were coming now from an area whose flora was unfamiliar to Ravenel, and so their identification was more taxing and, correspondingly, more interesting. His student's own growing expertise also meant that he sent fewer and fewer easily identified plants, while the proportion of new or ambiguous species increased. Even so, Ravenel identified the genera easily but often had to put off further study until the exsiccati was complete.[45] Ravenel anticipated sending the species he could not identify to Berkeley for his opinion. He therefore cautioned Ellis to exercise more care in the collection and organization of specimens. Ravenel suggested that he send two or three good specimens, each gummed down on a piece of white paper on which he should record the plant's assigned number, the matrix and locality, and his name as collector. By all means, too, he must poison his specimens or they would be lost.[46]

In the years that had passed since his confrontation with Curtis on the issue of authorship, Ravenel had become reconciled to the necessity of sending doubtful specimens abroad for determination and to the convention that the more advanced botanist who identified a new species would serve as author. Ravenel was himself no longer shut out by this rule, having issued several new species in the *Fungi Caroliniani Exsiccati*. In addition, an article published by Berkeley and Curtis in December 1853 in the British *Annals and Magazine of Natural History* recognized his contribution in a unique way. "We ought to observe," they wrote, "that a considerable portion of Mr. Ravenel's specimens were accompanied by copious notes, of which we have constantly availed ourselves. Indeed his name might almost uniformly have been associated with our own, were it not for the inconvenience of giving three authorities for each new species." Although his name did not appear as an author of the article, he was credited, alone or in conjunction with Berkeley, as author of a number of new species published there, and three new plants were named for him.[47] Ellis could not yet expect this sort of special treatment. When he began to demonstrate curiosity about Ravenel's foreign contacts, Ravenel did not discourage him from writing but gently explained the rules of the game.[48]

During the 1850s Ravenel became well known to other botanists in America and Europe because of his exsiccati and the frequent appearance of his name in Berkeley's writings. Therefore, from time to time new mycological correspondents wrote to him requesting help. Julien Marc Deby, a French-born botanist who lived in Georgia from 1854 until 1859, became interested in fungi and wrote, desiring to compare notes and hoping for some duplicates of Ravenel's specimens.[49] Berlin botanist Robert Caspary wrote in August 1855 to see if Ravenel could provide examples of potato leaves infested with the blight that a decade earlier had caused famine in Ireland. There was no potato blight in South Carolina, but Ravenel was able to supply the request through Ellis with reasonable dispatch.[50]

As the year 1856 began he was distracted from the exsiccati anew by collecting in other types of plants. Except for the discovery of a new species of *Baptisia*, a genus of the legume family, he had largely ignored everything but the fungi for several years. His paper on *Baptisia stipulacea* was read by Gibbes before the Elliott Society in January 1856. In 1879, however, *B. stipulacea* was identified by William Canby as a synonym of *B. microphylla* Nuttall.[51]

As spring came, Ravenel remained at Pooshee longer than usual to take advantage of the low country's richer botanical range. William

Starling Sullivant and his new associate, Leo Lesquereux, were preparing to issue a new moss exsiccati, and Ravenel was helping to procure some of their desired southern species. He was also putting together a set of freshwater shells for Lesquereux's son in repayment for a valuable set of European fungi sent by the father and a set of lichens that he had been promised.[52]

At the same time, Ravenel was recommencing his correspondence with Tuckerman, from whom he had heard nothing since shortly after his visit in 1853. Tuckerman in his study of lichens had one advantage that both Ravenel and Curtis lacked; he had been to Europe to study the type specimens of genera and species founded by European workers. He was, then, in a good position to pronounce upon new species with greater authority than the two mycologists. Ravenel urged him to go ahead with his study of the southern lichens before some European forestalled him in publication of American species. When in July he received a copy of Tuckerman's new volume of exsiccati, he noticed a few southern species and was puzzled as to why Tuckerman had never asked him to send any. Tuckerman's answer cleared up a misunderstanding of eight or ten years' duration. Of course Tuckerman wanted southern exsiccati specimens. He had simply not thought it necessary to ask for them. With his puzzlement relieved, Ravenel assured Tuckerman that he would be happy to collect for him if he would send a list of desiderata.[53]

Tuckerman sent not one list but several, at intervals, and Ravenel was well occupied collecting for him during his trips to Saint John's at Christmas 1856, 1857, and 1858. He assured Tuckerman that he had many opportunities to gather lichens while attending to his own fungal collecting, and that nothing pleased him more than an excuse to mount his horse and ride off into the woods for a few hours. He was also enthusiastic about the value of Tuckerman's work and suggested that he might be able to collect enough material to justify one fascicle of lichens peculiar to the Black Oak area.[54] This, however, was not to be. The last double fascicle of Tuckerman's exsiccati was issued in 1854. Cover sheets dated 1860 were printed for combined fascicles seven/eight and nine/ten, the former to have consisted largely of Ravenel's collections, but these were never issued. Between 1937 and 1942, however, the Farlow Herbarium of Harvard University gathered together 150 of Tuckerman's exsiccati specimens, including many contributed by Ravenel, and published them under the name *Reliquiae Tuckermanianae.*[55]

In June 1858 Ravenel announced in one of his letters to Tuckerman that he was engaged and hoped soon to be married again.[56] The bride-to-be was Mary Huger Dawson, daughter of Octavius Huger Dawson and Caroline Deas Dawson. Like Ravenel, the Dawsons were active members of Saint Thaddeus Church. Henry Ravenel and Mary Dawson were married August 12, 1858, at the home of her widowed mother in a simple ceremony, performed by Episcopal minister John Cornish.[57]

Mary, at the age of twenty-five, was young enough to be a daughter to her forty-four-year-old husband; she was only six years older than Ravenel's eldest child, Lydia, then nineteen. Mary apparently got along well with her husband's children. When she and Ravenel had Caroline, the first of their own five daughters, baptized in 1859, Lydia was one of the sponsors, and Ravenel's other children each served in turn as sponsor to a younger half sister.[58] The one person Mary could not win over was the ghost of her predecessor. Although he was fond of his new bride, Ravenel never forgot his love for Elizabeth or entirely ceased to mourn her. Beginning a diary in 1859, he left a blank page each February 5 in her memory, except during the Civil War when paper became very scarce. In 1866 when Frank Porcher's wife died, Ravenel wrote with knowing sympathy, "This is the greatest earthly calamity that can befall a man." Mary was, fortunately, wise and mature enough not to become jealous of Henry's memories. On her own initiative, she named the third of their daughters Elizabeth Gaillard in honor, as Ravenel recorded, "of my first beloved wife."[59]

Neither marriage nor the collecting he was doing for others represented the full reason Ravenel let several years go by between the issuance of fascicle four and the commencement of serious work on fascicle five. Two other problems hindered him. The first was that Aiken's flora was much less profuse and varied than that of Saint John's. In fungi, particularly, the new area was comparatively lacking, for Aiken's dry climate was less conducive to their growth than the moist atmosphere of the low country. Aiken had given him little in the way of interesting species, and his first year or two of exploration had been enough to exhaust the supply. Much of his collecting, therefore, was accomplished during Christmas visits to Saint John's, but several years of intensive winter collecting had nearly exhausted his old botanical range for that season. If he could still work with the energy he had had ten years earlier, he complained to Curtis in October 1856, one summer of collecting in Saint John's would be enough to bring two new fascicles to a speedy conclusion.[60]

Even Aiken's limited ecological range was only a secondary impediment. The period of concentrated botanical study that had followed his wife's death brought back in full force the dislike of microscopy that he had struggled against in 1854. "I cannot, cannot work at the microscope & this is the only eye with which we can look with any satisfaction at a fungus. Distaste is gradually growing into aversion, from the invariably depressing effect it has on my health & spirits."[61]

Ravenel's problems with the microscope were not unique to him. The short focal length of high-powered, simple microscopes required that the user's eye, the lens, and the object to be studied be very close together, and the close juxtaposition produced eye strain. Despite the discomfort, some botanists, particularly Englishmen, preferred the simple to the compound microscopes. By about 1830 compound microscopes were available with spherical and chromatic corrections. Their resolving power was a little higher than that of the simple microscopes (approximately one micron, compared to five or six), but the simple microscopes had been superior to the older compound ones for many years, and there remained even in the 1850s a lingering distrust of the compound instruments.[62] Berkeley was among those who preferred the simple microscope. In 1854 he reported to Ravenel, "I have just had a present of a fine compound microscope from my friend Dr. Hooker, which will be a great saving to my eyes," but he continued, "As far as they go I think doublets far preferable to the best compound microscope."[63]

Ravenel's inability to use the microscope did not improve as it had the last time he was bothered with the problem. He had to stop his work with the fungi and in April 1857 reported to Ellis that he had been unable to identify the last bundle of plants satisfactorily. He advised his student not to send any more specimens to him but to open correspondence with Tuckerman and the Englishman Christopher Broome instead.[64]

In October 1857 Ravenel made arrangements to deposit his herbarium with the Charleston Museum, though he retained the lichens and mosses until he should hear of the results of Tuckerman, Sullivant, and Lesquereux's ongoing work in those orders. The herbarium was intended as a loan, and he parted with it only reluctantly, but he was pleased that while he was unable to proceed with his work the herbarium was available to other scientists. The large number of authentic specimens among the cryptogams made it a very valuable collection.[65]

Curtis had recently transferred to the Episcopal parish at Hillsboro, North Carolina. A larger and more active church than the one in Society Hill, it required much more of his time, leaving him little leisure for mycology, and he, too, was retiring from botany. He was disappointed to learn that at the same time he must withdraw, Ravenel had also become unable to work. He had hoped to pass his own correspondents and unfinished work over to Ravenel. Nevertheless, he tried to look at the bright side of the situation. "There will be this satisfaction to us both—that we have pretty effectually opened the field, & have opened up many a treasure. I dont know but we have done our full share, & may justly take our rest." Yet he looked back wistfully at the ambitions of his youth, "Oh, that Mycologia Americana!"[66]

Peters was also disheartened to hear that Ravenel was giving up mycology. When he wrote, he spoke for all those whose dedication and skill in the science were of a lower order than Ravenel's or Curtis's but whose interest was sincere. "With yourself and Dr. Curtis out of the field, we shall be without guides, and must stop for want of leaders. I hope you will find it possible & agreeable to finish the V Fac of your excellent preparations of South Carolina Fungi." If Ravenel would continue with the exsiccati, he believed he could furnish some more specimens and would also enlist Beaumont's aid.[67] A letter in June 1859 from Allen Poe of Montreal, one of Curtis's correspondents, also nudged Ravenel towards a fifth fascicle. "If any of the specimens I have sent Dr. Curtis have sufficient interest for your Vth Fasc. and I can obtain the requisite number my services are at your disposal," he stated simply.[68]

Eventually Ravenel was persuaded to issue another volume. When he informed Ellis of the decision in September 1859, he already had much of the material ready, including some of the species provided by Ellis himself in prior years. He intended, however, to prepare an index to the set and so was not expecting to have it ready for distribution for several months.[69]

In the same letter that announced his return to work on the exsiccati, Ravenel shared with Ellis one of the interests that had lately absorbed much of the time once devoted to mycology. "I have become quite an amateur Pomologist & vintner," he confided, "taking great interest in my fruit trees & vines. . . . I am trying to procure all the varieties of grape I hear of, & if you could aid me in doing so, I would esteem it a great favour."[70] The interest was by no means new. Even in Saint John's, Ravenel had had some interest in horticulture. In 1850 or 1851 he had published a paper on the history of the Catawba grape, a popular native variety commonly planted in the southern states, and at the invitation of the Vine Growers' Association of Cincinnati had in December 1851 presented to them a paper on the same subject.[71]

Throughout South Carolina, Georgia, and Alabama enthusiasm for fruit culture was growing during the 1840s and 1850s. Peaches and grapes were the most popular and profitable of the fruit crops. Robert Nelson, a Danish refugee who established a nursery in Macon, Georgia, contributed greatly to the business of southern peach raising by developing in the early 1850s an improved variety of early peach intended for the New York markets. In 1853 he sent some of his improved peaches to market, where New Yorkers paid fifty cents a-piece for them, while the previous year ordinary peaches had sold for as little as twenty-five cents a bushel. Commercial grape culture had failed in the early 1830s, but soon growers developed valuable varieties of hardy native grapes, and in the Aiken area a number of successful vineyards were founded. A. de Caradeuc and J. C. W. McDonnald were the most successful of Aiken's vintners, and Jules Berckmans produced fine grapes at his nursery in Augusta, Georgia. Another Augustan, Jarvis Van Buren, developed a reputation for apples, as did Silas McDowell of North Carolina.[72]

On moving to Aiken, Ravenel became enthusiastic about horticulture. Even before he had moved his family to the farm at Hampton Hill, he was planning a peach orchard.[73] Nor was his orchard to be a pitiful half acre of scrawny trees. In 1862 he estimated that he had about four thousand peach trees and six to eight thousand bearing grape vines, as well as a few each of apple, pear, fig, pomegranate, plum, jujube, and cherry trees. A good harvest of peaches alone could bring him five or six thousand dollars on the New York markets.[74]

In a day when five thousand dollars a year meant wealth, Ravenel's success as a fruit grower was impressive indeed. His fruit crop was not his main source of income, however, and Ravenel's interest in the plants was clearly at least as much botanical as financial. His reference to himself as an amateur in his letter to Ellis indicates, in fact, that he regarded horticulture more as a hobby than as a business. He also made this apparent in a letter to Asa Gray in 1855. "I am somewhat of an amateur farmer," he wrote, "& take great interest in my farm & garden, for healthy & invigorating exercise, & for instructive experimenting."[75] Ravenel was probably not playing down his farming activities for the benefit of Ellis and Gray. In the context of nineteenth-century America's agricultural society and the still preprofessional state of scientific study, they were unlikely to think him less a botanist for his interest in cultivars. Indeed, his own early interest in fungal plant pathogens was reinforced by Caspary's interest in potato blight and by Berkeley's request in 1854 that he watch for mildew on native American or British grapes.[76]

As in Saint John's, Ravenel became active in the formation of a local agricultural society. The Aiken Vine-Growing and Horticultural Association was inaugurated in July 1858. The timing of its formation, as well as the sharp increase in Ravenel's horticultural correspondence during 1858 and 1859, indicate that the association and horticulture functioned as an emotional and intellectual substitute for mycology. Ravenel was one of the leaders of the agriculture society, serving terms as treasurer and as president. Other active members included Caradeuc, McDonnald, D. Redmond of Augusta's *Southern Cultivator* (a long-lived monthly for farmers), and John Cornish of Saint Thaddeus.

Ravenel brought to the Aiken vine growers' association his botanist's desire to promote among farmers an appreciation of science and its application to their art.[77] Many other horticulturists, he found, shared his interest in taxonomy. He recruited help from them in collecting varieties of grape vines and studying their relationship to the original, undomesticated plants. In September 1859 he read to the

Aiken group a paper giving a summary of his preliminary findings on the subject. The paper was very well received and was reprinted twice, once by the United States Patent Office and once by the *Southern Cultivator*.[78] A similar paper was submitted to the South Carolina State Agricultural Society. It was published in the *Farmer and Planter*, and for his contribution the state society awarded him six large silver forks.[79]

Like many other horticulturists, Ravenel was not content merely to study and grow the available varieties of fruit. He experimented with grafting foreign grapes onto hardy native stalks and also tried to develop new kinds of grapes.[80] These concerns brought to mind the question of the permanence or impermanence of species. Cultivated fruits, he wrote in July 1859, are all varieties of wild parent stock. Most are not capable of living except under a high degree of cultivation. Remove those favorable but artificial conditions, and the cultivars will die away or revert in future generations to the wild type. New varieties may be raised from the seeds of an established variety. This standard horticultural wisdom Ravenel mentioned while arguing another point. He did not bring up the subject of the possibility of change among the wild species from which the varieties arose, but he implied that, in contrast to the changing varieties, the species were constant.[81]

By the fall of 1860, when Ravenel prepared his second essay on the classification of fruit, he was familiar with Charles Darwin's *Origin of Species* (1859), at least through Asa Gray's review, which appeared in *Silliman's Journal* in March 1860. Ravenel decided to state his views on the subject of species more explicitly.

By *species* all naturalists understand those primordial forms which have existed, unchanged in essentials, for a period beyond all historic times, and which are capable of propagating their kind, *inter se.* . . . By *varieties* we understand all casual deviations from the typical form; sometimes so well marked and prominent as to be continued even in a state of nature, when the proper conditions are present.—These variations, however, never rise to the value of specific difference, and are liable (when the conditions under which they originated are withdrawn) to lapse again into the typical form of the species. *Species,* therefore, are constant and permanent in their character; *varieties,* inconstant, and liable to revert again to their respective species.[82]

Although he affirmed the constancy of species, Ravenel did not deny Darwin's theory and the possibility of evolution. Rather, he denied their relevance to taxonomy. In this way, Ravenel thought his definition of species as unchanging forms to be quite unobjectionable. It did not conflict with Darwin's theory, for by the English scientist's own admission, the time needed for important changes in species to occur must be measured in thousands and tens of thousands of years. "For all common purposes, . . ." he concluded, "we may consider species as immutable."[83]

Many years later Ravenel remained open-minded on the question of evolution, neither accepting nor rejecting it. Like many other scientists of his time, including Asa Gray and fellow southerner Joseph LeConte, Ravenel doubted not evolution per se but natural selection as the principal causal mechanism. In fact, Ravenel found evolution to have "a great degree of plausibility" as a creation account.[84] A long letter written in December 1879 to Thomas Meehan treated the subject in more detail. "Evolution *in some form,*" he began, "as an interpretation of natural phenomena, is so well substan[t]iated through all the range of the natural sciences, & reconciles & explains so much of what would otherwise remain obscure & inexplicable, that it is hard to resist so plausible an explanation."[85]

Yet Ravenel could not fully accept evolution. He felt that many of Darwin's disciples used the theory to explain too much. They would leave no room in nature for "a Directing, Supernatural Providence" but would instead leave all to the operation of blind forces. He found this point of view objectionable from the standpoints of both faith and science. How, he asked, could any environmental force account for the near equality in number of men and women in populations throughout the world? Environment would uniformly affect all children conceived in a given area, and its influence would logically be to create a preponderance of one sex or the other.[86]

There were, of course, valid and important scientific problems with the theory of evolution, particularly gaps in the fossil record and ignorance of the laws of heredity and mutation. Many of these objections did not begin to be eased until rediscovery of Gregor Mendel's work on heredity in 1900, thirteen years after Ravenel's death. Despite his objections, Ravenel neither rejected evolution nor allowed it to shake his faith. He was sure that errors in interpretation of nature, God's word, or both, would ultimately be corrected and science and religion would come into perfect harmony.[87] Ravenel's open-minded attitude toward evolution was an indication of the fair-minded conservatism of his character.

In Aiken, Ravenel continued to build upon the scientific foundation he laid in Saint John's in the 1840s. Collecting and taxonomy remained the central points of his approach to botany, unshaken by the passage of time, by personal calamities, or by Darwin. His most important work of the period, the *Fungi Caroliniani Exsiccati,* was a presentation to other taxonomists of standardized portions of his collection. While his outlook on botany was unchanging, his stature as a botanist increased. Both in the United States and in Europe, he became well known among scientists for his enthusiasm for and contributions to mycology. Once he had struggled to increase his circle of correspondents; now men wrote unbidden to him, seeking to establish an acquaintanceship. Of these correspondents, few by the end of the 1850s fit the mold of teachers, that status being, probably fairly, reserved to Berkeley and Montagne. Others were his scientific equals or his helpers. As the decade ended, however, Ravenel's dyspepsia and his inability to use the microscope dictated that he would have to make some changes in his approach to botany or give up the science altogether.

The Disruption of War, 1860–1865

6

In 1860 colorful uniforms and bright flags were a central part of the American public's image of war.[1] Throughout the American South and, to a lesser extent, the North, militia units parading in fanciful costume on the lawns of county courthouses reflected, as well as reinforced, the concept that war was a gallant adventure. Each Fourth of July the old veterans of the Revolution trooped together down dusty main streets to be honored once again for the part they had played in freeing the country from British rule. Old age and death gradually thinned their ranks. Younger Americans had no memory of British military occupation or the horrors of battle, but the glorious side of the Revolution lived on in yearly celebrations. The widespread cult of the Revolution contributed a bit to the circumstances that allowed young men to march off to war in 1861, convinced, as were many of their older and, presumably, wiser political leaders, that the conflict would be only a brief and grandly exciting interruption to their ordinary lives.

Ravenel was not fooled. In January 1861, as he watched state after state join South Carolina in secession, he worried about the future. "We may be on the very threshold of a bloody & desolating civil war," a war that, one month later, he predicted would "be one of the bloodiest the world has ever seen."[2] Concerned though he was, Ravenel saw reason to be optimistic. Until only days before his old acquaintance Edmund Ruffin fired the first shot against Fort Sumter, Ravenel hoped that war might be averted and that North and South might coexist peacefully. Even as war came to seem inevitable, faith in the southern Confederacy's eventual triumph was strong within him, and he looked ahead with confidence.[3] Even Ravenel, though alive to the gravity of the situation, was not immune to the charm of uniform and flag, and he became caught up in some of the excitement of the days just before Sumter. When Captain Mangum of Aiken's volunteer company, the Allen Guards, came calling in February, Ravenel gave him twenty dollars to help equip his men, some of whom could not afford uniforms. The ladies of Aiken donated a flag, and early on April 12, 1861, Ravenel joined other citizens of the town to see the troops off to Charleston. "I could not but think," he reflected, "what an answer it [the company] furnished to the poor deluded fanatics at the North who have been trying to sew [*sic*] dissension among our people. Three fourths of the men, I am very sure have never owned a slave. Many of them are foreigners. . . . They have buckled on their armor & are now perilling their lives in defence of their adopted country." At three in the afternoon of that same day, word reached Ravenel that the war had begun.[4]

Few people could really have been surprised at the commencement of hostilities. Trouble had been brewing for decades. The issue of high tariffs that had greater negative impact upon the South than upon the North caused tension throughout the 1820s. Attempts, led by southern spokesman John C. Calhoun, to persuade Congress to lower the tariffs failed, and in 1832 South Carolina seized the initiative. Hoping to be followed by other southern states, a state convention assembled in November and declared the offending law null and void with respect to the Palmetto State. The movement fizzled quickly. Other southern states criticized South Carolina's action, and President Andrew Jackson met it with firm condemnation, calling it treason. A compromise tariff took much wind out of the sails, and in March 1833 the convention reassembled and rescinded its Ordinance of Nullification. Nevertheless, the Nullification controversy began a noticeable shift in the patriotic loyalties of a number of South Carolina leaders from the United States to an idealized southern nation. Many talked of secession.[5]

Ravenel was a Union man in 1832 and for many years afterwards. Ten years later, when he addressed the State Agricultural Society, he touched on crop diversification, a favorite theme of secessionists, but he made no specific allusion to sectional tension.[6] The simple economic benefits of cushioning against a fall in the price of rice or cotton and of increased crop yield due to improved systems of crop rotation were obvious arguments for the diversification of crops. While the idea had certain appeal to those favoring southern independence, Ravenel evidently espoused it for the improvement it could effect in southern agricultural production, without concern for its value in the event of secession.

Political worries of the early 1850s growing out of the agitated feelings surrounding the Compromise of 1850 caused great concern in Saint John's. Citizens from that area joined with those of Saint James's and Saint Stephen's parishes to hold a political meeting November 2, 1850. They heard addresses from the well-known southern nationalist Robert Barnwell Rhett and from two less famous men, William Blanding and Louis F. Robertson. Their speeches fired their listeners with zeal, and on that day the men of Saint John's Berkeley and Saint Stephen's formed a Southern Rights Association and raised a volunteer company for the protection of the region. Ravenel joined the Southern Rights Association and served as its treasurer until April 1852 when he handed the position on to his younger brother Thomas.[7] Ravenel also joined the Middle Saint John's Company, which Thomas served as captain, but his enthusiasm for the venture was not great. He was not an officer but only a lowly private, and the roll book for 1852 shows him absent three times from drills. Three absences in a year might not seem many; yet he was gone more often than anyone else.[8]

Ravenel saw still another way to serve the South. In April 1852 he appeared before the Black Oak Agricultural Society to deliver the oration in honor of the anniversary of the society.[9] Three years earlier he had also delivered an address and had chosen as his topic an entirely apolitical subject, the relationship between agriculture and meteorology. The intervening years had brought such political turmoil to the South, however, that he was sure he would be speaking to an issue already on everyone's mind and that he would not need to apologize for bringing up politics at the anniversary meeting.

Ravenel hoped to calm prevailing fears and worries and, at the same time, to strengthen his neighbors' resolve to meet unwaveringly the daily insults to their way of life coming from abolitionists. He pursued these goals in as strongly positive and optimistic a way as possible by describing the South's elements of strength while treating charges brought against her by outsiders very lightly. The first such strength, he argued, was the essential conservatism of the southern people, which guarded the South from political excesses born of disrespect for government and also from encroachment by government upon the rights of the people. This conservatism was a natural outcome of a rural economy based on slavery. Control of the laboring class excluded from the South unruly free laborers, particularly foreign workers, who were unable to understand the delicate balance of personal freedom and social responsibility necessary to the smooth working of a democracy. An agricultural economy and slavery, then, gave the South the essential conservatism that Henry Ravenel saw as one of her greatest strengths.[10]

Ravenel cited as the second of the South's advantages the importance of her agricultural products to the world economy. Cotton, of course, was necessary to northern and English mills, but the South also produced significant crops of rice, sugar, and tobacco. The North and England also depended on her as a market for their manufactured goods, and this dependence would prevent them from destroying slavery, for to do so would be to destroy their own economy.[11]

Third and greatest of the South's strengths was the justice of her cause. Slavery was a necessity, for it was impossible that the two races should either become amalgamated into one or coexist on terms of equality. Whites, therefore, would always dominate blacks, and it was infinitely to the benefit of the latter that the relationship between the two races should be well defined, with mutual obligations established in law and social custom. Whites were thereby prevented from exploiting their slaves for labor, then leaving them unprotected in sickness and old age. Such, of course, could easily be the lot of northern laborers. Ravenel did not rest his argument with the assertion that slavery was expedient. Much good, he asserted, had fallen to blacks from enslavement. They had increased in number since coming to the United States, a sure sign of health and happiness, and were enabled here to be useful while daily making progress toward attaining a higher level of civilization. Ravenel's firm belief in progress served, on the one hand, to justify the collection of all kinds of scientific data, even though not immediately useful, and, on the other hand, as the cornerstone of Ravenel's acceptance of slavery. Progress, Ravenel wrote, applied to the physical world and also to the human community, both black and white, and he saw in slavery "an educational school for the improvement of the African race." As Anglo-American civilization had emerged from barbarian tribes of northern Europe, so would the blacks progress until they had reached the limits of their capacity to improve, and Ravenel did not speculate where those limits might be. Biblical sanctions with regard to slavery were also significant, but Ravenel refrained from elaborating on them.[12]

Dramatic, ringing, just slightly flowery, Ravenel's 1852 address probably had a stirring effect on his audience and made them feel, if only for a moment, "a firm and abiding conviction that all is not lost— that our position is strong—our defence unfailing, impregnable—and that, with united and manly efforts, we can yet roll back the furious tempest which threatens to sweep across our devoted land." When read carefully, however, the speech reveals disappointing gaps in thought and inconsistencies in logic. At one point, for example, Ravenel mentioned the pride which the South had taken in fulfilling her duty to the Union, "without any appeal to another law, exterior and foreign to, the written constitution which she has sworn to observe." This was an obvious swipe at New York's William Seward for his much-criticized 1850 invocation of "a higher law than the Constitution which regulates our authority over the domain." Unfortunately for the effectiveness of Ravenel's argument, however, Seward's higher law was God's law. The South Carolinian's denial that the South depended on any law other than the Constitution took on a hollow sound when Ravenel referred to the Bible's approval of slavery.[13]

Most striking of Ravenel's lapses, however, is his failure to make clear exactly what he was so concerned about. What was "the furious tempest"? Was he worried about the criticism of northern and European abolitionists, about abolition itself, or perhaps about an unnecessary or premature movement toward secession, always a possibility in South Carolina? More significantly, what was "our devoted land"? What did he mean by his occasional references to "our ship of State" or "the country"? Sometimes he seemed to have the South in mind; at other times it seemed to be the Union. Moreover, when obviously writing of the South, he alternated greatly in his use of pronouns. The South and her people were in turn she, we, or they. These uncertainties of prose were not mere symptoms of a general inability to write clear English. Although he made no claim to literary talent, Ravenel was quite capable of writing clearly. It would seem likely, rather, that his vagueness here indicated an uncertainty in his own mind as to where his loyalties lay. The onetime unionist was not yet a southern nationalist.

Answers to the questions raised by the 1852 *Anniversary Address* can be found in Ravenel's botanical correspondence. Like most scientists of the period, Ravenel generally kept politics out of his scientific letters, but he occasionally opened his mind to his Massachusetts correspondent Edward Tuckerman. To him he wrote on December 31, 1850, not quite two months after the Saint John's southern rights meeting, of his fear that northern demagoguery had overtaken the political power of the North and was leading the nation into disaster:

> I have never entertained a doubt that a large portion of the intelligent & patriotic citizens of the North, whatever they may think of our domestic institutions, are disposed to be faithful to the compromises of the constitution & the rights of the states—could the settlement of this distracting subject be left to them, I would have confidence in the issue—But I fear the decision of the question has passed beyond their power—. . .
> The South has loved the Union for the common glories of the past, & for what might have been the common glorious destiny of the future—. . . The future is dark and portentous,—& I almost despair of the integrity of the Union, but it may be that He who has hitherto so signally blessed & prospered our country, may overrule the wicked machinations of its foes.[14]

Northern extremism, then, was the enemy threatening both the South and the Union. The North and the northern people were old friends, with whom reconciliation might still be possible. Day by day, however, it became more apparent that the compromises had truly satisfied no one. Old tensions worsened, and the deaths of America's great elder statesmen left no strong leaders to fight for conciliation. Daniel Webster's death in 1852 particularly deepened Ravenel's concern, for the northern orator was the last of the trio who had fashioned compromise between free soil and slavery. Ravenel shared with his friend Tuckerman his feeling that the South as well as the North had suffered a loss in Webster's passing, speaking of him not by name but by allusion as "the *great Northern light*—The last of that brilliant triad, . . . the shining constellation in our political heavens." With Webster, Clay, and Calhoun gone, Ravenel knew not where the country could turn for leadership.[15]

Over the following eight years Ravenel completed his transition from unionist to southern nationalist. Just how the transformation was effected must remain unknown, for few of Ravenel's personal papers have survived from this period, and Ravenel did not begin his daily journal until 1859. No doubt, however, the change was not easy, for it involved setting aside deep feelings of attachment taught to him from childhood. Boyhood fascination with stories of the American Revolution had led to an adult realization of the depth of the South's stake in the Union. Southern blood had helped to win independence and had been shed in defense of the flag on many other battlefields. Of course he felt great reluctance at the thought of cutting these ties. Like most Americans of his generation, however, his attachment was always first to neighborhood, parish, and state and only then to the United States. His primary loyalties could, therefore, remain intact while national loyalty slowly swung from the United States to an unformed combination of the southern states. This was important to him, for his affection for the place of his birth was fierce. In a moment of reflection he wrote to Tuckerman of his feelings for Saint John's: "I have a peculiar love for this section of country—my native place, . . . & the home of my friends—Here, for six or eight generations, . . . have the ties of home attachment been growing & strengthening." Even the war stories so inspiring to national patriotism produced an even stronger loyalty to Saint John's. The heroes of these childhood tales were local men, and their sacred battlefields were the plantations of his neighbors.[16]

However strong his sectional loyalties, Ravenel's view of national politics remained remarkably thoughtful and fair-minded. His disdain of northern extremism did not blind him to the dangers posed by extremists in his own section. Robert Barnwell Rhett he characterized as untrustworthy, devoted to South Carolina and the South but lacking in judgment and statesmanship. On controversial issues, as well, Ravenel favored calm consideration and preferred to see the South continue to compromise on noncrucial points in order to work with the moderate elements of the North. As presidential politics heated tempers in the spring of 1860, for example, the question of slavery in the territories was brought sharply to his attention. He thought Stephen Douglas's views rather peculiar, in that Douglas admitted the theoretical right of slaveowners to bring their human property into the territories, yet would also allow territorial legislatures to throw up barriers that would make the importation of slavery effectively impossible. Ravenel did not by any means approve this view. He saw its unbecoming logical inconsistency and found it offensive that a territory should be able to refuse the admission of any kind of property. Yet an alternative proposed by some southerners, that the South must insist on congressional legislation to open the territories to slavery, he thought unwise. By insisting on congressional intervention the South would alienate the opinion of moderate northerners and would gain little. The more southerly territories, where slavery would, Ravenel thought, be profitable, would have slavery with or without congressional protection. In the northerly territories, however, slavery would languish no matter how well protected. "Our people do not reflect enough upon these things for themselves," he complained, "but are led on by politicians, & made to think that safety, honour, self respect & our very existence depend upon these issues."[17]

Perhaps as a curb to the ambitions of extremist politicians, of whom South Carolina had at least her fair share, Ravenel greatly hoped that the southern states would act together to secure protection of their rights. Public opinion in South Carolina he judged to be unanimous about the necessity of secession in case of Lincoln's election. Excitement intensified as election day drew near, and Ravenel worried that his state would leave the Union hastily, without due deliberation and without the support of the other southern states. Premature secession, he thought, could be a great mistake. It could deprive South Carolina and the entire South of needed unity in the face of nothern opposition and forever deny them any chance of effective resistance to northern encroachments. Election of the despised Republicans changed his view of the situation radically. Opinion in other southern states appeared to crystallize in favor of secession, and by the end of November, Ravenel was ready to see South Carolina take the lead. No longer did he fear her leadership would be spurned. Severance of the Palmetto State from the Union seemed a way to unite southern opinion and achieve a common deliverance.[18]

If Ravenel the citizen welcomed secession, Ravenel the scientist regretted its necessity. He did not want a rift to open between himself and his northern correspondents. When Gray and Tuckerman both wrote within days of each other to inquire about the political situation, he hastened to assure them of his continued personal esteem and respect. He did, however, set forth plainly his own opinion that the South was justified in feeling that there was no longer any safety in remaining in the Union. To accept rule by a political party whose very principles were founded upon opposition to the South and her institutions was an unacceptable degradation. Whatever happened, he wrote Tuckerman, he hoped that politics would not interfere with the botanical friendship that they had shared for many years.[19] Tuckerman was apparently willing to accept Ravenel's assurances and await the outcome of secession. Gray, however, could not forgo a last, though much too late, chance to reclaim Ravenel for the unionist cause. He sent down a pamphlet, *On the State of the Country,* by Professor Hodges of Princeton. Out of respect for Gray, Ravenel did try to read it with an open mind, but alas, the disagreement was total. Hodges's argument was based on the theory that the states had given up all sovereignty when they ratified the constitution. A position denied by many northerners, it was certainly not one to be admitted by a secessionist. Ravenel sent off another long letter on politics, hoping to help Gray understand the South's attitude.[20]

War is never truly friendly to science. Branches of science judged useful to the military effort may get a boost, but all other areas suffer. Manpower and money are drained away to help fight the war, and there is no solution to it but peace.[21] So it happened in America during the Civil War. The blockade cut southern scientists off from contemporary European and northern contributions, and no one could concentrate properly on research when the fate of the entire country was being played out on the fields of Virginia.

Ravenel was certainly not the only scientist who accomplished less between 1860 and 1865 than during any other five-year period of his career. The blockade and intense, distracting interest in military events were, of course, of major significance in restricting his work. Poor health also conspired to keep him from botany, however, and it is hard to resist the conclusion that even without the war the early 1860s would have been a slow period for Ravenel's scientific productivity. Dyspepsia, aggravated by eyestrain, continued to make it difficult or impossible for him to use the microscope. In addition, beginning in early 1860 his stomach ailments so sapped his strength that Ravenel began to refer to himself as an invalid. A ride of a few miles on horseback could make him feel unwell for hours, and at times even short walks fatigued him. On some days he had to confine himself to his house and garden, not going more than a few hundred yards from the door. Collecting, of course, became impossible. Anything that could not be gotten quickly and easily could simply not be gotten, and in December 1860 he had to turn down Tuckerman's request for several plants. Trips to Charleston by train were still possible, but walking around in town became difficult. A walk across the city to visit Lewis Gibbes was a luxury he could not afford.[22]

In addition to the problems it caused directly, the dyspepsia lowered Ravenel's resistance to other diseases. A cold caught in Charleston during the last days of March 1860 kept hold of him for more than three weeks before he began feeling better. Gradually, Ravenel learned to regulate his diet to keep the dyspepsia under control. By October 1864 he judged himself to enjoy fair health as long as he was careful about his diet.[23]

Loss of hearing was also a problem during the early 1860s and possibly for some time before. An ear infection contracted during Ravenel's collecting trip through Georgia had produced acute deafness, which had disappeared after four weeks, leaving his hearing unimpaired. By late 1860, however, he had become slightly hard of hearing. Apparently, his deafness varied in its severity from time to time. In December he was having a bad enough time that his friend Francis Peyre Porcher sent a pair of "auricles," but they provided no relief, and he returned them. In March, however, he sang with the Saint Thaddeus church choir to give his daughter Henrietta confidence as she played the organ for the first time. "We have too many young singers in the choir," he complained the following Sunday, "unpracticed in sacred music—ignorant of the necessity of keeping time, & with voices too loud & untrained." Three months later, his hearing again deteriorated, and Ravenel could only make out very loud voices, very close to the ear. He soon began to suffer from pain and discharge in one ear. The infection lasted for two weeks, and it was another two weeks before he could hear a normal conversation.[24] Even then, he continued for the rest of his life to suffer from a fluctuating deafness.

In May 1860 Ravenel's ill health prevented him from accepting an opportunity to deliver a series of lectures on botany in a school of natural history being formed by Professor John McCrady of the College of Charleston. The situation would have provided some income; five dollars was being asked of each person attending, the proceeds to go to the lecturers. Ordinarily Ravenel would have welcomed a chance to share his interest in botany with others, but his chronic weakness made him incapable of the physical and mental effort needed to prepare the lectures in the rather short period of time remaining before they were to begin.[25]

Despite his ill health, Ravenel labored doggedly on the fifth fascicle of the *Fungi Caroliniani Exsiccati* throughout the spring of 1860. With books and plants spread out in his study, he would work until he was tired, leave everything just as it was, and return to the task when he felt better. In this manner he glued down about four species a day, including three or four specimens of each species in each of the thirty volumes to be issued. The tedious job was finished by the middle of June, and he began distributing copies of what he was determined would be the last volume. As though to convince any doubters who might look for a sixth, he included a general index to all five fascicles.[26] Unfortunately, the ever-critical Curtis found the index wanting, and he confided to Gray that he thought it poorly arranged. Gray, however, published a favorable review, treating the five fascicles as a set, and Lewis Gibbes took the opportunity to praise Ravenel's work and to expound on his own ideas about fungi.[27]

Ravenel also lent a little help to Alvan Wentworth Chapman during early 1860. Chapman's botany of the southern states was nearly out of the printer's hands, but the family Eriocaulinaceae was causing some problems, and on Gray's advice Chapman wrote for specimens of a plant sent by Ravenel to Gray as *Eriocaulon flavidulum* but suspected by Gray of being a distinct species. Ravenel quickly sent off specimens and received for them a flattering thank-you from Chapman. The plant, he wrote, "proves to be a new species of Eriocaulon, which I have taken the liberty to dedicate to you. May it stand as long as the Pyramids!" A complementary copy of the flora was only to be expected, and after looking it over Ravenel sent off to the Charleston *Courier* a brief but favorable notice of its publication.[28]

With the issuance of the last fascicle of his exsiccati and the publication of Chapman's flora, Ravenel was ready to complete his withdrawal from active botany. His correspondence had already begun dropping off, and when in May 1861 he received from Montagne several French publications on crypotogamic botany, he filed them away without reading them. Political events seemed much more exciting at the time.[29]

Dropping active botany did not mean dropping all interest in science. Ravenel sought to use his knowledge to help his new country. Drawing on his own interest in meteorology, he suggested in July 1861 that the Confederate corps of meteorological observers retain duplicate copies of their monthly returns of observations and file them away for the use of the government in peace. Because of the federal blockade of southern ports, imported luxury articles such as coffee became scarce rather quickly. Ravenel wrote to the Charleston *Courier* in April 1862 to share a way to make "coffee" out of cottonseed. Another of his articles, entitled "A Plea for Justice to the Manufacturers," urged fair treatment of merchants who had to raise their prices to compensate for elevated wholesale costs. The resulting inflation was due solely to scarcity imposed by the war and not to unethical conduct on the part of most merchants. Ravenel's argument was a strong appeal to reason and patience in an issue more apt to trigger emotion than intellect.[30]

As the war progressed, Ravenel found another way to turn his scientific knowledge to good use. Mushrooms, whether sautéed, baked, fried, or raw, were a delicious and readily available food, free for the picking nearly year round. Ravenel and Curtis had both tried them before the war, Ravenel joking that it was truly a good way for a mycologist to enjoy the fruits of his knowledge. Wartime food shortages made mushrooms less of a joke. Ravenel found he had access to a valuable food supplement and wished to share the information with his neighbors. The meetings of the Aiken Vine-Growing and Horticultural Association provided Ravenel a modest forum. The association continued to have monthly meetings during the growing season at least through 1863, and members customarily brought in selections of their fresh fruit and vegetables for display. At the first meeting of 1862, in June, Ravenel and his wife brought in a large basket of mushrooms, and three other members brought vegetables. Evidently the mushrooms were well received, for at the adjournment of the meeting they brought 90 cents in an impromptu auction that netted $3.50 for the Ladies' Relief Association. Thus encouraged, Ravenel brought more to the next meeting, and in August he presented an essay on edible mushrooms.[31]

Ravenel's use of fungi as food reawakened a little of his old interest in mycology. He wrote in September 1862 to William Hume asking to have his cryptogamic herbarium packed up and sent back to him from the Charleston Museum, where it had been since 1858. The herbarium needed sorting and rearranging, and Ravenel thought he would keep it till the war was over.[32] He may have intended the move partly as a precaution lest the Yankees take Charleston, as they were threatening to do. With Port Royal and the Sea Islands in Federal hands, the possibility of Charleston's falling was not unthinkable.

Curtis, too, was experimenting with mushrooms for the table and was actually more adventurous in this way than his South Carolina friend. He wrote to Ravenel in October 1863 to tell about three or four species that he had found palatable. Far from encouraging Ravenel, though, the letter seems to have brought to his mind the risk of accidental poisoning. This possibility had occurred to him before, and in 1850 he had published an article in the *Southern Quarterly Review* that touched on the subject. Not even mycologists were immune from this danger, of course, and Ravenel was probably a bit concerned when he learned that his friend was eating *Agaricus pubecens*. The species had been described by Berkeley, but he was certain that what he and Curtis had been calling *A. pubecens* was not the same plant. When he learned the following year that Curtis had by then tried twenty-four species and was still alive and well, he decided to expand his horizons beyond the mere two types he had tried so far. Soon he was writing to Curtis to describe the pleasures of eating the giant puffball, *Lycoperdon giganteum,* and to confess that the perils involved in his cooking experiments made them exciting.[33]

Ravenel's major opportunity to serve the Confederacy as a scientist came in the summer of 1862. Former Elliott Society member Francis Holmes approached him about the possibility of supervising nitre production at three plants, to be established in Aiken, Hamburg, and Edgefield. Ravenel's health had improved, and so the Aiken scientist seriously considered Holmes's offer. He visited Holmes in Columbia to talk the matter over and also went to inspect the state nitre works, directed by Dr. William H. Ford. Soon, however, he turned the responsibility down and recommended John Sims to take his place. He had not enough time to give proper attention to the nitre works without abandoning his family and farm. Such a sacrifice, he believed, was unnecessary when Sims could willingly do the same job as well or better.[34]

Ravenel never became directly involved in the Confederate war effort. Brothers, brothers-in-law, and friends went off to join the military, but Ravenel's health left him on the sidelines. Twice, as the Confederacy raised the draft age to include older men, he was ordered to report for active duty. Both times, however, he was excused as being too frail for the military. On the first occasion, having been ordered to report before January 1, 1863, he merely sent in a certificate from his physician, Amory Coffin, stating that he was too unwell to travel. This strategy did not impress the military authorities, who in February ordered him to appear before a court-martial to explain his absence. He was acquitted of wrongdoing, and a military examining board granted him official dispensation from service, but the experience was nonetheless intensely humiliating.[35] Lessons learned in 1863 helped him in April 1864 when he was again called up. That time he took Coffin's certificate in hand and rode over to see the examining board in Edgefield, where he was dismissed with no hesitation.[36]

Although active military service was beyond his ability, Ravenel did try to help in other ways. Three times, in the first flush of war excitement, in 1863, and again in 1864 amid rumors of a possible invasion of Aiken, he joined the home guard. Unable to stand the exertion of drilling, he intended only to present himself in the event the troop was called into the field.[37]

He saw another chance to help in April 1862 when the Confederate Bureau of Ordnance published in the *Courier* a plea for church and plantation bells to be cast into cannon. As chairman of the vestry of Saint Thaddeus Church, Ravenel responded to the Confederacy's need, proposing that the congregation offer their church bell to the government. The congregation accepted Ravenel's proposal, and he wrote to F. L. Childs of the Charleston Arsenal to offer the bell. The government graciously accepted the gesture, but informed Ravenel that enough material was currently available. It would let the congregation know if the bell were ever needed. The summons never came, however, and the bell still hangs in the belfry.[38]

Ravenel made still another gesture in support of the Richmond government, a gesture that eventually ruined him financially. When the war opened, Ravenel derived most of his income from interest-producing investments. He had almost twenty-five thousand dollars, a large amount indeed, out at interest, including fourteen thousand dollars owed to him by private individuals. As these debts came due and were paid, or as inflation ate away at the value of the Confederate dollar and debtors stepped forward to pay with inflated currency, again and again he reinvested in Confederate bonds. In March 1864 he even instructed his broker to sell sixteen shares of the Farmers' and Exchange Bank and $350 worth of City of Charleston stock, yielding 6 percent. He reinvested all of it in Confederate bonds yielding only 4 percent.[39]

Finally, Ravenel's only son, Harry, was called into the military. Although only sixteen, he had joined the militia of Abbeville District while he was away at school. The Confederacy's manpower shortage was so acute by late 1864 that South Carolina was forced to call even such young militiamen into active service. Ravenel fitted Harry up with a blanket and simple eating and cooking utensils and drove him to the depot in Aiken to board the train for Hamburg and join his company. Though it was apparent to him that the Confederacy was fast sliding into the abyss, he sent his son off to the war and was glad Harry could do something in defense of his country.[40]

Christmas 1864 was so gloomy as to be an absolute mockery of the crowded, laughing, joking holidays of the prewar years. Ravenel and his family went, as always, to Pooshee, but few others joined the somber celebration at his father's house. Thomas and his family had to stay away because his wife was recovering from typhoid. Ravenel's sister Maria stayed away, too. Her husband Percival had been killed in action not long before, and she had no heart for celebrating.[41] Just days after Christmas, Ravenel began trying, to no avail, to persuade his father to begin preparing to move. The fall of Charleston was imminent, but the old man would do nothing. The idea of leaving his home was much too painful.[42]

War closed in on the Ravenels swiftly in 1865.[43] Ravenel heard on January 22, while he was still at Pooshee, that Harry had been stricken with typhoid fever. Riding to Charleston, he searched for his son in the various hospitals, finally finding him at the Citadel. Ravenel applied for a furlough to take him home and accepted a medical discharge for Harry only when it was pressed upon him by the surgeon in command and the colonel of Harry's regiment. Their report that Harry had been offered a discharge because of his age and small size but had refused it was highly gratifying to Ravenel, and he proudly took his boy home where he hoped that careful and tender nursing would restore him. As he did whenever any of his children were ill, Ravenel paid close attention to the progress of the illness. Within just a few days Harry seemed better, but on the afternoon of February 2 he took a sudden turn for the worse. His pulse was very feeble, he could not speak, and he gave no sign of recognizing anyone in the family. Ravenel sat by Harry's side and watched his only son weaken. Yet as always Ravenel found comfort in his, and Harry's, trust in God, and he reflected that Harry was all he could want in a son in righteousness, integrity, obedience, and affection. The acute anxiety was over quickly. By the morning of February 4 Harry was decidedly better, and he continued to improve steadily.

As one crisis passed, another took its place. The military situation deteriorated with frightening rapidity. Sherman's forces were nearing Charleston, and on February 18 the Ravenels were informed that Confederate troops were abandoning the Saint John's area. Left without military defense in the face of imminent invasion, Ravenel felt his responsibilities heavily. His own family, his father, his sister Maria, his sister-in-law Liz, and their families all looked to him for guidance. He thought of taking them, and many of their neighbors, to Aiken, but Harry's illness, the problem of finding provisions on the road, and the awful possibility that the house in Aiken might not even be standing made him decide to stay at Pooshee and await the Yankees. The silver and valuable papers had already been buried, and the family made such additional preparations as they could. Four months' rations were distributed to the slaves, and food supplies were taken into the plantation house. Two of Ravenel's daughters, Henrietta and Charlotte, stayed up till 2:00 A.M. one night, stuffing personal valuables into a mattress. The next morning they were back at the job, squirreling things away in a hiding place they had found in their room.

Raiding parties began troubling nearby plantations within days of the Confederates' withdrawal, but it was not until March 1 that they descended on Pooshee. Horses, wagons, buggies, harness, the contents of smokehouse and root cellar, wine, guns, and poultry were all taken, but no one was hurt, no buildings were burned, and Ravenel found comfort in the loyalty exhibited by the Pooshee slaves during the incursion. One small pony and her colt were left behind by the raiders, and the northern troops did not touch the family's indoor food supply or sack the house.

Following the harrowing night of March 1, life calmed down again and even became routine. By March 14, things seemed secure enough to leave Pooshee for a morning's visit with Henrietta Stevens and the Jervey family at Northampton. "To our delight," recorded Susan Jervey, "part of the Pooshee colony ventured over this morning; a party of women and children headed by Cousin Henry's patriarchal figure mounted on old Uncle's little white pony."[44] It was a good test of Ravenel's dignity to look patriarchal with his lanky, five-foot, ten-inch body mounted on a little pony.[45] Ten days later he started back to Aiken with his family in a hired wagon pulled by mules. Arriving safely, they found already in residence friends who were refugees from other parts of South Carolina. House and outbuildings were safe, but many small mementos, including some of Ravenel's scientific correspondence, had been taken by a marauding party of Confederate troops. The two eldest daughters, Lydia and Charlotte, were left behind in Saint John's, but in mid-April Ravenel went back to retrieve them. United once again, the family gloomily followed the news as best they could, while one Confederate army after another surrendered. Four years of war were over; it was spring and time for a new beginning.

Getting By, 1865–1869   7

Widespread destruction faced southerners after their defeat. In South Carolina alone, thirteen towns were burned, as well as much of the state capital, Columbia. Resources for rebuilding were not readily available, for the South's war effort had consumed much of the food and other goods, and greenbacks were scarce.[1]

Henry Ravenel was more fortunate than many. Aiken was still standing. His own property was in relatively good shape, and in his fields thousands of peach trees and grape vines were standing unmolested. Amid fresh green leaves were the small globular swellings of forming fruit, promising a bumper crop come July.[2]

War did not leave Ravenel untouched, however. It wrecked his personal finances and forced him and his family into unfamiliar poverty. They never recovered their prewar prosperity, and everything that Ravenel did after May 1865 was tied to his unaccustomed financial need. Yet the need must not be exaggerated. Though he was sometimes anxious about providing even the most basic necessities for his large family, something always came along to keep them from actual want. Small Christmas and birthday gifts, at least for the younger children, remained customary, and occasional trips to Augusta or Charleston were not beyond the family's means. Ravenel was never forced to step outside the behavioral bounds of Victorian gentlemen in coping with the situation, and the family clung successfully to many of the trappings of nineteenth-century gentility. The piano and the silver were never sold, for example, despite the occasional necessity of paying personal property taxes on them. Ravenel willingly worked to bring in money, and he allowed his older daughters to help by teaching school, while his wife took in boarders for a short time. It never occurred to any of them, however, that the daughters could help care for the garden or orchard; indeed, not until 1871 did they do the family's cooking.

Poverty forced its way to Ravenel's attention very soon after the war. He took stock of his financial position May 22, 1865, and found his investments, from which he had derived the greater part of his income, nearly obliterated.[3] He had lost $24,000 in Confederate bonds and cash, but he had 146 bank shares, whose value he rightly doubted; $1,060 in City of Charleston bonds yielding 6 percent; $1,050 in State of South Carolina bonds yielding 6 percent; and $1,500 in bonds of the Charleston and Savannah Railroad Company also yielding 6 percent. This, he wrote, "with my farm (& 32 negro slaves?) is the total amount of my property."[4] One week later, May 29, 1865, Ravenel knew without doubt that his slaves were slaves no longer. The loss of their labor was a serious blow, and emancipation also entailed loss of bonds from his first wife's brothers, Charles and Peter Snowden, amounting to $7,770 for slaves purchased. Ravenel knew they could no longer repay him and cancelled the debt.[5] He worried about both how he would get along without his slaves and how they would get along without him. Although his former slaves all expressed a desire to remain with him, he knew he could no longer afford to employ them all and that they would eventually have to leave. Even so, he continued to feel a sense of responsibility for them. As long as possible he planned to support one old woman and her two grandchildren, and he prayed that emancipation might be successful, "a blessing & not a curse" for the freedmen.[6]

Ravenel had little trouble arranging terms with his former bondsmen for such work as he needed and could afford to have done. His first impulse was to place the system on a footing as similar as possible to the old one. Those freedmen whose full-time labor was needed would receive in return housing, food, clothing, and medical care, while the others would have to find work elsewhere but could still lodge at Hampton Hill, paying rent with a portion of their work time.[7]

His proposal was accepted, none of the freedmen expressing any dissatisfaction with the work arrangement. By the end of June, however, Ravenel had reconsidered and concluded that in fairness to his employees, he should begin paying them wages and leaving to them the responsibility of providing for their own clothing, blankets, shoes, medical care, and whatever luxuries they might desire. He was well aware of the injustice of continuing to treat former slaves as though they were slaves still. The same arrangements, he thought, should be made with them as might fairly be made with white men.[8]

Ravenel's desire to pay his laborers cash wages was hindered by his own lack of cash. His income from investments was halted, and during the first year after the war he was just able to meet his family's few needs for cash by selling garden vegetables and cutting timber for the railroad.[9] Not even the once lucrative peach crops could be counted on for income. With South Carolina's railways in shambles, Ravenel could not get the fruit to northern markets; other southerners had little cash to spend on such luxuries, and so the rich peach harvest of 1865 was wasted. What the Ravenels could not eat, dry for future use, or give to friends fell from the trees to rot on the ground.[10] Spring frosts destroyed the crop in 1866 and 1867.[11] The following year the trees bore well, but Ravenel's inadequate work force, consisting that year chiefly of himself and his son Harry, could not keep up with the swiftly ripening peaches. Though they boxed up as many as possible for marketing in New York, there was much wastage, and again the orchard ground was strewn with rotting fruit. The produce that reached New York arrived in poor condition, bruised from traveling, and brought low prices.[12] In response to such bad luck, Ravenel began digging up and selling the trees themselves in December 1867.[13]

Failure of cash income from the usual sources, investments and the fruit crops, induced Ravenel to find other ways to compensate his workers. Like many other southern planters, he eventually turned to a combination of cash payment for housework and sharecropping for work around the farm. If the examples of such arrangements that he noted in his journal can be taken as typical, he was inclined to be fairly generous. In February 1866 he struck a bargain with two men to clear the brush out of the peach orchard and plough it twice in return for a sixth of the profits of the peach crop.[14] The hard freeze in the spring of that year ruined the crop, however; so neither Ravenel nor the men made any profit. On other occasions, in the springs of 1871 and 1873, he contracted with former slave Jimmy for planting corn the first year and corn and cotton the second. Ravenel would supply the land and use of a mule and cart; Jimmy would supply the labor. The corn crops were to be split fifty-fifty, and Ravenel was to receive a fourth of the cotton wool and all the seed.[15] The success with which Ravenel and his former slaves worked together after the war contrasted markedly with the experiences of many other southerners. Ravenel's relatives in Saint John's had a wretched time trying to arrange terms with former slaves. The first summer it was difficult even to get them to plant enough food crops to see everyone through the winter, and René complained that he, William, and their neighbors had lost much property through theft.[16] In 1866 things went a little more smoothly. A written contract defined labor terms at Pooshee, but disputes still arose. Richard Dwight, Ravenel's brother-in-law and manager of the plantation, had to consult the military authorities before dismissing some workers accused of shooting livestock and again over the issue of whether building fences around unplanted land was included in the hands' contract duties or must be compensated separately. Northern officers attempted to be fair to both sides, with the result that Dwight was frustrated by the outcome both times.[17]

For Ravenel a more important worry was finding something he could do to ensure a steady, even if small, income for his large family. Two daughters had been added to the household during the war. Susan Stevens, born July 20, 1861, and Elizabeth Gaillard, born July 4, 1864, brought the number of children to eight.[18] The responsibility of providing for them all was a depressing burden. In the first weeks after the end of the war he often tortured himself by recalling times when he might have foreseen the Confederacy's collapse and saved his property. He might, he thought, have sold his slaves and invested the proceeds in specie or land, or he might have placed his capital in safer securities than Confederate bonds, but he had let the chances slip past. "I even aggravated the evil," he confessed to his journal, "by avariciously selling articles because they brought me a large profit (as I supposed) & which I might now have owned, had I not disposed of them."[19]

Spurred by need, Ravenel impatiently cast about for employment.

Even as he watched his fine crop of peaches ripen in 1865, he knew well that spring frosts would make peach growing a precarious living and that woodcutting could last only as long as the timber supply. That fall he thrust aside his dislike of cities and began to consider selling Hampton Hill and moving to Charleston or Columbia. Letters to James Wilson in the capital and Frank Porcher and Peter Gaillard in Charleston brought back discouraging news about business in the cities,[20] and he looked for other opportunities.

At this point Ravenel intended to find wage labor for long-term income and to sell assets to meet short-term needs. Accordingly he wrote in August 1865 to Edward Tuckerman to renew their botanical friendship and to spread the word that his valuable herbarium and botanical library were on the market. He also had thirty to forty unsold volumes of *Fungi Caroliniani Exsiccati* available.[21] In November he wrote in similar vein to Paul Ansel Chadbourne of Bowdoin College, to whom he had owed a letter since just before the war, and also to Thomas P. James in Philadelphia. By November, though, Ravenel had half relented with regard to the herbarium's sale, and when William Canby wrote to enquire what terms he would be willing to accept, he replied that he would rather not sell it unless circumstances forced him to do so. Christmastime brought from Chadbourne an order for a set of the exsiccati with another enquiry about the herbarium. Ravenel countered with an offer of the first twelve fascicles of Jean Baptiste Mougeot and Christian Gottfried Nestler's *Stirpes Cryptogamae Vogesorum* (1810–1843) for $100 in specie or $124 in currency, Greville's *Scottish Cryptogamic Flora* for $40, and twelve volumes of de Candolle's *Prodromus* and five volumes of Karl Kunth's *Enumeratio Plantarum Omnium Cogitarum* (Stuttgart, 1833–1850) for $50.[22]

Although he kept the herbarium, Ravenel's microscope was soon sacrificed. In November he gave it to Amory Coffin, the family physician, in payment of the past year's medical bill of sixty-five dollars. He had been little able to use it for the past seven or eight years but parted with it reluctantly even so. Coffin was also rather reluctant to take it, but he kept it, and in future years he always made it available when Ravenel needed it.[23]

In the spring of 1866 George Engelmann, the talented German-born botanist who specialized in midwestern flowering plants, re-cruited Ravenel's help collecting specimens of the phanerogamic genus *Juncus* for an exsiccati. When Ravenel protested that he was willing to help but could not afford a collecting trip to the coast and could not devote much time to the venture, Engelmann offered to pay Ravenel for his efforts. Ravenel accepted the offer and spent spring and early summer collecting more than a hundred specimens of each species he could find. His enjoyment of phanerogamic botany re-turned, and he learned a great deal through his correspondence with Engelmann. The experience gave Ravenel an idea. In July he began writing to other botanists, asking all of them the same question: Would there be enough demand for collections of plants to furnish Ravenel a living? As he reminded Gray, his collecting grounds in South Carolina contained a rich and interesting flora, and his previous experience would enable him to collect in all the orders of cryptogams except the algae. Collecting native American seeds for European seed dealers was another possibility, as was the issuance of fascicles of plants with an index.[24]

Reponses came within a month or two. Gray wrote back less than two weeks after Ravenel had written him. He was glad to hear from Ravenel again; it was the first letter from him since the war. Gray reported that good specimens of phanerogams would bring about eight dollars per hundred, and seeds would pay better. Tree seeds were wanted for Victoria Colony, Australia, and Dr. Ferdinand Muller of the Melbourne botanical garden needed seeds of southern pines and oaks. He also suggested that the Royal Botanical Gardens at Kew might buy some seeds. Gray assured Ravenel he might "Rely on my sympathy and zeal, in all these things—especially when I am to serve my best foreign correspondents as well as yourself." Despite his en-couraging tone, Gray did not think Ravenel could make enough to live on by his collecting, but he did believe the proceeds might be a good supplement to other income.[25]

Curtis was even less hopeful than Gray. He pointed out a problem of which Ravenel was already aware, that most botanists acquired their exotic plants by exchange and would have little need to buy specimens. Engelmann was also less than encouraging. Ferdinand Jakob Lindheimer, Engelmann's friend and a fellow German immigrant, had traveled extensively in Texas between 1843 and 1852 collecting sets of plants for distribution at eight dollars per hundred. Though fourteen years had gone by since Lindheimer quit collecting to become a newspaper editor in New Braunfels, Engelmann still had great quantities of Lindheimer's plants on hand with no purchaser in sight. Tuckerman and Berkeley both had more positive comments to make. Tuckerman suggested B. Westermann & Co., German booksellers in New York, for help in setting up European sales, and Berkeley wrote that he had placed an advertisement in the *Gardener's Chronicle*.[26]

Berkeley's advertisement caught the attention of several botanists, including Mordecai Cubitt Cooke, a talented Englishman whose efforts in mycology were fast placing him on Berkeley's own level. His prominence had increased sharply during the Civil War years with the publication of three books, the *Manual of Botanic Terms* (1862), *Plain and Easy Account of British Fungi* (1862), and *Index Fungorum Britannicorum* (1865). In August 1866 Cooke wrote to Ravenel that he had "often & unsuccessfully" tried to obtain copies of the *Fungi Caroliniani Exsiccati* and now was encouraged by Berkeley's notice to see whether he could obtain South Carolina fungi and on what terms.[27]

Business relations between Engelmann and Ravenel and between Cooke and Ravenel reveal the depths of Ravenel's naïveté in matters of commerce. In his cotton, rice, and peach operations, he had always left the business matters to a factor, and brokers similarly had handled the details of investments. Now Ravenel had to devise a marketing system himself, and he found the task more complicated than he had expected.

As his first mistake, Ravenel failed to understand the subtle change that had to occur in his relationship with Engelmann upon his acceptance of Engelmann's offer to pay. He declined to name a price for his collections, saying he would be willing to accept whatever Engelmann thought they were worth. This, of course, placed some pressure on Engelmann to be generous. Next, rather than insisting that Engelmann tell him what he wanted, he collected large quantities of everything he thought might be of interest. Since payment for specimens was customarily made on the basis of the number supplied, this put still more pressure on Engelmann's generosity. Finally, Ravenel did not seem to realize that Engelmann might expect him to take greater care than usual with the collections. He did try to obtain good specimens of *Juncus* for Engelmann, collecting them in flower that summer and going back to the same sources in September to collect them in fruit, but apparently he used no more than his usual care in assembling the material. When a check for $140 came in November, accompanied by criticism of the collections, Ravenel was stung. The money was more than he expected, but the words hurt. He accused Engelmann of not fully appreciating the difficulties under which he worked and told him how he had nearly prostrated himself by walking two or three miles in the blazing sun to collect *Juncus canadensis.*[28]

Ravenel's arrangements for the first set of plants Cooke ordered were also made awkwardly and left the Englishman rather disgruntled. Finding it difficult to transmit cash to Ravenel, Cooke placed his order through a New York bookseller, Trubner & Co., just as he had proposed in his August letter. When that order failed to yield results, he placed it again through a second firm, Williams and Norgale, again with no success. Finally, in August 1867 he asked the Reverend Edwin Cortlandt Bolles of Portland, Maine, to contact Ravenel and have him send on as many numbers of the exsiccati as Ravenel had available, with loose specimens of the species contained in the other fascicles.[29]

Not until early October did Ravenel get around to sending through Bolles the material Cooke had ordered. On the same day Ravenel sent Cooke two separate proposals for the sale of his duplicate collection of fungi. One proposal was that Ravenel should arrange his duplicates, counting the specimens and making sure they were good representations of the species, then send them to Cooke, asking about three dollars per hundred for them. Under the other proposal Ravenel would box up all his duplicates and send them "as is," Cooke to pay whatever he thought they were worth upon their arrival. Ravenel's letter reached Cooke first, and he was still thinking about the proposals when the package arrived. Unfortunately, the contents were disappointing. Evidently, Ravenel had not packed the specimens with his usual care or the collection had deteriorated in storage or both, for the fleshy fungi arrived in very bad condition, moldy and broken. Cooke reported that some were so poor that he could only throw the fragments on the fire.[30]

Unimpressed though he was with the first package, Cooke was cautiously willing to consider taking the rest of Ravenel's duplicates. There were obvious business objections, however, to both of Ravenel's proposals, and he proceeded to point them out to Ravenel. First, Cooke could in no way consider the arranged fungi at three dollars per hundred without having more information about the collection. In addition, he thought the price rather high. Ordinarily, fungi in good condition could be had for about two dollars per hundred, but transportation costs would bring the price of Ravenel's specimens to nearly twice that. For that much money Cooke would expect a rather extraordinary collection. He had, for example, recently purchased at four dollars per hundred a fine set of two thousand German species "in beautiful condition arranged and mounted in cases with classified indices &c."[31]

Ravenel's second proposal Cooke thought unfair to the South Carolinian himself, who was certain to be disappointed if Cooke should happen to remit less than Ravenel had hoped for the collection. As an alternative Cooke would promise ten pounds (about fifty dollars), and if on examination he thought it worth more, he would pay up to an additional ten pounds. This proposal Ravenel accepted, and by March 1868 arrangements were made to send his plants and Cooke's remittance through Bolles.[32] Before the exchange could occur, however, a new plan was formed at Ravenel's suggestion. Ravenel divided his duplicates into ten sets of varying sizes. The largest, 810 species, was for Cooke, who would pay four dollars gold for it and who would also undertake the sale of two more sets to other European botanists.[33]

Seven other sets Ravenel sent to Horace Mann in Cambridge, Massachusetts. Mann had written to him in February 1868 to enquire about some books and plants. He had since bought Mougeot and Nestler's *Stirpes* for a hundred dollars and had disposed of Ravenel's two volumes of Louis Agassiz's *Contributions to the Natural History of the United States* (4 vols.; Boston, 1857–1862) to someone else. At Ravenel's request, Mann also agreed to take one set of fungi for himself and dispose of the remaining six to other American botanists. In a similar fashion Ravenel had made the acquaintance of William Wallace Denslow of New York, who now promised to sell for him some of his books and phanerogamic plants.[34] Once more Ravenel was able to do business through factors.

Before May 1868 when he made his arrangements with Denslow, Mann, and Cooke, Ravenel had been receiving a very low percentage of his income from botany. Gray's prediction had come true. The money from the sale of specimens was insufficient to live on but did supplement other income. Because collecting botanical specimens paid so poorly, Ravenel did not feel justified in devoting much time to botany. In January and again in February 1868 he complained to Edward Tuckerman that though his interest in botany had been considerably revived since the war, he was having to neglect it in order to make a living.[35]

If botany did not pay, Ravenel hoped that horticulture would. In July 1866 Ravenel received a letter from Thomas Meehan, an established nurseryman in Philadelphia and editor of the *Gardener's Monthly and Horticultural Advertiser,* inquiring about seeds of native southern forest trees. Ravenel asked Meehan what he thought of the prospects of selling seeds to European nurseries and seedhouses. The Philadelphian replied that he had been in touch for many years with the large dealers of England, France, and Germany and had found the demand for seeds to be rather limited. European nurseries and seedhouses were already quite well stocked with American plants. Meehan would, however, take three barrels of cypress seeds and twenty pounds of the seeds of each pine species if Ravenel could supply them.[36]

Within two weeks of writing his discouraging letter on seed collecting, Meehan had decided upon a new and better cure for Ravenel's money problems. The nursery business, he wrote, could be quite profitable, particularly if Ravenel grew young roses and grapes, which should do better in the South than the North. The superior quality of the plants would give him an edge over northern competitors. Meehan promised to supply Ravenel with starting stock for which he could pay whenever convenient, or never, if the business failed. Ravenel hesitated. John Cornish, pastor at Saint Thaddeus, urged him to try the nursery, but Jules Berckmans wrote from the standpoint of several years experience in the field and warned Ravenel that it was not easy to be successful as a nurseryman.[37] By the middle of September, Ravenel had reached a decision, and he set about turning Hampton Hill into a nursery. Beginning capital was hard to find, but Cornish loaned Ravenel five hundred dollars that he had in trust for investment purposes. Meehan sent a large box of evergreens, roses, and other plants along with instructions and advice, all of which he said Ravenel should take as a gift and not attempt to pay for. Mrs. William Gregg, a friend and neighbor of the Ravenels', donated a large quantity of rose clippings, and before November's end, Ravenel was in the nursery business. "I am glad that I have at last begun to do something that looks like work for a living," he noted.[38] Like his other money-making ideas, Ravenel's nursery was only moderately successful. He continued to operate it, however, as long as he remained on the farm.

Just as he was launching the nursery, Ravenel found another way to turn horticulture to profit. On November 26, 1866, a letter came from former Confederate general Daniel Harvey Hill, now editor of a magazine in Charlotte, North Carolina, the *Land We Love.* The magazine was to include a department of agriculture, and Hill hoped to get Ravenel to write the botanical articles. "We pay from $2 to $3 per printed page for all accepted articles," Hill wrote, but "To gentlemen of science, the latter sum always." He concluded the letter by writing, "It would be a source of pride to enroll your name on our list of contributors."[39]

Hill's request fell on fertile ground. It had occurred to Ravenel some weeks prior to receiving the proposal that horticultural writing might be profitable. He had, in fact, been working on a short, practical guide to gardening that he intended for publication. A chart entitled "Vegetables All the Year Round," which he devised for inclusion in the article, brought him fifty dollars the following spring from Francis Holmes, who used it in a third edition of his little book *The Southern Farmer and Market Gardener* (Charleston, 1866). Ravenel did not hesitate to accept Hill's offer. When he saw a copy of the first number, issued in May, he was impressed by its neat preparation and good articles. He especially admired Hill's editorials. "He wields his pen as gracefully as the sword," Ravenel commented, and in December he sent a notice of the magazine to the *Courier* by way of Frank Porcher.[40]

Like many other southern periodicals, the *Land We Love* had a short life, its last issue appearing in March 1869. It carried a variety of articles, including essays, poetry, and a large amount of material dealing with the Civil War. Ravenel provided agricultural articles for five issues between May 1867 and March 1868.[41]

Ravenel's articles written for the *Land We Love* dealt with diverse topics of practical interest to farmers, including the raising of peaches and grapes and the more esoteric subject of the function of leaf stomata in regulating water loss in plants. All conformed with a major desideratum of such pay-per-page magazine articles in dealing with topics he knew intimately and could write up quickly. With the work of only a few hours bringing in twenty dollars or more, Ravenel was not badly paid for his time, and Harvey Hill did have a reputation for paying his writers promptly.[42]

In addition to what he was paid directly for the articles, Ravenel received a welcome bonus in connection with an article on *Lespedeza striata,* Japan clover. This legume was clearly a foreign plant introduced to the United States two or three decades earlier. Ravenel had first noticed it in South Carolina in 1849 or 1850, and could find no mention of it by earlier American botanists, though it had been known from Japanese specimens as early as 1784. In the eighteen years since he first found it, he had heard of its spread to a number of new localities where it was gaining a favorable reputation for hardiness and for excellence as cattle fodder. Although he cautioned against hasty judgment, he hoped Japan clover, which could remain green through hot, dry summers that killed other plants, would prove a godsend to worn-out lands.[43]

Such magnificent qualities combined in one plant were sure to arouse the interest of southern farmers. During the fall following publication of the *Lespedeza* article, Ravenel received a steady flow of inquiries, many enclosing fifty cents or a dollar or two to purchase some seeds. Ravenel was quite prepared for this influx of orders. He had considered *Lespedeza* seed a possible item of commerce for months before he published the article, having received at least one request for it as early as the previous November. As the seeds of the little plant ripened the following October, he and Harry collected large quantities to fill orders.[44]

Publication of the *Lespedeza* article, to the extent that it was a deliberate attempt to attract orders, was one of the few truly clever things Ravenel ever did in connection with his postwar commercial activities. It was an imaginative use of advertising by one who otherwise neglected that aspect of business almost entirely. On two occasions others had placed advertisements for him. Denslow and Mann, with Ravenel's approbation, had advertised in the *American Naturalist* some books that he intended to sell.[45] Berkeley's advertisement in the *Gardener's Chronicle* had been, of course, quite successful in attracting attention. Despite the lessons presented by Berkeley's notice and the *Lespedeza* article, however, Ravenel never formulated an advertising program.[46] He was embarrassed to be charging money for things that he would once have given away and preferred to let others know of his services discretely, by word of mouth only.

Chronologically, Ravenel's successful exploitation of *Lespedeza striata* closely coincided with the progress of his arrangements with Denslow, Mann, and Cooke for the sale of his collections. During the late summer and fall of 1868, as requests for seed came in, he was also receiving from time to time reports on the sale of collections. Denslow sold two sets of plants for Ravenel before he died June 30, 1868, of tuberculosis.[47] Horace Mann also met an early death from tuberculosis, November 11, 1868, but not before he had sold two sets of fungi and a set of Volumes 4 and 5 of the *Fungi Caroliniani Exsiccati*. Soon after his death his brother settled accounts with Ravenel, sending him a check for $75.63.[48] Cooke did not share the fate of Ravenel's other factors but did share their success. By late August he had sold a set of fungi and had gotten a commission for Ravenel from Joseph Hooker to collect up to £5 worth of seeds of American trees and shrubs. The last of Cooke's fungi collections was sold by early November.[49]

For Ravenel, the happy outcome of both ventures at once confirmed his hope that he could make a significant contribution to his family's welfare through botany. His feeling in January and February 1868 that he could not afford to devote time to botany melted with the last spring frosts. In May he wrote hopefully, but with some lingering reservations, to Curtis of his agreement with Cooke. "I have some hope of turning these things to profit. If I could meet with a ready sale, or could have several sets engaged it would pay me very well to devote some time to collecting, but of course one or two sets only at five or six dollars per 100 would scarcely be worth the while."[50]

For the first time since the outbreak of war Ravenel began to go out collecting on a regular basis. Seven years of inactivity in botany had taken their toll on his knowledge. He was rusty. With renewed practice, though, he improved quickly. "The old interest is reviving—" he wrote Curtis in June. "Long forgotten impressions are restored, & memories of things long since faded away are gradually coming out again like the features of an old picture on which the dust of time had been settling."[51]

Personal worries cast occasional shadows on Ravenel's new happiness. His elderly father sickened and died in October 1867, and in August 1868 Ravenel's wife Mary was extremely ill for several days as a result of a miscarriage.[52]

These were fleeting problems, but politics were a different matter. The deep interest with which Ravenel had followed political and military events during the war did not evaporate on the coming of peace. Rather, he remained as passionately interested as ever. With a pragmatism born of his belief in the wisdom and goodness of God, Ravenel intellectually accepted defeat as a chastisement administered to the southern people by a loving father. Soon after the war he declared himself ready to become again a loyal citizen of the United States and showed his readiness in little symbolic ways such as taking the oath of loyalty and attending a church service to mourn Lincoln's death. Yet, Ravenel's rational acceptance of the South's defeat contrasted sharply with his emotional fury and humiliation, and in the first years after the war his journal and letters presented an unharmonious mixture of feelings. Pious reflections on the will of God were interspersed with outpourings of indignation, as though, having given vent to his anger, he felt the need to reassert the dominance of his mind.

In his scientific correspondence, particularly with northern botanists, Ravenel presented the piously Christian aspect of his feelings. In his first letter to Tuckerman after the war, Ravenel wrote: "It has pleased the great Umpire of Nations in the order of His Providence, that the Southern Confederacy should not accomplish the object for which they sought. So be it. I accept the issue as from His hands,— & am content. . . . I submit without discontent, because I know that infinite wisdom cannot err."[53] The same day he wrote these words, he inscribed in his diary a long, bitter diatribe on the inhumanity and poor judgment of federal officers. Its tone was a mixture of outrage and perverse pleasure at the confirmation of his antebellum opinion of northern abolitionists, and its words were not those of a man who was content.[54]

Realizing that he was not in a position to do much to alter the political situation, Ravenel tried to develop a more accepting emotional attitude. It was not an easy task, though botany helped by providing another outlet for his emotional energy. By 1868 he had made considerable progress. "I never let politics worry me," he wrote to Curtis in June of that year. "Sometimes when I allow myself to brood over some flagrant act of despotism, my blood begins to boil up, but I soon dismiss the matter."[55]

Annoyance at governmental policies did not prevent Ravenel from developing in 1868 and 1869 a happy working relationship with Dr. John Shaw Billings of the library of the surgeon general. Their correspondence apparently began at the end of December 1868 when one of Ravenel's acquaintances in Augusta forwarded a letter he had received from Billings on the subject of cryptogamic botany. It was also fostered by officials at the Department of Agriculture. In November 1868 the federal commissioner of agriculture had ordered from Ravenel six pounds of *Lespedeza* seed at five dollars per pound. The South Carolinian quickly filled the order and wrote back to tempt the department with fungi, offering the *Fungi Caroliniani Exsiccati* at eight dollars per volume. That letter was forwarded to Billings, and by early January of 1869 he and Ravenel were in direct correspondence.[56]

Billings was, he informed Ravenel, only a beginner at the cryptogams, having taken up their study in September. He was especially interested in the microscopic fungi but was also in correspondence with Horatio Charles Wood. Wood sent him algae, and he sent Wood fungi. Billings proved from the first a warm friend to Ravenel. The two men found they shared much the same opinion on the overreaching theory of evolution. Writing of contemporary German and French ideas about the causation of disease by fungi, Billings exclaimed, "They are very amusing certainly—and if one were to believe Hallier—a Penicillium Spore and the Darwinian theory will account for pretty nearly every natural Phenomenon hitherto observed."[57]

Billings was also generous in providing Ravenel with business. He accepted Ravenel's offer to collect algae for him, saying they would make fine returns for some of Wood's specimens, and in February he obtained Department of Agriculture funding to purchase a set of Ravenel's exsiccati for forty dollars.[58] These two acts were of small consequence compared with another of his proposals, also made in February. The federal government, he wrote early that month, was preparing to launch a small expedition to Texas to investigate the causes of Texas fever, a prevalent disease of cattle. Although Congress had not yet appropriated the necessary funds, plans were already being made with the intention of beginning the investigation as soon as money came available. British veterinarian John Gamgee had been hired as the principal investigator, and he wanted a botanist to examine the Texas fungi to determine whether they might be causing the disease. Despite his own amusedly skeptical opinion of the fungal theory of disease origin, Billings was willing to go along with the idea and to throw the benefit of the job in Ravenel's direction.[59]

Ravenel's opinion on the subject was also cautiously skeptical. He had been aware for a long time of this early cousin of the germ theory of disease, having reviewed an American book on the subject in 1850 in the *Southern Quarterly Review.* He had then believed that insufficient data existed to decide the issue one way or the other, and though he countered the author's anecdotal accounts of occasions on which he had become ill while studying fungi with his own contrary experience, he was also intrigued by a suggested association between fungi and epidemics and urged further research on the topic.[60] He quickly decided to join the expedition.[61]

Ravenel's excursion to Texas began with a trip to Washington, where he arrived on March 19. He spent a few days with Billings, being given tours of the Surgeon General's Offices; the Army Medical Museum, where he was shown the machinery and techniques for making microphotographs; and the offices and museum of the Bureau of Agriculture. He arrived in Houston on March 29, via New Orleans and Galveston, and there he met Gamgee, whom he liked immediately. During the following weeks the two worked together closely, Gamgee doing internal examinations of slaughtered cattle while Ravenel went out frequently to examine the local flora and make large collections. He took his responsibility seriously and concentrated his efforts on the fungi and grasses, bypassing many new and interesting phanerogams, taking only those he could manage while traveling about.[62]

Except for an occasional touch of homesickness, Ravenel enjoyed the trip. He found Gamgee and his companion David Gaillard to be interesting company, and he took pleasure in a short visit with Ashbel Smith, the onetime London representative of the Republic of Texas, at his farm near Houston. As was often the case when Ravenel had engrossing and worthwhile work to do, his health remained good throughout most of his time in Texas. During the third week in April, Ravenel began feeling slightly ill, and the sensation lingered for a day or two. He began morbidly contemplating the thought of a serious illness. "To one of my domestic habits, & surrounded always with a large family any of whom are ready & anxious to add to my comforts, the thoughts of being sick at a hotel among strangers, a thousand miles from home, are not pleasant," he wrote self-pityingly.[63] After dwelling on these thoughts for a little while, he quickly got well.

Ravenel's time in Texas was relatively brief. He left less than six weeks after arriving and was back in Aiken on May 11. Billings met him in New Orleans and came along to spend a day with him in Aiken, where they were joined on May 12 by William Canby.[64] When the visitors left, Ravenel assessed the results of his trip and found it productive, botanically, medically, and financially.

Ravenel spent the remainder of May sorting through and arranging the large collections he brought back with him. Though he kept many specimens himself, he sent many more away to friends. Ravenel gave John Torrey the grasses and sedges, and Torrey in turn passed some of the grasses on to George Thurber and the sedges to Olney, who, Torrey said, had developed "unmitigated *Carex-on-the-brain.*" Ravenel sent lichens to Tuckerman, mosses and hepatics to Sullivant, phanerogams to Engelmann, and fungi to Billings.[65] In June he wrote a report for the commissioner of agriculture, in which he concluded that, despite as careful a search as time would permit, he had found the Texas grasses remarkably free of parasitic fungi, and had, in fact, found nothing to excite suspicion. In short, he found nothing to support the theory of Ernst Hallier that the disease was caused by a fungus that Hallier had named *Coniothecium stilesiannum,* which he had hypothesized was taken in by the cattle with their food.[66] Ravenel's conclusion was correct. In 1893 Theobald Smith and Francis Kilborne showed that Texas fever is caused by a protozoan spread by cattle ticks.[67]

To Ravenel and his family the financial rewards of the trip were at least as exciting as its scientific rewards. Soon after his return he went with Mary and Lydia to Augusta, where they spent a day making some long-neglected purchases for the house and where Ravenel had his photograph taken to repay friends who had sent him theirs. About two weeks later his family surprised him with a beautiful photo album to accommodate the twenty-one photographs of friends and botanical correspondents that made up an expanding collection.[68]

Although it provided a welcome influx of money for some extras, the onetime cash payment of $284.25 that he received for his work in Texas did not go very far towards providing any permanent security. That fall the family rearranged their living quarters to rent out the three eastern rooms.[69] As a by-product of the Texas expedition, however, and of his resulting resumption of correspondence with Torrey, an opportunity for financial security was laid before Ravenel, but he rejected it. A myth crops up in some of the older sketches of Ravenel's life that the only thing that prevented him from taking a teaching position at a university during this period was his deafness.[70] Some authors say that he was offered positions by two unnamed colleges, one in Baltimore and one in California.[71] What actually happened was that in the spring of 1869 Torrey heard about two possible openings and, having Ravenel in his thoughts at the time, wrote to him about them: "I have been informed that they mean to have a professor of Botany in the new University of California & one of the Professors of Washington College, Lexington Va. informs me that they will do the same in that institution. He asks me to nominate a candidate for the Chair. How would you like a place in either of these Colleges?"[72] Ravenel thought the matter over for a fortnight before making his reply, and even then had some difficulty in expressing himself to Torrey, writing the letter twice before getting the wording just as he wanted it. He was grateful for Torrey's friendly interest and realized the value of his proposal. A teaching position would give him an opportunity to be useful to the measure of his ability, while securing a permanent income for his family. At the same time, he felt "a becoming distrust" of his own ability, for he had never taught botany in school or college, but his main reason for turning down the preferment, he said, was his hardness of hearing. "Perhaps you are not aware that I suffer from partial deafness,—to such an extent, that I am in a measure cut off from ordinary social intercourse. In my family & among my friends; this is well known,—& provided for,—but I fear it would be an obstacle in a lecture room & before a class of students."[73]

Was deafness a reason for turning down Torrey's proposal or an excuse? Ravenel certainly had cause to be concerned about his deafness; yet he seems to have exaggerated the problem, perhaps presenting it in the place of other reasons why he did not wish to be a candidate for the two positions. Ravenel's hardness of hearing was noticeable to others. Billings, for example, sent him a gift of seven or eight patterns for ear trumpets a few months after their visits.[74] Deafness had not prevented Ravenel's successful interaction with a large number of strangers in Texas, however, and he seldom complained of difficulty hearing another person. One notable exception was Catharine Beecher, of the famous northern abolitionist family, who came out with Ravenel's realtor to look over the farm. Ravenel evidently found her unpleasant and noted that he could not hear a word she said.[75]

It seems likely that Ravenel, taught by his father at an early age to consider his own health delicate and since then nursed through his sicknesses by a loving wife and doting children who were constantly "ready & anxious" to comfort him, had come to consider poor health, including his deafness, normal and an acceptable excuse for avoiding unpleasantness. This is not to suggest that he was feigning. Though perhaps partly of psychosomatic origin, the illnesses and deafness were evidently real enough. It is to suggest that alongside the attractive modesty of character displayed in his letter to Torrey, there existed a less attractive tendency to give in to his physical weaknesses or even to exploit them rather than to try to rise above them.

On the other hand, the situation also suggests that at the moment Torrey's offer arrived Ravenel was feeling optimistic about his life and was not greatly desiring a change. His financial situation probably seemed better to him then than it had since the war. He was anticipating payment for his botanical explorations in Texas, and on July 6 he received notice that Cooke had disposed of three additional sets of fungi for him.[76] He and Harry, following several unsuccessful attempts by the latter to find gainful employment, were working hard at the nursery and hoping to make something of it. Daughter Emily was anticipating marriage to Edward G. Cain of Saint John's, Lydia was teaching school in Aiken, and all the children were healthy, including the newest daughter, Mary Huger, born January 4, 1867.[77] Ravenel was also becoming more accepting of the political situation, and he had cause to believe that in his capacity as a warden of Saint Thaddeus parish he was making strides toward solving an acrimonious dispute between Pastor Cornish and his discontented parishioners.[78] Having passed successfully beyond the panic of financial uncertainty and preoccupation with politics that had weighed heavily on his spirit at the close of the Civil War, Henry Ravenel was a botanist once more.

A Botanist Once More, 1869–1887

8

Both because his hobby had become a business and because he had to conform to an austere budget, Ravenel the professional plant collector found he had to approach botany through a new set of rules that had been unknown to the mycologist of the 1850s. He could no longer afford foreign books, which he had once purchased almost carelessly. Time was no longer an overabundant commodity to be filled up with botany as recreation, but had to bring a return. Finally, Ravenel had to change his relationships with other botanists, and as his dealings with Engelmann and Cooke showed, this was a hard adjustment to make. While others freely traded specimens and publications, Ravenel alone had to turn down the trades and request cash payment for his help, usually with an awkward and apologetic explanation of his circumstances.

Success in transforming former correspondents into paying customers was almost nil; indeed, in most cases Ravenel did not even try. To ask Curtis who helped with doubtful fungi and was supporting his family on a slim salary to pay for the collections he sent was unthinkable. Tuckerman, too, continued to receive his lichens free. Ravenel included lichens among the named collections he made for sale; so Tuckerman's help with nomenclature was repayment enough for specimens. In the last months of 1869 and January 1870 Tuckerman reexamined specimens sent by Ravenel from South Carolina and

132

studied his new Texas lichens, sending him notes on the specimens in light of his mature thoughts on the taxonomy of the order. In 1872 he sent a copy of his important new treatise *Genera Lichenum* to Ravenel, whom he called his "valued friend, the accomplished explorer and illustrator of the Lichens and Fungi of South Carolina."[1] Long friendship also forbade that Lewis Gibbes be asked money for scientific favors. When the Charleston polymath developed an interest in butterflies, Ravenel's nine-year-old daughter Sue helped provide collections. No payment was mentioned, though Ravenel did accept an offer of a return of named duplicates.[2]

Asa Gray was the major exception among Ravenel's earlier correspondents. He considerately offered to pay for collections. In June 1870, for example, he sent fifteen dollars in payment for a set of lichens, at the same time requesting some seeds for which he offered payment. A few weeks later and again the following summer, he passed on to Ravenel the needs of some of his foreign correspondents for additional seeds.[3] The roots of this relationship were twofold. Gray's specialty, the phanerogamic plants of the North and West, was so far from Ravenel's own that he could do very little to help him in trade. At the same time Gray's role as a clearinghouse for Europeans interested in American botany gave him many opportunities to be of financial assistance with no outlay of his own funds.

With Job B. Ellis, also, Ravenel had more luck in superimposing a commercial relationship over an older scientific friendship. A great difference separating Ellis from Curtis or Tuckerman was that Ravenel was under no debt of gratitude to him for assistance in the early part of his career. The debt, in fact, lay in the other direction. Even so, it took some kind but firm persistence on Ravenel's part to make Ellis understand, when they resumed their correspondence in 1872, how his new circumstances must affect their relations.[4]

New correspondents were a special problem. The number of American botanists, including those interested in cryptogams, had expanded dramatically in the years since Ravenel had begun his work. In his first cryptogamic publication in 1849 it had taken less than two pages to describe the work of all contemporary American cryptogamists. By the 1870s the number was at least four times as large, and within Ravenel's lifetime mycologists grew so numerous as to be able to support a separate specialists' journal, the *Journal of Mycology,* now *Mycologia,* founded in 1885. A few years later, in 1903, at the St. Louis meeting of the American Association for the Advancement of Science, mycologists began a short-lived experiment in the organization of an American Mycological Society.[5] As one of the veteran American cryptogamists, Ravenel was inevitably destined to receive pleas for help from many of these newcomers.

Circumstances conspired to send a larger share of these cries for help his way than he might otherwise have expected. His old correspondent Moses Curtis began by 1869 to suffer from failing health. Vertigo and dizziness bothered him for months at a time, and even when he felt well, he was unable to do much reading or writing without a return of his symptoms. He was inclined to blame his problems on long use of the microscope and began to require all his correspondents to send him sketches of the fructification whenever that was necessary to determine species. He became slow in his responses and inaccurate in his determinations with the welcome result that by December 1870 all but two of his correspondents had ceased sending material for identification. As these scientists stopped corresponding with Curtis, some sought to establish a relationship with Ravenel instead.[6]

Curtis died April 10, 1872. Although sudden, his death had not been unexpected, and Ravenel, who heard of it from Curtis's wife, wrote that his friend's letters of the past two years had made him anticipate a sudden death. His own health was not good enough to allow him to go up to Hillsboro to help arrange Curtis's herbarium and library for sale, but he wrote letters to Curtis's wife to give her advice on the disposal of the herbarium, and in return she sent him some pamphlets and a list of Curtis's species with the internal identification numbers assigned to specimens sent to Berkeley.[7]

Until Curtis's death Ravenel had worked somewhat in his friend's shadow. Though Ravenel enjoyed at least as good a reputation as Curtis among the older cryptogamic specialists, Gray apparently had held Curtis in higher esteem. After all, he shared with Curtis a New England heritage and remembered a very pleasant collecting trip in the North Carolina mountains that had been greatly facilitated by information from Curtis. Also, the North Carolinian's outspoken letters freely conveyed his habitual criticisms of other botanists, Ravenel included, in such a way as to belittle others' reputations as compared with his own. His readers could only wonder how much to take at face value, as may be illustrated by the bemused reaction of Elliot Calvin Howe to one of Curtis's letters:

Yesterday, quite unexpectedly, I rec'd a long letter from Dr. Curtis. Besides a brief *report* & a lengthy criticism on Prof. Tuckerman, he gives the following unique & conclusive reply to my query about Ravenel's skill in Mycology.

"As he comes to me for aid, I suppose I may place myself somewhat in advance of him. With this admission, you may put him as among the best Mycologists, such as they are, in the U.S., though I believe there are no others who make any pretentions in this line."

Curtis also told Howe about the help he and Berkeley had given Ravenel in preparing the *Fungi Caroliniani Exsiccati*. "So we have it *ex Cathedra* that Dr. C., in this country at least, is autocrat in the realm of Fungi," Howe concluded.[8] On another recent occasion Curtis had, immodestly but not necessarily untruthfully, asserted to Stephen T. Olney the superiority of his own cryptogamic herbarium over Ravenel's, ranking the latter's, in fact, behind Schweinitz's collection at the Academy of Natural Sciences of Philadelphia.[9]

On Curtis's death Ravenel rightly mourned a good friend and a generous correspondent, for in his frequent help, his well-meant advice and sympathy, Curtis had more than once proved himself to be such. Yet he had also lost his harshest critic and detractor and the only man to vie with him for the position of dean of American mycologists.

Soon after Curtis's death, Berkeley recommenced a long-delayed task, the publication of a great quantity of the combined collections of Curtis and Ravenel that he had examined in the 1850s. Some of the species discussed in his new series of articles were previously established taxa, but many new species were attributed to Berkeley and Curtis or to Berkeley and Ravenel. The new articles brought Ravenel's name into a renewed and favorable prominence before the world's mycologists.[10]

Perhaps of more importance in attracting the notice of beginning American botanists was the fact that Ravenel was a southerner. Soon after the war, death claimed several of the older generation of southern naturalists, including Ravenel's old teacher Robert Gibbes in 1865, Charleston comparative anatomist John Holbrook, and conchologist Edmund Ravenel in 1871. At the same time, younger men fled the South for other places not afflicted with defeat and Reconstruction. Matthew Fontaine Maury spent several years in self-imposed exile in Mexico and Europe.[11] John and Joseph LeConte left South Carolina College for positions at the University of California.[12] Eugene Hilgard, a promising young agricultural scientist at the University of Mississippi, went in 1872 to the University of Michigan for two years before joining the LeConte brothers in California.[13]

Of the three southerners who had been nationally known before the war specifically as botanists, Ravenel alone remained active. Curtis was now dead, and Alvan Chapman, whose work on southern phanerogamous plants had established him as a leading authority in that field, had temporarily abandoned botany and dropped out of sight to run a drugstore in Rome, Georgia.[14] Of course, there were other botanists in the South, including Ravenel's old friend Francis Peyre Porcher, but none of them had attained as wide a reputation as Ravenel, Curtis, or Chapman. The many young botanists not privy to Chapman's whereabouts therefore considered Ravenel the best possibility not only for fungi, but for all southern plants. To make matters worse, because of the bleak economic conditions in the South following the war and the resultant emphasis on business and commerce, a greatly disproportionate number of promising botanists of this generation were northerners, so their opportunities for establishing correspondence with southerners of their own age was very limited. "Really I know of no one to whom I could recommend you to apply for Southern plants," Ravenel wrote one hopeful botanist. "Our people have had to struggle so hard for the necessaries of life of late years, that scientific recreation is not much thought of."[15]

Ravenel had a sincere desire to help these younger men, but their needs often conflicted with his own need to make a living from his collecting. If they were willing to buy a ready-made collection or if they wanted enough of just a few types of plant to make it worth his while to collect expressly for them, he could accommodate them. If, however, they wanted to establish an exchange or desired only a sprig or two of some particular species not already in the herbarium, so small an amount that Ravenel could not graciously ask payment but must still expend considerable time in gathering it, then he sometimes refused, particularly if the request came from someone unknown to him or an apparent dilettante.

Ravenel's new approach to botany both reflected and was facilitated by a change in his perception of himself. Though he partly made his living through botany, he no longer considered himself a student of the science. "I have in a great measure given up botanical studies. I have neither the time or [*sic*] means now to prosecute these studies as formerly,—& only look into them occasionally," he wrote to Job B. Ellis in January 1872.[16] Turning down George Davenport's request for an exchange of specimens nearly two years later, he made reference to the same feeling. "I am not now actively at work in Botany," he wrote, "having been obliged from force of circumstance of late years to give it but slight attention."[17]

These remarks are perplexing in light of the unquestionable fact that Ravenel was working quite hard at botany. Except when periods of ill health kept him confined to the house, he went out frequently to collect, and he wrote in March 1870 to Tuckerman that he believed his field work was more scrutinizing than it had been twenty years before. Many smaller forms that had escaped his attention then, now caught his eye. Ravenel's son Harry had also become interested in botany, and before Harry's departure in March 1871 to try farming in Georgia, the two often went botanizing together. Again, on his long yearly visits to Harry, Ravenel spent much time in the field.[18]

Even when ill, Ravenel would turn his attention to plants. During a period of relatively poor health in the spring of 1871, for example, some sedentary observation of growing plants yielded new and interesting analyses of the patterns of growth of *Baptisia perfoliata* and of certain common garden plants including squash, gourds, watermelon, and mango. At question was the number of leaves necessary to complete a rotation of the stem, the direction in which the leaf spiral ascended the stem, and the relative spacing of leaf and tendril. Gray read the papers for him at the 1871 meeting of the American Association for the Advancement of Science in Indianapolis but reported that no one in attendance was competent to discuss the topics. At his repeated suggestion the *Baptisia* paper was reprinted where it would be more generally available.[19]

Articles written during this period for the popular agricultural press also betrayed Ravenel's botanical outlook. A series of "Notes on our Native Flora" appearing in 1873 and 1874 in the *Rural Carolinian,* an organ of the South Carolina chapter of the national Grange, gave short descriptions of a number of South Carolina's wild flowers. They stressed the aspects of gross morphology most interesting to Sunday afternoon flower-pickers, including the color and size of flowers, shape of leaves, and the general habit of growth.[20]

Given the apparent fallacy of Ravenel's proclamations that he was not actively engaged in botany, there are two possible explanations. He may have made the statements merely as a gentle way of refusing help when he was unable to comply with a request for plants, or more likely, the statements were made sincerely and reveal something about what it meant to him to be actively studying botany. As an active student in the 1850s he had gone to considerable trouble and expense to obtain up-to-date botanical literature and a good microscope and had spent much time in their use among his specimens. In this way he was able to expand his knowledge daily and to bring his ability in taxonomy to a level very near that of his English mentor, Berkeley. No longer was any of this possible, however, and this lack understandably constituted a critical difference in Ravenel's eyes. "I have never resumed active work since the interruption caused by the war," he wrote to Tuckerman in 1877, "—& the condition of affairs in which we were left afterwards, was not favorable. I have been so much pressed however on all sides for Southern plants, that I still do what I can in the way of collecting for my friends—nothing more than collecting. I have neither the time or [*sic*] inclination to go any further."[21] Collecting, then, was not enough to count as "active work" so far as Ravenel was concerned. Ironically, because the truth of the situation was so far from Ravenel's own perception of it, he stood in the early 1870s on the threshold of a long period of very productive labor, based solidly on the scorned collecting. From 1869 through the rest of his life, Ravenel worked at his collecting with a greater steadiness than had characterized his work in the 1850s. Lacking now were the times of intense activity, like the year that followed his first wife's death in 1855, but lacking, too, were the frequent, total interruptions of several months' duration that had slowed his pace in that earlier period. Of course, there were slumps even now. Besides occasional ill health or slowdowns in orders for plants, personal worries sometimes distracted him, and he found it difficult, as he had in the past, to pay attention to botany when such problems were upon him.

Middle and late 1873, for example, brought distractions aplenty. In June, Sue, then eleven, contracted the measles and developed complications resembling typhoid fever. She was bedridden for more than a month, and at one point Ravenel was afraid they would lose her. At the same time, Ravenel's involvement with the *Rural Carolinian,* whose editor, Daniel Harrison Jacques, was first deputy of the national Grange for South Carolina, led to his appointment as the master of a newly formed Aiken chapter, a somewhat time-consuming office. There were additional financial worries, too, increased slightly by the birth February 17, 1870, of Ravenel's last child, another daughter, Tiphaine. In the fall of 1873 money became so tight that he again considered selling the herbarium but sold the farm instead and purchased a house in Aiken, "rather smaller than the other, but large enough, with garden room enough for my purposes," where he moved his family in November.[22]

June through December of 1875 was also a very stressful period. In June the financial failure of the convalescent home that had located at Hampton Hill forced Ravenel to take the farm back and cancel the remainder of the debt. Inspection of the premises revealed that in the year and a half since it had passed out of his hands some welcome improvements had been made to the house, but the orchard, vegetable garden, and asparagus field were choked with weeds. No crop of any kind had been planted. Ravenel contracted with former slave Jimmy to move his family out to the farm, assume the duties of caretaker, and resume planting. The farm came back when he still owed $600 on his house in town and when more than $6,000 had been owing on Hampton Hill. He had counted on that money to pay his house note and to provide future income from investment. Within days of taking back the farm he learned that the *Rural Carolinian* could no longer afford regular paid contributors and must sever its business connection with him. As a result, his annual income was cut by $175 to $200.[23]

October brought further trouble. Eleven-year-old Lizzie became seriously ill. Amory Coffin, Ravenel's friend and physician, called it autumnal fever, a form of typhoid. Extreme weakness and fever were

House reputed to have been Ravenel's residence in Aiken (Photo ca. 1970, courtesy of Dorothy MacDowell, Aiken, South Carolina)

followed by a skin eruption, mental confusion, lung congestion, and a troublesome cough that sapped Lizzie's strength. After less than two weeks of illness she had declined so far that she seemed to hold on to life by only a thread. Finally she began to improve. She gained consciousness and seemed to be gaining strength.[24]

Lizzie's recovery was short-lived. Two weeks later she began losing ground and by December 1 was once more too weak to get out of bed. On December 12 Charlotte suddenly became ill also. A violent headache was followed by convulsions and unconsciousness. Charlotte's illness, like Lizzie's, was pronounced typhoid fever, but it ran a different course from the beginning, coming on suddenly and progessing rapidly to a crisis. On December 22 Lizzie was back on the road to recovery, but Charlotte died. She was buried the next day in the cemetery of Saint Thaddeus Church, and Ravenel, as always in times of sorrow, turned to the Lord for comfort. *"Christmas Day!"* read his journal entry two days later. "For a period of twenty years, I have been privileged to record annually with a thankful heart, that our loving family are all spared to be together. Now one has been taken. Shall we not still believe that all is done in mercy & kindness?"[25]

Despite the troubles and sadness that 1875 brought to Ravenel, the year also brought some expansion of his botanical correspondence. He began collecting fungi for the German mycologist, Baron Felix von Thuemen. Thuemen had written him as early as 1872 at the suggestion of Mordecai Cooke to advertise an exsiccati series that he had just begun to issue, the *Fungi Austriaci,* and to propose that Ravenel trade American plants for Thuemen's centuries of fungi.[26] Not surprisingly, Ravenel apparently turned down the proposal, and Thuemen, who expressed himself very eager to form a partnership with an American botanist, began to correspond with Ellis instead. Ellis prevailed upon Ravenel to send fungi as well, and in March 1875 the South Carolina mycologist packed up some fungi to be shipped through Ellis. This transaction was on a purely cash basis, six dollars per one hundred species. As troubles mounted that year, Ravenel felt he could not continue collecting and wrote to Thuemen that he must stop.[27]

At the same time, however, Thuemen started to edit another, more ambitious exsiccati, this one not limited to Austrian fungi. The *Mycotheca Universalis* was to contain fungi from every continent. Thuemen promptly recruited Ellis and two other young American mycologists, Charles Horton Peck and William Ruggles Gerard, to provide American specimens. In March 1876 he also wrote to Ravenel imploring him, despite his desire to stop sending fungi, to make collections for the exsiccati. Any species at all would be welcome, he assured Ravenel, and if the South Carolinian would send 125–130 good specimens of each species, Thuemen promised two shillings sterling per species. The offer was generous, for Thuemen was principally interested in parasitic leaf fungi, which are easy to gather. Ravenel accepted and began sending fungi, including undescribed species, quite regularly to Thuemen. Beginning with the sixth century, or set of a hundred species, published in 1876, through the last, issued in 1884, every century of the *Mycotheca Universalis* contained at least a few Ravenel specimens. Those that Theumen did not use in this exsiccati he placed in another, smaller one issued contemporaneously, the *Herbarium Mycologicum Oeconomicum.*[28]

Also in 1875 Ravenel received the first of many letters from William
G. Farlow. Farlow had studied botany under Asa Gray, then, after
taking a medical degree as a sort of employment insurance policy and
working for a short time as Gray's assistant, had spent the years 1872–
1874 in Strasbourg studying with Anton De Bary. Now he was back
at Harvard to introduce cryptogamic botany to the curriculum. He
was reasonably well supplied with the necessary books and herbarium
material, for Gray, hoping to keep him at Harvard, had been active in
his absence. In 1873 he had purchased Curtis's herbarium, with some
help from Ravenel, who had assured his friend's widow of the suita-
bility of Harvard as a repository. Now, however, Farlow found that
Gray's collection was missing the first two fascicles of the *Fungi
Caroliniani Exsiccati* and wrote to see if Ravenel could supply them
and whether he knew where Farlow could obtain Schweinitz's *Synopsis
Fungorum.*[29]

Farlow's letter came during the troubled December of 1875, but
Ravenel made time to answer it. He only had a few copies of the first
fascicle besides his own full set but provided names of two people
who might be willing to sell theirs to Farlow.[30] With this exchange
began a correspondence ending only at Ravenel's death. The nature of
the relationship between Ravenel and Farlow scarcely changed from
that established by these first letters. Farlow, though well trained in
German laboratory technique and knowledgeable in botany generally,
lacked the depth of experience in the taxonomy of American fungi
that Ravenel possessed. When specific questions or needs arose in this
area a letter to Ravenel often produced the desired information. In
1878, for example, when Farlow had questions about Berkeley's *Ravenelia glanduloformis* and *Phallus ravenelii,* he wrote to Ravenel and
received specimens of *Ravenelia* and a loan of the original notes that
Ravenel had taken in the 1850s when he first discovered *Phallus ravenelii.*[31] In return for this sort of help, Farlow wrote news-filled letters
sharing with Ravenel the use he had made of specimens or other
materials sent, and telling him about his other research. He was
prompt with his thank-yous, frequently sent and more frequently
offered specimens in return for Ravenel's, and was courteous, even
deferential, in his approach to the older man. As a result, Ravenel was
more than willing to go the extra mile to help him, even in matters

not strictly botanical. In July 1878 Farlow asked for a photograph of Ravenel, suitable for framing, to be hung in his laboratory as part of a gallery of important cryptogamists. He presumed Ravenel had only small card photographs available but pleaded for a copy if Ravenel ever had a larger photograph taken.[32] Indeed Ravenel had no large photos on hand, but he recalled one that he had given to a friend, who had recently died. Ravenel got the photo back from the friend's family and sent it up to Cambridge where it arrived in time for Christmas.[33] Farlow's request had been a compliment not easily ignored.

There was nothing very unusual in the small favors Ravenel did for Farlow. He did the same from time to time for many others, for when the favor requested did not involve a long exchange and came from someone who seemed truly dedicated to botany, Ravenel was usually happy to oblige. Peck, for example, in 1878 successfully prevailed upon Ravenel to send a sketch and even more detailed notes on *Phallus ravenelii* than Farlow had received, and also in 1878, Canby had requested and received specimens of several species of *Baptisia* that he needed for a study of the genus.[34] The distinguishing feature of Ravenel and Farlow's relationship, rather, was its length and intensity.

Only once did their long correspondence hit a sour note. Ravenel had for some years been sending Farlow algae, more for the sake of helping Farlow with his interest than out of any interest Ravenel himself had in the little plants. He also sent algae to Francis Wolle, a minister and teacher in Pennsylvania whose acquaintance he had made at about the same time as Farlow's, and both men were courteous in sending him reports on the species he gathered for them. This dual correspondence caused no problem until December 1881 when he sent duplicates of the same collection to both Farlow and Wolle. Both sent back their determinations, and on comparing lists, Ravenel found some differences of opinion. He mentioned the discrepancies to Farlow, particularly pointing out one specimen, which Wolle had thought to be a new species of *Draparnaldia* and proposed to call *D. ravenelii* but which Farlow had identified as *Batrachospermum vagum*. "Of course I have no opinion in the matter," he remarked, "not having given any microscopical examination, nor being sufficiently familiar with the species of Algae to offer any opinion." He was sure, though, that Farlow would see the need to eliminate such discrepancies and generously offered to send Farlow his other Wolle specimens to increase his collection.[35]

No doubt Ravenel's mild but plain assumption that Farlow was wrong in his identification was somewhat embarrassing to the Massachusetts botanist. Farlow knew the algae quite well, having just recently completed a study entitled "Marine Algae of New England and Adjacent Coast" for the United States Fish Commission Report of 1879. Furthermore, Farlow's opinion of Wolle was low enough that he was not going to concede easily; yet to attack *Draparnaldia ravenelii* would be churlish. Instead Farlow resorted to personal criticism of Wolle, who, he wrote, was not a scientific man. If he did any good at all for botany it was by sending some things to Veit Brecher Wittrock and Carl Otto Nordstedt, who made the appropriate corrections in otherwise worthless descriptions and published them in their exsiccati series of Scandinavian algae (Stockholm, 1877–1889). At one time, he continued, Wolle had had a plant that both Farlow and Tuckerman said was a lichen, yet Wolle published it as a new alga. Worst of all, he once sent Farlow a mounted preparation of a plant that he said was a marine alga from Florida along with colored drawings to show the development of sporangia, which are not found in algae. The prepared slide turned out to be a hair of *Drosera,* a genus of flowering plant, with the central vascular bundle quite plain. Farlow kept both drawings and slide to amuse visiting botanists. He would be glad, he concluded, to see any of Ravenel's Wolle specimens; their determinations were often entirely wrong.[36]

If Farlow hoped Ravenel would enjoy his stories at Wolle's expense, he was disappointed. Ravenel evidently was not inclined to find humor in criticizing others, and in this situation he reacted true to character. He sent off by return mail, "in justice to Mr. Wolle," a short note letting Farlow know that Wolle had just written to change his opinion. *Draparnaldia ravenelli* was indeed a *Batrachospermum.* Yet even as Ravenel wrote this, Farlow was writing again to admit he had reexamined the doubtful sample and found a *Draparnaldia* mixed in with the *Batrachospermum.* With this admission made, Ravenel was inclined to be forgiving of Farlow's slip. The difference of opinion he attributed to the natural result of working among a little-known class of plants in a country still but poorly explored. With regard to the report on

Wolle's incompetence, Ravenel replied, "Of course it will be strictly confidential."[37]

As Ravenel entered into correspondence with talented young men like Farlow, he found the informal rules he had set for himself with regard to selling his collections slipping farther into the background. These young botanists so often and so earnestly implored only small favors. He helped them, and though he very often received their collections in return,[38] seldom did he make money.

In 1877 the South Carolinian decided he must redouble his efforts to make some profit from botany. Ravenel wrote to Cooke, who in former years had so successfully disposed of a number of sets of fungi. He proposed a trip to Florida for the special purpose of collecting fungi and other plants for distribution in sets. Cooke reacted with alacrity and enthusiasm. Ravenel, he wrote, could count on him "to enter fully and heartily into" the project and to give it his "best attention."[39] With this assurance received, Ravenel contacted others to arrange for distribution of other cryptogamic plants that he might collect. Coe Finch Austin agreed to take the mosses and hepatics, while Tuckerman would take the lichens, and Wolle the algae. The trip through Georgia and as far into Florida as Gainesville, required only about three weeks. So from the middle of November until December 11, Ravenel worked hard to make good use of his time. He stayed with a friend who had moved to Florida from South Carolina, and by thus reducing the expenses of his trip found that he was able to collect enough fungi to repay his expenses. The twenty-five dollars Tuckerman sent for lichens and any money received from Austin and Wolle was profit, so the new venture was launched with reasonable success.[40]

Ravenel left the distribution of sets entirely to their recipients. He sent Tuckerman, Austin, and Wolle relatively small parcels. They either used the materials themselves or distributed them informally. To Cooke, on the other hand, Ravenel sent massive quantities of fungi from Florida, from a trip the following spring to Darien, Georgia, and of course, from South Carolina. The English botanist intended from the beginning that Ravenel's fungi should be issued in formal sets as an exsiccati. To ensure a profit from them, Cooke advertised in advance in *Grevillea,* a British journal of cryptogamic botany, which he edited. As the advertisement made clear, Cooke took care of the format and preparation of the exsiccati, and he also was in charge of collecting payment for sets and distributing them. Specimens in the *Fungi Americani Exsiccati,* as the new set was called, were issued on loose sheets, rather than bound into books as in Ravenel's earlier exsiccati, but they, like the first, were carefully glued down individually on their pages. Cooke had a very poor, though by modern thinking unjustified, opinion of those botanists who had lately fallen into "the idle habit" of issuing exsiccati specimens enclosed in envelopes, "a most vicious practice and one likely to produce very serious consequences."[41]

In exchange for relief from the microscopic examination of the fungi he sent Cooke and from the tedious work of assembling the exsiccati sheets, Ravenel had to take in good grace both the form of the new work, which he did not quite like, and Cooke's occasional errors. Ravenel pointed out to Farlow a number of cases where species published by him and Berkeley were referred to Berkeley and Curtis, as well as some other errors. "Personally, I lay no great stress," he wrote, not entirely convincingly, "on having my name appended to a species, but priority in description, & exactness of authorship are necessary to avoid endless confusion." He was for the most part willing to excuse Cooke's occasional slips on the basis of the great amount of other work the Englishman had before him.[42]

In addition to preparing the exsiccati, Cooke published several articles in *Grevillea* or other cryptogamic journals commenting on Ravenel's fungi. He also described a large number of new species from them. Moved, so it seemed to Ravenel, by simple generosity, Cooke occasionally credited his American collaborator with coauthorship of the new species, even though, Ravenel admitted to Farlow, he sent at least the microscopic species entirely without notes or description. Both the commencement of the exsiccati itself and South Carolina's release from Republican domination in the same year, 1877, had added fuel to the fire of Ravenel's interest in mycology, already burning ever more brightly since the close of the war. Even so, he had not the slightest inclination to recommence his studies with the microscope.[43]

Cooke's original advertisement for the exsiccati anticipated the issuance of about four centuries of fungi. So much material was gath-

ered, however, that the work eventually expanded to eight, the first
issued in 1878 and the last in 1882. With the exception of just a few
specimens, Ravenel collected all the contents himself. At the same
time, he was helping his old correspondent Ellis with his exsiccati,
North American Fungi. The seventh century, issued in 1881, contained
thirty-three Ravenel specimens, and many other centuries also included a few.[44]

As Ravenel looked back over his life's work he could feel satisfaction
at his own accomplishments and those of the men he had aided and
was aiding still.[45] There was more work left in him, but as he reached
his late sixties, he began to slow down a little. The desire to take off
into the woods on hours' long expeditions was as strong as ever, but
tramping about became progressively more difficult, and his deafness
also worsened. In August 1883 at the urging of Tuckerman, who
offered to pay Ravenel's expenses, Ravenel undertook a trip to Salem,
North Carolina, to find a particular plant previously collected by
Schweinitz. He found that his deafness made travel among strangers
very difficult. In Aiken he rarely went anywhere except to visit his
most intimate friends.[46]

As Ravenel grew older, money problems became a little less wor-
risome. In February 1882 he accepted an offer from the Charleston
News and Courier to take over the agriculture column in their Tuesday
evening weekly, and at the same time accepted a commission to prepare
a list of South Carolina plants to be appended to a handbook of the
state's resources then in preparation by Harry Hammond, the eldest
son of former governor James Henry Hammond. For this he was paid
$100, and further commissions from the state agricultural department
followed. Finally in November, Hampton Hill was sold. The purchase
price, $2,500, clear of commissions, was pitifully small compared
with the $15,000 he had hoped to get for it soon after the war, but it
provided a welcome cushion for his old age.[47]

Ravenel knew he still had one financial ace up his sleeve: the herbarium. He had played with the idea of selling it for years, but now
with old age coming upon him, he gave the possibility renewed
attention. He wished to ensure the collection a place where it would
be available to other scholars after he was gone. He may also have
wanted to spare his family the problems Curtis's wife had faced in

disposing of his herbarium a decade before. Hoping to locate it at a school or scientific institution in the United States, preferably in South Carolina, he approached in turn Johns Hopkins University, the College of Charleston, and South Carolina College but was turned down by all of them. Johns Hopkins had no botany teacher and needed no collection, and neither of the South Carolina schools could afford the one thousand to fifteen hundred dollars that Ravenel was asking.[48] The collection was a large and valuable one. In October 1881 Ravenel inventoried it and found he had plants representing over eleven thousand separate species, about half of which were fungi, including approximately a thousand type specimens of species of Berkeley and Ravenel, Berkeley and Curtis, or Cooke.[49] In fairness to his family he knew he could not dispose of the collection for less than it was worth, but he became discouraged by the refusals of these colleges and never got around to offering it elsewhere.

His family had always been a pleasure to Ravenel, and now he watched his children grow up strong and healthy. Lizzie, who had nearly died in 1875 from typhoid, turned nineteen in 1883 and began teaching school with her elder half sister Lydia. Emily and Edward in Florence had a full house; Ravenel lived to greet the arrival of the ninth of their children. Carrie, who had married Edward H. Lucas in 1877, had several children too, and like Emily, had named one son Henry Ravenel. Harry, after much struggling and ill fortune, was doing well in Darien, Georgia, and he too was married and had a family.[50] Other cares gradually faded from Ravenel's mind in the mid 1880s. Diary entries were largely given over to brief notes on the weather, letters sent or received, the state of the garden. The old bugbear of his younger days, politics, was accorded scarcely a mention.

Botany, however, still held his interest. He continued to receive letters from young botanists wanting advice or specimens, and he complied to the best of his ability. In September 1886 he had to turn down Ellis's request for some plants. "I would gladly comply with your request," he wrote, "but I fear my active working days are over. In the latter part of June I had a warning attack—some head trouble, which was quite serious for the time, & left me so weak that I have scarcely been out of the house since. . . . If the opportunity comes I will remember your wants."[51]

In the following weeks he found specimens or fragments in his herbarium and sent them on, and he procured some other fungi on peach leaves but could not be entirely sure what they were. "My head is not strong enough to do anything that requires close attention," he confessed.[52]

Among the letters were occasional compliments and honors of the type that scholars bestow on one another. The day before he turned sixty-nine a diploma arrived most unexpectedly from Austria certifying Ravenel's election to the Imperial Zoologic-Botanic Society of Vienna, and on his seventy-second birthday came word that he had been elected a member of the Elisha Mitchell Scientific Society at the University of North Carolina. Less than two months later, in July 1886, the university at Chapel Hill bestowed honorary LL.D. degrees on both Ravenel and Alvan W. Chapman, Ravenel's nomination having come from a botanist named Thomas Wood.[53]

A year passed, and another birthday came, bringing honors of a more personal kind. Harry came to spend the day, and all Ravenel's children, except Emily and Carrie, were with him. Others, too, remembered him. "I have received from friends several tokens of affectionate remembrance which have moved me deeply," he wrote. "I am very weak today & cannot write much, but I wish to record this acknowledgment of my great thankfulness to a merciful Providence for all these blessings & also for the blessings that have fallen to my lot during the whole course of my life."[54] In this peaceful faith Ravenel lived the remaining days of his life, enjoying the love of his family, the memories of his career, and the honors due, in the words of Thomas Wood, "a devoted student of the fungi" and a "very high authority on the subject."[55]

Epilogue

Henry Ravenel died July 17, 1887. He had experienced two mild strokes, one in January and one in June of the previous year, but his death was attributed to dropsy. He was buried in the churchyard of Saint Thaddeus Parish, where he had served so long as a warden, near his daughter Charlotte.[1]

Ravenel's will, made out two years earlier, was simple and concise.

Being desirous of leaving a home at least to my wife & unmarried daughters, & as I have but little worldly property besides the house & lot in Aiken, I therefore direct that my property remain as an undivided estate for their use & benefit, until my youngest daughter become of lawful age. That then it be sold or disposed of, & the proceeds thereof be divided equally, share & share alike, between my wife & my children that may then be living.[2]

A separate note written several years previously expressed his wishes regarding the disposition of several family heirlooms, carefully kept through the lean years, and gave advice on the disposal of his real treasure, the herbarium. The cryptogamic portion alone was worth fully a thousand dollars and should be kept together, he wrote. The phanerogams should be kept with the rest, unless any member of the family developed enough interest in them to desire to keep them.[3]

Soon after her husband's death Mary Ravenel began to receive enquiries about the herbarium, and she found she had little idea how to go about selling it, not even knowing what price to place on it. Ravenel's note had suggested a thousand dollars for the cryptogams alone, and so, on the advice of her friends, she doubled the amount for the entire collection. When it had not yet been sold a year later, she began to suspect the price might be too high and wrote to Farlow who helped her place a more reasonable value on it. Still she had no luck; the southern schools where she would prefer to place it could not afford it. Finally she began to sell some sets separately, and in 1891 sold a large part of the cryptogamic portion to the British Museum (Natural History) for six hundred dollars.[4]

Henry Edmund Ravenel, a distant relation, purchased the phanerogams for an unknown sum and gave them to Converse College, a school for women that he had been instrumental in founding in Spartanburg, South Carolina. The collection at Spartanburg has had a checkered history. It was cared for lovingly by biology teacher Elizabeth Williams, but at one point the school, needing money, sold a portion to George Vanderbilt for the Biltmore Estate in Asheville, North Carolina. Along with much of the rest of Biltmore's botanical collection, it was destroyed by a flood. Anxious to save the remainder of Ravenel's collection, Williams spirited it away to her attic, whence it was rescued soon after her death by Robert Powell, present head of the biology department at Converse.[5]

Conclusion

What effect did Henry Ravenel, southerner, have upon Henry Ravenel, botanist, and what conclusions can be drawn from his experiences upon the state of science in the South as a whole?

Ravenel's career may be considered to have encompassed three distinct periods, 1839–1860, 1861–1865, and 1865–1887. These periods differ from each other in the level and type of scientific activity carried on by Ravenel and conform, as well, to different eras of southern political life.

Of these three periods the first was the most important for Ravenel as a scientist. To describe him as a "professional" botanist during this period would be, of course, to apply a twentieth-century concept to a nineteenth-century man, and the fit would be awkward at best. Although Ravenel referred to himself as a botanist, he never tacked on the adjective "professional," and it is doubtful that he thought of himself in such terms. At the same time, however, his activities during this early period corresponded to a level of commitment but little short of what could be considered professional. He approached botany in a decidedly scholarly manner, not only collecting plants but also studying them in the light of current literature. He was in touch through correspondence with a number of the most important cryptogamic botanists of his time, and though he was not of the inner circle, the masters, particularly Berkeley, recognized the high level of

152

his ability and devotion to botany and awarded him a greater status than many of their other correspondents. By the end of the 1850s he had built up his own small network of collectors who helped him with specimens for the *Fungi Caroliniani Exsiccati* and sent material for identification. Most important, in planning his scientific collecting and research, he kept the standards and needs of botany foremost in his mind, rather than following the mere dictates of his own desires. Ravenel never clearly stated his choice between specialization in one area of botany and taking a broad overview of the subject, nor did he make a clear and consistent move in one direction or the other. During the 1850s, however, he moved towards a commitment to mycology over other types of botany. At all times his work was restricted to botany; never did he display the fragmented efforts of the seventeenth- or eighteenth-century naturalists. In this way he was like other leading botanists of his time.

The 1840s and 1850s also correspond with a period of intensifying conservatism and political closed-mindedness throughout the South, a trend reflected in Ravenel's own political thought. His approval of slavery cannot be doubted, and if his views on that subject, on North-South relations, and on eventual secession were somewhat milder and opener than many others', they were still well within the range of views held by the majority of South Carolinians. He did not accept the views of the majority blindly but, as much thoughtful analysis in his journal reveals, acceded to them with eyes open. Ravenel's religious views were also quite ordinary. His Episcopal inclinations were un-usual in the South as a whole, but they were common enough among wealthy South Carolinians.

It is clear that Ravenel suffered no social pressure because of his interest in botany or his views on slavery or religion. Other, less direct effects of these opinions were also minimal. Slave labor provided him with the leisure he needed to botanize and did not interfere with his relations with northern botanists, with whom he remained on cordial terms until the very eve of war. Similarly, religious faith presented no barrier to his scientific interests. In his attitude toward the connection between religion and science, Ravenel followed the tradition that as there was one God, so there was one truth, which both theologian and scientist strove to reveal. He saw God's hand in the beauty of each plant, and his belief that scripture and science must be in accord allowed him to shrug his shoulders philosophically at apparent contradictions. These would be worked out by correction of the errors of human theologians or scientists, all in God's good time.

Limits on Ravenel's growth as a scientist during this period were intrinsic to his own personality or circumstances. Ill health was one of the chief limitations. In 1852, 1853, 1855, and again from 1858 through 1860, he suffered attacks of dyspepsia that were disabling in their severity. The attacks may have been linked to his use of the microscope, for while they seemed related to general psychological and physical stress, they were exacerbated by microscopic work. They were probably at least partly of psychosomatic origin, leaving open the possibility that they were related to social attitudes toward health and illness. The nineteenth century is well known for a certain preoccupation with health, and the possibility that southern feelings on the subject were measurably different from those of other areas has not been explored adequately for further speculation. It presents an inviting avenue for future research.

Another limitation, or perhaps the result of an unseen limitation, was that Ravenel never made a trip to Europe. The opportunity to study a wider range of European literature and to see herbarium specimens from the four corners of the earth might have done for him what it did for Gray and Tuckerman, raising their work to the same level as European botany. Ravenel, though he apparently aspired to be more, remained a second-rank mycologist compared with Fries, Berkeley, or Montagne. His failure to travel to Europe does not indicate a lack of understanding of the possible benefits of such a trip, as may be witnessed by his vicarious pleasure and excitement when Tuckerman planned a voyage. Instead, it apparently demarcates the extent of his commitment to botany. He never seriously contemplated the possibility. It is doubtful that financial considerations were important, especially after he moved to Hampton Hill, where he had a fairly large cash income from investments and large, though irregular supplements from his fruit crops. The fact is that Ravenel, faced with the expense and bother of a long trip in foreign countries, simply chose not to go.

During the second part of his career, spanning the Civil War and the months immediately afterward, Ravenel did very little in botany.

His withdrawal was occasioned both by poor health and by preoccupation with political and military events. The poor health itself was
probably aggravated by worry over politics. Even had he desired to
continue scientific activities, it would have been impossible to keep
abreast of new developments, cut off as he and other southerners were
from scientific news.

For the remainder of his life Ravenel was again active in botany,
this time, however, without scholarly ambitions. He confined himself
to collecting. The influence of his environment during this time is
subtle and difficult to analyze. Continued delicate health helped limit
him to collecting. He found that by avoiding use of the microscope
he could eliminate a significant source of stress and so keep his dyspepsia under control. Collecting, on the other hand, provided gentle
outdoor exercise and was generally beneficial to his physical condition.
At the same time, however, the poverty resulting from the war was
also a major restriction on his botanical activities. He was no longer
able to buy books but instead had to sell portions of his earlier library,
and the leisure hours he had once devoted to study now were directed,
as much as possible, to income-producing activities.

Reconstruction did not have a purely pernicious influence upon
Ravenel's work. Indeed, he returned to botany following the war
largely as a means of making money. Without that spur it is possible
that he might never have returned to the science. The question is
unanswerable, but the dual nature of the influence of postwar need
upon his work must be recognized.

Despite the new, nonscholarly focus of Ravenel's own work following the war, he maintained his earlier concern with the progress of
botany and tried to do what he could by helping others. Especially
significant was his aid to younger men like Peck and Farlow. German
postgraduate education in the sciences, as well as the greater prevalence
of botany in American college curricula, by the 1870s and 1880s
prophesied the decline of the importance of correspondence networks
as a means of botanical education. Informal instruction of this type,
however, has never entirely lost its usefulness, and during the final
period of Ravenel's life it retained comparatively greater importance
than it was to have in the following century. Within this context,
Ravenel served these younger scientists as a teacher and guide.

Except for the interruption in correspondence caused by the war itself, the postwar period presents the only known time when North-South political animosity marred Ravenel's relations with another botanist. Most northern botanists allowed correspondence to pick up where it left off with very little change. Tuckerman even sympathized with Ravenel over Republican rule in South Carolina and rejoiced with him at its end in 1877.[1] Yet, at least one man allowed the Civil War to color his impression of Ravenel, and it would be strange if others had not done so as well. "I will send [specimens for identification] to Ravenel this week," Howe wrote to Peck in 1868, "though I confess to a feeling akin to horror at the thought of addressing a South Carolinian! But our science must not suffer though we be compelled to invoke the aid of *Le Diable* himself."[2]

Although the effect of Reconstruction on Ravenel's career remains uncertain, his life attests to the generally depressing effect that period had on science in the South. Gains made by southern education during Reconstruction were offset by the frequent impoverishment of the former leisured class. Neither those who, like Ravenel, clung to their earlier life by whatever threads remained nor the forward-looking businessmen of the New South had time for the serious pursuit of nonpractical arts or sciences. It is, perhaps, symbolic that Ravenel's son, though interested in botany, became a businessman.

There is a limit to how far conclusions drawn from the life of one man may be expanded to serve as general principles for dealing with science in the South. Nevertheless, Henry Ravenel's life has much to teach us about what some have argued was the intrinsic unsuitability of the South for scientific pursuits.

First, intelligence and energy applied to science do not in any way guarantee that an individual will formulate political or social principles different from or better than those of other members of his society. Southern scientists had as much likelihood as anyone else of subscribing to social outlooks now condemned but then broadly accepted. Nor did slavery or the holding of pro-slavery opinions have an intrinsically negative impact on the work of southern scientists.

Furthermore, the South's increasing political conservatism during the later antebellum period was not necessarily mirrored by increasing scientific conservatism or resistance to theoretical innovation. Ravenel, in fact, reacted in 1860 to Darwin's theory of evolution with considerable open-mindedness.

Second, many scholars have shown with regard to other societies or other times that religious piety, either in the individual scientist or in the society as a whole, may be more likely to spur scientific research than to hinder it. There is a form of religious piety that asserts the oneness of God's creation and the duty of scientists to glorify God by studying his works, and it is to this doctrine that Henry Ravenel subscribed. To the extent that it was shared by other southerners, the theme of the supposed enmity between southern piety and southern science has been overplayed.

Third, those other, supposedly negative factors, including romanticism, a rural environment, and a hot climate, all had some slight, interesting effects on Ravenel, and presumably on other southern naturalists, but none of these effects could be considered entirely negative. Ravenel possessed in full measure one trait of romanticism, that is, an appreciation of the wild outdoors and an ability to see beauty in unfettered nature. He admitted that these feelings caused him to prefer field work over close, microscopic examination of his collections, but they did not prevent him from carrying on his closet botany with patience and perseverance for fifteen years, until forced by nervous dyspepsia to desist.

As for the agricultural environment, which he vastly preferred to that of the cities, Ravenel was able to rise above a barrier of isolation that did annoy many others. In addition, his rural surroundings colored his work with a concern for the promotion of scientific agriculture that might have been lacking had he lived in a city or a less agriculturally oriented society. Nearby Charleston, and Curtis's frequent letters and occasional visits were, of course, of immense help. The stimulation of others was necessary at the beginning of his career, but once it was fairly launched, he complained of isolation not from other scientists in general but from other mycologists, and this deficiency he could not hope to cure anywhere in America. He desired closer contact with other members of his own tightly specialized subcommunity of botanists. In this sense Tuckerman in Massachusetts suffered more from isolation than did Ravenel, who was close enough to Curtis to enjoy his companionship.

Ravenel complained upon rare occasions of summer heat, but as we would expect, he was accustomed to it and seldom let it prevent him from working. In the winter he reaped the benefit of the region's mild climate when he found there were plants to be gathered all year round, and never did he pen the complaints of William Farlow, who wrote at Christmas one year that it was too cold to stay in the herbarium long enough to do anything.[3] Nonetheless, it must be admitted that he moved from Saint John's rich botanical fields to the sparse collecting range of Aiken to escape the heat and humidity of the low country, which he felt had a debilitating effect on his health. No doubt this heat and humidity would have seemed even less pleasant to a scientist coming to Charleston from the North or from England than to a native like Ravenel.

To say that certain factors in southern society often cited as inimical to the advance of science were not always so is not to deny their negative impact upon some scientists. Nor does it support T. Cary Johnson's implicit message that science in the South was on a parity with science in the North. Rather, the lessons taught by an examination of Henry Ravenel's life lend weight to the assumption that both Johnson's and Eaton's views of southern science suffered a lack of depth and perspective due to the infant state of development of the history of American science in 1936, when Johnson wrote, and even in the 1960s, when *The Mind of the Old South* was published.

Further investigations into the nature of American, and particularly southern, science will likely reveal that during the antebellum period southern science was often quite comparable to the science practiced in the North, outside of certain exceptional institutions such as Harvard and the Smithsonian. The life and career of Henry William Ravenel suggest that in botany this was true. Harvard's Asa Gray was clearly a leader, but Curtis and Ravenel were comparable to Tuckerman and Sullivant, Chapman and Engelmann to Oakes and Olney, Peters and Beaumont to Michener and Sartwell. It was after the war that the South lagged behind noticeably. Certainly in cryptogamic botany there were no young postbellum southerners to compare with Farlow, Peck, or Ellis.

Notes

Introduction

1. Thomas Cary Johnson, Jr., *Scientific Interests in the Old South* (New York: D. Appleton-Century Co., 1936).
2. Clement Eaton, *Freedom of Thought in the Old South* (New York: Peter Smith, 1951, reprint of 1940 edition), 196–217, 199 (quotation).
3. Clement Eaton, *The Mind of the Old South* (revised ed.; Baton Rouge: Louisiana State University Press, 1967), 224–44, 243 (quotation).
4. William B. Hesseltine, *The South in American History* (2nd ed.; New York: Prentice-Hall, 1943), 296; Francis Butler Simkins, *A History of the South* (2nd ed.; New York: Alfred A. Knopf, 1953), 153, 161; Clement Eaton, *A History of the Old South: The Emergence of a Reluctant Nation* (3rd ed.; New York: Macmillan Publishing Co., 1975), 456; I. A. Newby, *The South, A History* (New York: Holt, Rinehart, and Winston, 1978), 163, 181.
5. Joseph Ewan, "The Growth of Learned and Scientific Societies in the Southeastern United States to 1860," in Alexandra Oleson and Sanborn C. Brown (eds.), *The Pursuit of Knowledge in the Early American Republic: American Scientific and Learned Societies from Colonial Times to the Civil War* (Baltimore: Johns Hopkins University Press, 1976), 210; Robert V. Bruce, "A Statistical Profile of American Scientists, 1846–1876," in George H. Daniels (ed.), *Nineteenth-Century American Science: A Reappraisal* (Evanston: Northwestern University Press, 1972), 79.
6. Todd L. Savitt, *Medicine and Slavery: The Diseases and Health Care of Blacks in Antebellum Virginia* (Urbana: University of Illinois Press, 1978); Todd L. Savitt, "The Use of Blacks for Medical Experimentation and Demonstration in the Old South," *Journal of Southern History* XLVIII (August 1982), 331–48; Ronald L. Numbers and Janet S. Numbers, "Science in the Old South: A Reappraisal," *Journal of Southern History* XLVIII (May 1982), 163–84, 184 (quotation).
7. Brooke Hindle, *The Pursuit of Science in Revolutionary America, 1735–1789* (Chapel Hill: For the Institute of Early American History and Culture, Williamsburg,

Virginia, by the University of North Carolina Press, 1956), 16–17; William
Martin Smallwood, *Natural History and the American Mind* (New York: Columbia
University Press, 1941), 129.

8. The manuscript diary (Private Journal of Henry William Ravenel) is available at
the South Caroliniana Library, University of South Carolina, Columbia. The
edited version is Arney Robinson Childs (ed.), *The Private Journal of Henry William
Ravenel, 1859–1887* (Columbia: University of South Carolina Press, 1947).

9. Neil E. Stevens, "The Mycological Work of Henry W. Ravenel," *Isis* XVIII (1932),
133–49.

10. Simkins, *History of the South*, 161, 162; Kenneth M. Stampp, *The Era of Recon-
struction, 1865–1877* (New York: Alfred A. Knopf, 1975), 69; Steven A. Channing,
Crisis of Fear: Secession in South Carolina (New York: W. W. Norton & Co., 1970),
28–29, 63, 67, 271–72; Eaton, *Freedom of Thought*, 308, 330; Herbert Ravenel
Sass, *The Story of the South Carolina Lowcountry* (3 vols.; West Columbia, S.C.:
J. F. Hyer Publishing Co., n.d.), I, 208.

Chapter 1: Growing Up in the Low Country, 1814–1829

1. G. A. Rothrock, *The Huguenots: A Biography of a Minority* (Chicago: Nelson-
Hall, 1979); John T. McNeill, *The History and Character of Calvinism* (London:
Oxford University Press, 1954), 237–54; N. M. Sutherland, *The Huguenot Struggle
for Recognition* (New Haven: Yale University Press, 1980); Arthur Henry Hirsch,
The Huguenots of Colonial South Carolina (Hamden: Archon Books, 1962), 10–13;
[Theodore Gaillard Thomas (ed. and comp.)], *"Liste des François et Suisses" from
an Old Manuscript List of French and Swiss Protestants Settled in Charleston, on the
Santee and at the Orange Quarter in Carolina Who Desired Naturalization Prepared
Probably About 1695–6* (Baltimore: Genealogical Publishing Co., 1968, reprint of
Charleston, 1868 edition), 57; Henry Edmund Ravenel, *Ravenel Records: A History
and Genealogy of the Huguenot Family of Ravenel, of South Carolina; with Some
Incidental Account of the Parish of St. John's, Berkeley, Which Was Their Principal
Location* (Atlanta: Franklin Printing and Publishing Co., 1898), 131, 141.

2. René Ravenel Diary, May 23, 1790, September 23, 1790, Box 1, Thomas Porcher
Ravenel Collection (South Carolina Historical Society, Charleston); Frederick
Dalcho, *An Historical Account of the Protestant Episcopal Church, in South-Carolina,
from the First Settlement of the Province, to the War of the Revolution;. . .* (New York:
Arno Press, 1970, reprint of Charleston, 1820 edition), 214–19.

3. René Ravenel Diary, June 23, November 17, 1794; May 24, 1802; October 31,
1804, and *passim.*

4. Ibid., January 14, November 18, December 3, 1809, March 11, October 21, June
15, 1810. Joseph Ioor Waring, *A History of Medicine in South Carolina, 1670–1825*
(Columbia: South Carolina Medical Association, 1964), 329–30.

5. René Ravenel Diary, June 17, 21, 1813, May 19, 1814; William Montgomery
Clemens, *North and South Carolina Marriage Records from the Earliest Colonial Days
to the Civil War* (New York: E. P. Dutton & Co., 1927), 228; H. E. Ravenel,
Ravenel Records, 165.

6. René Ravenel Diary, September 25, 1814.

7. Ibid., April 5, June 8, 12, 1816; H. E. Ravenel, *Ravenel Records*, 165; Brent H.
Holcomb, *Marriage and Death Notices from the (Charleston) "Times," 1800–1821*
(Baltimore: Genealogical Publishing Co., 1979), 298.

8. Childs (ed.), *Private Journal of HWR,* xiv–x.
9. Ibid., xv; H. E. Ravenel, *Ravenel Records,* 165–66; Clemens, *Carolina Marriage Records,* 228.
10. René Ravenel Diary, October 31, 1816; H. E. Ravenel, *Ravenel Records,* 174; Frederick A. Porcher, "Upper Beat of St. John's, Berkeley," Huguenot Society of South Carolina, *Transactions* XIII (1906), 50–51.
11. H. W. Ravenel to Edward Tuckerman, March 23, 1857, Octavo Volume 4, Edward Tuckerman Correspondence (American Antiquarian Society, Worcester, Mass.), hereinafter cited as Tuckerman Correspondence, AAS. Parts of the letter are quoted in Childs (ed.), *Private Journal of HWR,* xiv; and Neil E. Stevens, "Two Southern Botanists and the Civil War," *Scientific Monthly* IX (August 1919), 157–58. Henry William Ravenel, "Recollections of Southern Plantation Life," *Yale Review* XXV (Summer 1936), 750 (quotation); Frederick A. Porcher, "Upper Beat," 73.
12. Frederick A. Porcher, "Upper Beat," 72–73; George D. Terry, "Eighteenth Century Plantation Names in Upper St. John's, Berkeley," *Names in South Carolina* XXVI (Winter 1979), 17. The description of Pooshee is from Samuel Wilson Ravenel, "Christmas at Pooshee" (1903, typescript), Box 5, T. P. Ravenel Collection, 2–3; Harriette Kershaw Leiding, *Historic Houses of South Carolina* (Philadelphia: J. B. Lippincott Co., 1921), 131–54; Childs (ed.), *Private Journal of HWR,* 35; H. W. Ravenel, "Recollections," 750–51.
13. René Ravenel Diary, June 23, 1818; Childs (ed.), *Private Journal of HWR,* xiii–xiv; Elizabeth Teague, "Henry W. Ravenel" (typescript memoir kindly furnished by Harry Shealy, University of South Carolina at Aiken), 2, 3; James Henry Rice, Jr., *The Aftermath of Glory* (Charleston: Walker, Evans, & Cogswell, 1934), 179–84.
14. René Ravenel Diary, June 1, 1813; June 25, 1820.
15. Edgar W. Knight, *A Documentary History of Education in the South before 1860* (5 vols.; Chapel Hill: University of North Carolina Press, 1949–53), V, 24–26, 122; William H. Trescott, "The States Duties in Regard to Popular Education," *De Bow's Review,* n.s., X (February 1856), 148; Colyer Meriwether, *History of Higher Education in South Carolina with a Sketch of the Free School System* (Washington: Government Printing Office, 1889), 111–12; B. James Ramage, "Local Government and Free Schools in South Carolina," in Herbert B. Adams (ed.), *Johns Hopkins University Studies in Historical and Political Science* I, no. 12 (October 1883), 34–38.
16. Meriwether, *Higher Education,* 29–44.
17. René Ravenel Diary, June 25, 1820.
18. Ibid.; Samuel Gaillard Stoney (ed.), "The Memoirs of Frederick Adolphus Porcher," *South Carolina Historical Magazine* XLIV (October 1943), 214–18.
19. W. H. Heck, *Mental Discipline & Educational Values* (New York: John Lane Co., 1909); Walter B. Kolesnik, *Mental Discipline in Modern Education* (Madison: University of Wisconsin Press, 1958), 10–23; Stoney (ed.), "Memoirs of F. A. Porcher," XLIV (October 1943), 215–18.
20. Johnson, *Scientific Interests,* 126–31; Smallwood, *Natural History,* 102–9; Kenneth W. Hunt, "The Charleston Woody Flora," *American Midland Naturalist* XXXVII (May 1947), 671–74; Hindle, *Pursuit of Science,* 51, 53, 177; Edmund Berkeley and Dorothy Smith Berkeley, *Dr. Alexander Garden of Charles Town* (Chapel Hill: University of North Carolina Press, 1969).

21. David H. Rembert, *Thomas Walter, Carolina Botanist* (Columbia: South Carolina Museum Commission, 1980).
22. Albert E. Sanders, "The Charleston Museum and the Promotion of Science in Antebellum South Carolina" (Paper presented at the third Citadel Conference on the South, April 25, 1981), 5–8, cited by permission of the author.

Chapter 2: College and Young Manhood, 1829–1839

1. Diary Notes of Dr. Henry Ravenel, January 12, 1829, Box 1, T. P. Ravenel Collection; Childs (ed.), *Private Journal of HWR*, xv.
2. Daniel Walker Hollis, *University of South Carolina* (2 vols.; Columbia: University of South Carolina Press, 1951 and 1956), I, 16–19, quotation 18.
3. Ibid., I, 22–24; John Morrill Bryan, *An Architectural History of the South Carolina College, 1801–1855* (Columbia: University of South Carolina Press, 1976), 27–42.
4. Minutes of the Faculty of the South Carolina College Commencing on the Thirtieth of May, 1814, entries dated December 1, 2, 1829 (University Archives, University of South Carolina, Columbia), hereinafter cited as Faculty Minutes, USC.
5. Proceedings of the Board of Trustees, University of South Carolina, November 24, 1813–November 27, 1837, entry dated November 30, 1831 (University Archives, University of South Carolina), hereinafter cited as Trustees' Proceedings, USC.
6. Ibid., April 26, 1821.
7. Faculty Minutes, USC, November 14, 22, 1831, November 26, 1832.
8. Bryan, *Architectural History*, 59–63.
9. Stanley M. Guralnick, *Science and the Ante-bellum American College* (Philadelphia: American Philosophical Society, 1975), 142–43; Hollis, *University*, I, 79; Seymour E. Harris, *Economics of Harvard* (New York: McGraw-Hill Book Co., 1970), 157; Walter C. Bronson, *The History of Brown University, 1764–1914* (Providence: Brown University, 1914), 231–32; Brooks Mather Kelley, *Yale: A History* (New Haven: Yale University Press, 1974), 143.
10. Hollis, *University*, I, 78–79; M. LaBorde, *History of the South Carolina College, from Its Incorporation, Dec. 19, 1801, to Dec. 19, 1865, Including Sketches of Its Presidents and Professors* (Charleston: Walker, Evans & Cogswell, 1874), 527–28.
11. Hollis, *University*, I, 80; J. Marion Sims, *The Story of My Life* (New York: D. Appleton & Co., 1884), 82.
12. Knight, *Education in the South*, III, 220–21; Trustees' Proceedings, USC, December 16, 1829; November 24, 1830.
13. Knight, *Education in the South*, III, 220.
14. Guralnick, *Science and the Antebellum College*, 3–14; Howard Miller, *The Revolutionary College: American Presbyterian Higher Education, 1707–1837* (New York: New York University Press, 1976), 92–94.
15. Joseph Carson, *A History of the Medical Department of the University of Pennsylvania from Its Foundation in 1765. With Sketches of the Lives of Deceased Professors* (Philadelphia: Lindsay and Blakiston, 1869), 134.
16. T. J. Fitzpatrick, *Rafinesque: A Sketch of His Life with Bibliography* (Des Moines: Historical Department of Iowa, 1911), 27–31; David Starr Jordan, *Science Sketches* (Chicago: A. C. McClurg and Co., 1896), 158–60; James X. Corgan, "Some Firsts? In the Colleges of Tennessee," Tennessee Academy of Science, *Journal* LV

(July 1980), 89; Henry Grady Rooker, "A Sketch of the Life and Work of Dr. Gerard Troost," *Tennessee Historical Magazine,* ser. 2, III (October 1932), 3–19.

17. Corgan, "Some Firsts?" 87–88.

18. James Allen Cabaniss, *A History of the University of Mississippi* (University, Miss.: University of Mississippi, 1949), 9–11.

19. LaBorde, *History of South Carolina College,* 528; Wilson Gee, "South Carolina Botanists: Biography and Bibliography," University of South Carolina, *Bulletin,* no. 72 (September 1918), 42–43; Hollis, *University,* I, 119–21; J. H. Easterby, *A History of the College of Charleston, Founded 1770* (Charleston: Trustees of the College of Charleston, 1935), 123; Lewis R. Gibbes, *A Catalogue of the Phoenagamous [sic] Plants of Columbia, S.C., and Its Vicinity* (Columbia: Printed at the Telescope Office, 1835) (copy in Box 10, Natural History Pamphlet Collection, Charleston Museum); H. W. Ravenel to L. R. Gibbes, December 9, 1854, Letters to Prof. Lewis R. Gibbes from Dr. Henry W. Ravenel, 1850–84, from transcriptions of the originals in possession of the Charleston Museum, 2 vols. (South Caroliniana Library, University of South Carolina, Columbia), hereinafter cited as Gibbes Letters.

20. Richard M. Jellison and Phillip S. Swartz, "The Scientific Interests of Robert W. Gibbes," *South Carolina Historical Magazine* LXVI (April 1965), 77–79.

21. Charles Stevens to H. W. Ravenel, June 11, 1829, Henry William Ravenel Correspondence, 1841–86 (Special Collections, Robert Muldrow Cooper Library, Clemson University, Clemson, S.C.), hereinafter cited as Ravenel Correspondence, Clemson.

22. Childs (ed.), *Private Journal of HWR,* 289; Faculty Minutes, USC, June 14–18, October 18, December 9, 1830, June 17, December 12–16, 1831; November 27–30, 1832.

23. Frederick Rudolph, *The American College and University: A History* (New York: Alfred A. Knopf, 1962), 96–99.

24. Knight, *Education in the South,* III, 128.

25. Hollis, *University,* I, 90–96; Knight, *Education in the South,* III, 81.

26. Hollis, *University,* I, 91.

27. Faculty Minutes, USC, December 1829–December 1832.

28. Bryan, *Architectural History,* 74; LaBorde, *History of South Carolina College,* 132–34.

29. Sims, *Story,* 83–86.

30. Faculty Minutes, USC, December 1829–December 1832.

31. Clariosophic Society Minutes, 1826–1831, entries for November 28, 1829, December 5, 1829, Accession No. 167, Record Group 13SL, Vice President, Student Affairs–Student Activities and Organizations (University Archives, University of South Carolina).

32. Clariosophic Society Membership List, 1806–92, p. 140, Accession No. 171, ibid.

33. Clariosophic Society Minutes, December 5, 1829, February 27, January 16, 1830.

34. Clariosophic Society Minutes, pp. 174, 175, 189, 198, 208, 224, 225, 236, 239, 242–43, 248–49, 253, 258, 268, 273.

35. Stoney (ed.), "Memoirs of F. A. Porcher," XLVI (April 1945), 85–86.

36. Dumas Malone, *The Public Life of Thomas Cooper, 1783–1839* (Columbia: University of South Carolina Press, 1961, reprint of Hartford, 1923 edition), 336–39, 362–63, 368–71.

37. Ibid., 259–60, 282–84, 307 (quotation), 331, 285–89.

38. Hollis, *University,* I, 95.

39. H. W. Ravenel to M. A. Curtis, July 3, 1847, in Folder 22, Box 2, Moses Ashley Curtis Papers (Southern Historical Collection, University of North Carolina, Chapel Hill), hereinafter cited as Curtis Papers, UNC.

40. Faculty Minutes, USC, December 1, 17, 1832.

41. Childs (ed.), *Private Journal of HWR,* 289–90.

42. H. E. Ravenel, *Ravenel Records,* 165–66; Childs (ed.), *Private Journal of HWR,* xv; René Ravenel Diary, June 8–12, 1816.

43. D. E. Huger Smith, *A Charlestonian's Recollections, 1846–1913* (Charleston: Carolina Art Association, 1950), 30.

44. Frederick A. Porcher, "Upper Beat," 73; Robert Wilson, *An Address Delivered before the St. John's Hunting Club, at Indianfield Plantation, St. John's, Berkeley, July 4, 1907, Together with an Historical Sketch of the Club, Rules, and List of Members* (Charleston: Walker, Evans & Cogswell, 1907), 24; U.S. Bureau of the Census, *Population Schedules of the United States, 1850,* Microcopy 432, Roll 850, South Carolina, Charleston County (Washington: National Archives, Microfilm Publications, 1964), p. 397, family 61.

45. A. Hunter Dupree, *Asa Gray, 1810–1888* (Cambridge, Mass.: Belknap Press of Harvard University Press, 1959), 11–18; Gee, "South Carolina Botanists," 46; Howard A. Kelly, *Some American Medical Botanists Commemorated in Our Botanical Nomenclature* (Boston: Longwood Press, 1977, reprint of Troy, N. Y., 1914 edition).

46. Childs (ed.), *Private Journal of HWR,* 290.

47. Wilson, *Address,* 3, 17–19, 23–25; Francis Marion Kirk, *A History of the St. John's Hunting Club. An Address Delivered by Francis Marion Kirk at the Sesquicentennial Celebration held April 29, 1950, at the Club House, Pooshee Plantation, St. John's, Berkeley* (N.p.: St. John's Hunting Club, 1950), 3–5.

48. Wilson, *Address,* 20–22; Stoney (ed.), "Memoirs of F. A. Porcher," XLV (January 1944), 37.

49. Wilson, *Address,* 13, 20; MS Private Journal of HWR, December 13, 1860, January 10, 1861.

50. Stoney (ed.), "Memoirs of F. A. Porcher," XLV (January 1944), 37; Leiding, *Historic Houses,* 144.

51. St. Stephen's Jockey Club—the Santee Jockey Club, Rules and Minutes, Collection 34–111, and Pineville Police Association Minutes, 1823–1840, Collection 34–301 (South Carolina Historical Society).

52. Stoney (ed.), "Memoirs of F. A. Porcher," XLVI (April 1945), 85.

53. From a rather confused handwritten family tree in a volume called "Genealogical Notes and Clippings, Yates and Snowden Families and Connected Families, Seiler (Saylor), Leiber, Atman, Drake, Blair, Lequeux, Laurence, Jones, Warley," in Kirkland-Withers-Snowden-Trotter Families Papers (South Caroliniana Library).

54. *Population Schedules, 1850,* p. 397, family 60, p. 403, family 163, p. 403, family 164.

55. Childs (ed.), *Private Journal of HWR,* xv; Albert Sidney Thomas, *A Historical Account of the Protestant Episcopal Church in South Carolina, 1820–1957; Being a Continuation of Dalcho's Account, 1670–1820* (Columbia: R. L. Bryan Co., 1957), 705–6.

56. List of property, in Ravenel's handwriting, Folder 4, Ravenel, Henry William (1814–1887), Papers, Apr. 1844–25 July 1887, and n.d. (South Caroliniana Library), hereinafter cited as H. W. Ravenel Papers, SCL.

57. Dr. Henry Ravenel, Will, dated November 19, 1856, Folder 15, Box 3, T. P. Ravenel Collection.
58. U.S. Bureau of the Census, Original Agriculture, Industry, Social Statistics, and Mortality Schedules for South Carolina, 1850–1880, Agriculture, Seventh Census, 1850 (South Carolina Archives Microcopy Number 2), Roll 1, Abbeville–Lancaster; Frederick A. Porcher, "Upper Beat," 70–71; Whitemarsh B. Seabrook, *A Memoir on the Origin, Cultivation, and Uses of Cotton, from the Earliest Ages to the Present Time, with Especial Reference to the Sea-Island Cotton Plant,* . . . (Charleston: Miller & Browne, 1844), 18–20; Henry Savage, Jr., *River of the Carolinas: The Santee* (Chapel Hill: University of North Carolina Press, 1968), 258; Samuel Gaillard Stoney, *Plantations of the Carolina Low Country* (3rd ed.; Charleston: Carolina Art Association, 1945), 39.
59. Childs (ed.), *Private Journal of HWR,* xv.
60. H. E. Ravenel, *Ravenel Records,* 166.
61. Jane Searles Misenhelter, *St. Stephen's Episcopal Church, St. Stephen's, S.C., Including Church of the Epiphany, Upper St. John's, Berkeley, and Chapel of Ease, Pineville, S.C.* . . . (Columbia: State Printing Co., 1977), 77, 78; Childs (ed.), *Private Journal of HWR,* xvi.
62. Childs (ed.), *Private Journal of HWR,* xv, xvi; "The Days of Long Ago," memoirs in folder labeled "Thomas Walter," Box 11–318, Porcher Family Papers (South Carolina Historical Society); Stoney, "Memoirs of F. A. Porcher," XLIV (April 1943), 72.
63. Childs (ed.), *Private Journal of HWR,* 290.
64. Stoney (ed.), "Memoirs of F. A. Porcher," XLVI (July 1945), 144; Porcher, "Upper Beat," 40; Terry, "Eighteenth Century Plantation Names," 16.
65. Stoney (ed.), "Memoirs of F. A. Porcher," XLVI (July 1945), 144; "The Days of Long Ago," 2, 17.
66. Stoney (ed.), "Memoirs of F. A. Porcher," XLVI (April 1945), 87.
67. Stoney (ed.), "Memoirs of F. A. Porcher," XLVI (July 1945), 144 (April 1946), 102; Wanda Leeper Flint, Cleo Corley Flint, and Linda Flint Powell, "Readings from the Stones . . . Inscriptions from St. Stephen's Protestant Episcopal Church Cemetery" (Typescript, St. Stephen's, S.C., February, 1970, photocopy in Clayton Library, Houston, Tex.), 57. William Porcher is not mentioned in John Hendley Barnhart (comp.), *The New York Botanical Garden Biographical Notes upon Botanists* (3 vols.; Boston: G. K. Hall & Co., 1965), a comprehensive source for biographical references occurring before 1945, later references being treated less thoroughly; nor is Porcher mentioned in Max Meisel's dependable *Bibliography of American Natural History: Pioneer Century, 1789–1865* (3 vols.; New York: Hafner, 1967, reprint of New York, 1924–29 edition).
68. On Francis Peyre Porcher see Joseph Ioor Waring, *A History of Medicine in South Carolina, 1825–1900* (Columbia: South Carolina Medical Association, 1967), 282; Francis Peyre Porcher Biography, 2, typescript, ca. 1935 (South Caroliniana Library).

Chapter 3: American Scientist, 1839–1849

1. See, for example, Thomas Walter Peyre (1812–51) Plantation Journal (1834–51), microfiche 50–7 (South Carolina Historical Society).
2. Bill of Sale and Bond, each dated April 15, 1840, Folder 9, Box 11–331, Henry

Ravenel Papers (South Carolina Historical Society), hereinafter cited as Henry Ravenel Papers, SCHS.

3. Lewis Cecil Gray, *History of Agriculture in the Southern United States to 1860* (2 vols.; New York: Peter Smith, 1941), II, 726,738; Seabrook, *Origin, Cultivation, and Uses of Cotton,* 18–19; H. W. Ravenel to M. A. Curtis, May 14, 1847, Folder 21, Box 2, Curtis Papers, UNC.

4. *The Constitution, Acts and Proceedings of the Black Oak Agricultural Society, During the Past Year, Published by Order of the Society* (Charleston: Walker & Browne, 1843), 2.

5. Ibid.; Frederick A. Porcher, "Upper Beat," 43–46; Wilson, *Address,* 12–13.

6. *Constitution, Acts, and Proceedings of the BOAS* (1843), 2.

7. *The Constitution and Proceedings of the Black Oak Agricultural Society, for 1848 & 1849* (Charleston: Miller & Browne, 1849), 8–9, 10–12.

8. *Constitution, Acts, and Proceedings of the BOAS* (1843), 6–8; Margaret W. Rossiter, *The Emergence of Agricultural Science: Justus Liebig and the Americans, 1840–1880* (New Haven: Yale University Press, 1975), 23–25; C. U. Shepard, *Report of an Analysis of Cotton-Wool, Cotton-Seed, Indian Corn, and the Yam Potato, Made for the Black Oak Agricultural Society* (Charleston: Miller & Browne, 1846).

9. H. W. Ravenel, *A Memoir from the Black Oak Agricultural Society, Read before the State Agricultural Society, at Its Meeting in December 1842 at Columbia* (Charleston: Miller & Browne, 1843), passim, quotation 4, also printed as Wm. H. Ravenel [sic], "Agricultural Memoir," *Southern Agriculturist, Horticulturist, & Register of Rural Affairs* (April 1843), 131–47.

10. Avery Craven, *Edmund Ruffin, Southerner: A Study in Secession* (Baton Rouge: Louisiana State University Press, 1966), 77–82; Betty L. Mitchell, *Edmund Ruffin: A Biography* (Bloomington: Indiana University Press, 1981), 44–48.

11. Edmund Ruffin, *Report of the Commencement and Progress of the Agricultural Survey of South Carolina for 1843* (Columbia: A. H. Pemberton, State Printer, 1843), 4, 12, 36, and acknowledgements appearing on unnumbered back page; Edmund Ruffin to H. W. Ravenel, May 13, 1843, Folder 1, Box 1, Botany Department of the University of North Carolina Historical Collection (Southern Historical Collection), hereinafter cited as Botany Department Historical Collection, UNC.

12. H. W. Ravenel, "Mr. Ravenel's Letter on Marlling," in *Proceedings of the Agricultural Convention and of the State Agricultural Society of South Carolina, from 1839 to 1845—Inclusive . . .* (Columbia: Summer & Carroll, 1846), 289–91, quotation 290.

13. Peyre Plantation Journal, 233–43; F. A. Porcher, *Report on Manures, Read before the Black Oak Agricultural Society, by F. A. Porcher, Chairman of the Committee on Manures* (Charleston: Miller & Browne, 1844).

14. B. L. Mitchell, *Ruffin,* 55; Ruffin, *Report.*

15. Edmund Ravenel, *Echinidae, Recent and Fossil, of South Carolina, January 1848* (Charleston: Burges & James, 1848); Edmund Ravenel, "On the Medical Topography of St. John's, Berkeley, S.C., and Its Relations to Geology," *Charleston Medical Journal and Review* IV (November 1849), 701–3; Waring, *Medicine in South Carolina, 1825–1900,* 287–88; H. E. Ravenel, *Ravenel Records,* 144; Peyre Plantation Journal, diarylike entries on unnumbered page near the front, dated April 8, 16, 1834; Edmund Ravenel to H. W. Ravenel, April 8, 1844 (quotations), Folder 1, H. W. Ravenel Papers, SCL.

16. Childs (ed.), *Private Journal of HWR,* 290.

17. Stevens, "Mycological Work of Ravenel," 146. I myself know of no significant botanist named Olmstead, nor do Barnhart's few entries under that name indicate anyone of importance. Barnhart (comp.), *Biographical Notes upon Botanists*.
18. A. Hunter Dupree, "The National Pattern of American Learned Societies, 1769–1863," in Alexandra Oleson and Sanborn C. Brown (eds.), *The Pursuit of Knowledge in the Early American Republic: American Scientific and Learned Societies from Colonial Times to the Civil War* (Baltimore: Johns Hopkins University Press, 1976), 25; H. W. Ravenel to Edward Tuckerman, December 16, 1851, February 24, 1852, Octavo Volume 4, Tuckerman Correspondence, AAS.
19. "Reminiscences of Mrs. Richard Y. Dwight (Rowena Ravenel), Pinopolis, March 23, 1924," in Neil E. Stevens's collection entitled "Henry W. Ravenel" (South Caroliniana Library); Frederick A. Porcher, "Upper Beat," 38; Stoney (ed.), "Memoirs of F. A. Porcher," XLVII (April 1946), 101–2.
20. Laura M. Bragg, "The Museum Herbaria," Charleston Museum, *Bulletin,* VIII (May 1912), 47; A. S. Thomas, *Protestant Episcopal Church in South Carolina,* 187, 403–4. Bragg and Thomas disagree on the year when Wallace took over at St. Stephen's; Bragg says 1841.
21. Bragg, "Museum Herbaria," 47–48.
22. Cranmore Wallace to M. A. Curtis, March 19, 1846, Folder 17, Box 1, Curtis Papers, UNC.
23. H. W. Ravenel, "Some North American Botanists; VII. Stephen Elliott," *Botanical Gazette* VIII (July 1883), 253.
24. A. W. Chapman to H. W. Ravenel, June 13, 1885, Ravenel Correspondence, Clemson; Stoney (ed.), "Memoirs of F. A. Porcher," XLVII (April 1946), 101–2.
25. Childs (ed.), *Private Journal of HWR,* 290; "Reminiscences of Mrs. Dwight"; C. Wallace to M. A. Curtis, August 29, 1846, Folder 18, H. W. Ravenel to Curtis, December 11, 1846, Folder 19, both in Box 1, Curtis Papers, UNC.
26. E. Ravenel to H. W. Ravenel, December 14, 1846, Ravenel Correspondence, Clemson.
27. J. Bachman to H. W. Ravenel, December 17, 1846, ibid.
28. Ruffin, *Report,* 41; Michael Tuomey, *Report on the Geology of South Carolina* (Columbia: A. S. Johnston, 1848), 156; M. Tuomey to H. W. Ravenel, November 25, 1845, Folder 2, Box 1, Botany Department Historical Collection, UNC; M. Tuomey to M. A. Curtis, July 9, 1846, Folder 18, Box 1, Curtis Papers, UNC.
29. A. Gray to H. W. Ravenel, August 24, 1846, Folder 2, Box 1, Botany Department Historical Collection, UNC; H. W. Ravenel to A. Gray, September 7, 1846, Historic Letters, H. W. Ravenel (Gray Herbarium, Harvard University, Cambridge, Mass.).
30. M. A. Curtis, "Enumeration of Plants Growing Spontaneously around Wilmington, North Carolina, with Remarks on Some New and Obscure Species," Boston Society of Natural History, *Journal* I (May 1835), 82–141; M. A. Curtis, "An Account of Some New and Rare Plants of North Carolina," *American Journal of Science and Arts* XLIV (January 1843), 80–84; E. Tuckerman to M. A. Curtis, October 29, 1845, Folder 17, Box 1, Curtis Papers, UNC; M. A. Curtis to A. Gray, December 22, 1845, Historic Letters, M. A. Curtis (Gray Herbarium).
31. M. A. Curtis to A. Gray, January 13, 1846, Historic Letters, M. A. Curtis.
32. A. Gray to H. W. Ravenel, August 24, 1846, Folder 2, Box 1, Botany Department Historical Collection, UNC; M. Tuomey to M. A. Curtis, October 24, 1846,

Folder 19, C. Wallace to M. A. Curtis, August 29, 1846, H. W. Ravenel to M. A. Curtis, September 8, 1846, both in Folder 18, all in Box 1, Curtis Papers, UNC.

33. C. Wallace to M. A. Curtis, August 29, 1846, Folder 18, Box 1, Curtis Papers, UNC.

34. Ibid., September 19, 1846.

35. M. A. Curtis to H. W. Ravenel, September 17, [1846], Ravenel Correspondence, Clemson. A notation in Ravenel's handwriting, as well as the subject matter of the letter, clearly identify this as Curtis's first letter to Ravenel.

36. Ibid.; quotation from M. A. Curtis to A. Gray, November 23, 1846, Historic Letters, M. A. Curtis.

37. A. Gray to H. W. Ravenel, December 23, 1846, Botany Department Historical Collection, UNC.

38. M. A. Curtis to H. W. Ravenel, September 17, [1846], Ravenel Correspondence, Clemson.

39. Ibid.

40. M. A. Curtis to A. Gray, June 24, 1847, Historic Letters, M. A. Curtis.

41. H. W. Ravenel to M. A. Curtis, June 8, 1847, Folder 21, May 5, 1848, Folder 25, December 17, November 22, 1847, both in Folder 23, June 1, 1847, (quotation), Folder 21, November 3, 1847, Folder 23, all in Box 2, Curtis Papers, UNC.

42. H. W. Ravenel to M. A. Curtis, July 31, 1847, (quotations), Folder 22, November 3, 13, 1847, both in Folder 23, August 8, October 31, December 29, 1848, all in Folder 26, all in Box 2, ibid.

43. H. W. Ravenel to M.A. Curtis, September 13, 1847, July 3 (quotation), [?], 23 (quotation), 1847, all in Folder 22, Box 2, ibid.

44. Asa Gray, "A Monograph of the North American Species of Rhynchospora," *Lyceum of Natural History of New-York, Annals* III (1828–36), 191–219. H. W. Ravenel to M. A. Curtis, December 22, 1847 (quotation), Folder 23, February 22, 1848 (quotation), Folder 24, May 5, 1848, Folder 25, all in Box 2, Curtis Papers, UNC.

45. H. W. Ravenel to M. A. Curtis, February 22, 1847, Folder 20, Box 2, Curtis Papers, UNC.

46. M. A. Curtis to M. J. Berkeley, n.d. (postmarked February 5, 1848), April 27, 1848 (quotations), M. J. Berkeley Correspondence (Botany Library, Department of Library Services, British Museum [Natural History], London). See also Ronald H. Petersen, *"B. & C.": The Mycological Association of M. J. Berkeley and M. A. Curtis* (Vaduz: J. Cramer, 1980), 47.

47. H. W. Ravenel to M. A. Curtis, May 5, July 11, 1848, both in Folder 25, October 17, 31, 1848, both in Folder 26, all in Box 2, Curtis Papers, UNC.

48. H. W. Ravenel to M. A. Curtis, November 25, 1848, Folder 26, Box 2, ibid; M. A. Curtis, "Contributions to the Mycology of North America," *American Journal of Science and Arts,* 2nd ser., VI (November 1848), 349–53.

49. H. W. Ravenel to M. A. Curtis, December 15, 1848, Folder 26, Box 2, Curtis Papers, UNC.

50. Ibid., December 29, 1848.

51. H. W. Ravenel to Job Bicknell Ellis, November 14, 1855, Job B. Ellis Collection (New York Botanical Garden Library, New York City), hereinafter cited as Ellis Collection, NYBG Library.

52. E. Tuckerman to M. A. Curtis, October 29, 1845, Folder 17, Box 1, Curtis Papers, UNC. Edward Tuckerman, Jr., "An Enumeration of Some Lichenes of New England, with Remarks," "A Further Enumeration of Some New England Lichenes," and "Further Notices of Some New England Lichenes," in *Boston Journal of Natural History* II (February 1839), 245–62, III (July 1840), 281–306, and III (November 1840), 438–64, respectively.

53. Edward Tuckerman, "A Synopsis of the Lichenes of the Northern United States and British America," American Academy of Arts and Sciences, *Proceedings* I (1846–48), 195–285, esp. 213–14, 226, 249, 252, 261; M. A. Curtis to E. Tuckerman, November 15, 1845, January 8, April 12, 27, 1846, August 4, 1848, typescripts in box labeled "Letters of Dr. Moses A. Curtis, Dr. J. H. Mellichamp, Gilbert Rossignol," Letters and Diaries, South Carolina Collection (Charleston Museum, Charleston); A. Gray to H. W. Ravenel, December 14, 23, 1846, both in Folder 2, Box 1, Botany Department Historical Collection, UNC; H. W. Ravenel to E. Tuckerman, July 12, 1848, Octavo Volume 7, Tuckerman Correspondence, AAS.

54. H. W. Ravenel to E. Tuckerman, June 14, 1849, Tuckerman Papers, AAS.

55. A. Gray to H. W. Ravenel, August 24, 1846, Folder 2, Box 1, Botany Department Historical Collection; H. W. Ravenel to A. Gray, March 19, 1847, Gray Correspondence; F. P. Porcher, "A Medico-Botanical Catalogue of the Plants and Ferns of St. John's, Berkeley, South Carolina," *Charleston Medical Journal and Review* II (May 1847), 257; H. W. Ravenel to M. A. Curtis, August 20, 1847, Folder 22, Box 2, Curtis Papers, UNC.

56. H. W. Ravenel, "Polygonum Punctatum," *Southern Journal of Medicine & Pharmacy* I (1846), 629–30. Dr. Harry Shealy kindly called my attention to this publication. H. W. Ravenel, "An Enumeration of Some Few Phanegamous Plants, Not Heretofore Published as Inhabiting This State, Found in the Vicinity of the Santee Canal," *Charleston Medical Journal and Review* IV (1849), 32–38.

57. H. W. Ravenel to J. Torrey, November 14, 1848; January 12, 1849; August 17, 1849, John Torrey Correspondence (New York Botanical Garden Library), hereinafter cited as Torrey Correspondence, NYBG Library; S. B. Mead to H. W. Ravenel, February 28, 1848, E. Tatnall to H. W. Ravenel, February 18, 1848, both in Ravenel Correspondence, Clemson.

58. A. S. Thomas *Protestant Episcopal Church in South Carolina*, 187, 263.

59. H. W. Ravenel to M. A. Curtis, May 22, 1849 (quotation), Folder 27, July 23, 1847 (quotation), Folder 22, both in Box 2, Curtis Papers, UNC.

60. H. W. Ravenel, "Enumeration of Some Few Phanegamous Plants," 36; P. C. Gaillard to H. W. Ravenel, November 20, 1848, Ravenel Correspondence, Clemson.

61. *Constitution and Proceedings of the Black Oak Agricultural Society, for 1844 & 1845* (Charleston: Miller & Browne, 1845), 11; Ruffin, *Report,* 79; H. W. Ravenel to M. A. Curtis, July 3, 1847, Folder 22, Box 2, Curtis Papers; H. W. Ravenel, *A Meteorological Journal for the Year 1848. Kept in St. John's, Berkley, So. Ca. for the Black Oak Agricultural Society* (Charleston: Miller & Browne, 1849) (similar papers appeared for 1849, 1850, and 1851); H. W. Ravenel, "A Paper on the Subject of Meteorology in Its Connection with Agriculture &c.," in *Constitution and Proceedings of the BOAS for 1848 & 1849*, 14–20, 19 (quotation).

Chapter 4: Watershed Years, 1850–1853

1. .Letter quoted in Petersen, "*B. & C.*," 47.
2. H. W. Ravenel to M. J. Berkeley, March 27, 1850, Berkeley Correspondence.
3. R. W. Gibbes to H. W. Ravenel, January 16, 1850, Ravenel Correspondence, Clemson.
4. H. W. Ravenel to M. A. Curtis, March 2, 1849, Folder 27, January 15, 1850, Folder 29, both in Box 2, Curtis Papers, UNC.
5. Thomas Porcher Ravenel Diary, 1845–54, entries dated February 17, 18, 24, 1850, Box 2, T. P. Ravenel Collection; A. S. Thomas, *Protestant Episcopal Church in South Carolina,* 650. On the meeting between Bachman and Curtis, see Smallwood, *Natural History,* 118.
6. H. W. Ravenel to M. A. Curtis, December 29, 1848, Folder 26, May 22, 1849, Folder 27, September 11, November 27, 1849, both in Folder 28, all in Box 2, Curtis Papers, UNC; H. W. Ravenel to J. B. Ellis, June 21, July 12, 1855, November 3, 1856, Ellis Collection, NYBG Library; Reginald S. Clay and Thomas H. Court, *The History of the Microscope: Compiled from Original Instruments and Documents, up to the Introduction of the Achromatic Microscope* (Boston: Longwood Press, 1978), 32–77; S. Bradbury, *The Evolution of the Microscope* (Oxford: Pergamon Press, 1967), 182–205.
7. For an example of the emphasis placed by Berkeley on characteristics of the spore sacs, see M. J. Berkeley, "On the Fructification of the Pileate and Clavate Tribes of Hymenomycetous Fungi," *Annals and Magazine of Natural History* I (April 1838), 80–101; Petersen, "*B. & C.*," 15.
8. H. W. Ravenel to E. Tuckerman, April 19, 1858, Octavo Volume 4, Tuckerman Correspondence, AAS; M. A. Curtis to A. Gray, March 15, 1850, Historic Letters, Curtis; George Engelmann, "Revision of the Genus Pinus, and Description of Pinus Elliottii," St. Louis Accademy of Science, *Transactions* IV (1880), reprinted in William Trelease and Asa Gray (eds.), *The Botanical Works of the Late George Engelmann, Collected for Henry Shaw, Esq.* (Cambridge: John Wilson and Son, 1887), 373.
9. H. W. Ravenel to A. Gray, May 4, 1849, Historic Letters, H. W. Ravenel; M. A. Curtis, "New and Rare Plants, Chiefly of the Carolinas," *American Journal of Science and Arts,* 2nd ser., VII (May 1849), 408; Charles Sprague Sargent, *The Silva of North America: A Description of the Trees Which Grow Naturally in North America Exclusive of Mexico* (14 vols. in 7, New York: Peter Smith, 1947), VIII, 159–60.
10. H. W. Ravenel to M. A. Curtis, May 22, 1849, Folder 27, Box 2, Curtis Papers, UNC; H. W. Ravenel to E. Tuckerman, April 19, 1858, Octavo Volume 4, Tuckerman Correspondence, AAS.
11. H. W. Ravenel, "A Catalogue of the Natural Orders of Plants, Inhabiting the Vicinity of the Santee Canal, S.C., as Represented by Genera and Species; with Observations on the Meteorological and Topographical Conditions of that Section of Country," American Association for the Advancement of Science, *Proceedings* III (1850), 2–17.
12. Ibid., 2–5.
13. A. Hunter Dupree, "The Measuring Behavior of Americans," in George H. Daniels (ed.), *Nineteenth-Century American Science* (Evanston: Northwestern University Press, 1972,), 31–35.

14. H. W. Ravenel to M. A. Curtis, July 3, 1847, Folder 22, Box 2, Curtis Papers, UNC; 8-page manuscript fragment in Ravenel's handwriting, dated 1850 by archivists, Botany Department Historical Collection, UNC. See also [H. W. Ravenel?], "Physical Science, in Its Relation to Natural and Revealed Religion," *Southern Quarterly Review,* n.s., III (April 1851), 420–55; William Gilmore Simms to H. W. Ravenel, July 28, 1852, Folder 7, Box 1, Botany Department Historical Collection, UNC.

15. Childs (ed.), *Private Journal of HWR,* 275; M. F. Maury to H. W. Ravenel, May 4, 1850, Folder 5, Box 1, Botany Department Historical Collection, UNC.

16. R. Lloyd Praeger, "William Henry Harvey, 1811–1866," in F. W. Oliver (ed.), *Makers of British Botany: A Collection of Biographies by Living Botanists* (Cambridge: Cambridge University Press, 1913), 204–24; AAAS, *Proceedings* (1850), 2; W. H. Harvey to W. J. Hooker, May 23, 1850, XXIX, 329, W. J. Hooker Correspondence (Kew Gardens, London). Reference kindly provided by Joseph Ewan, Professor Emeritus, Tulane University, New Orleans, La.

17. W. H. Harvey to H. W. Ravenel, August 1, 1850, Ravenel Correspondence, Clemson; Praeger, "W. H. Harvey," 216.

18. H. W. Ravenel to M. A. Curtis, November 27, 1849, Folder 28, Box 2, Curtis Papers, UNC.

19. L. R. Gibbes to Ravenel, November 15, 1850, Ravenel Correspondence, Clemson.

20. M. A. Curtis (first article), M. J. Berkeley and M. A. Curtis (second, third and fourth articles), "Contributions to the Mycology of North America," *American Journal of Science and Arts,* 2nd ser., VI (November 1848), 349–53, VIII (November 1849), 401–403, IX (March 1850), 171–75, X (September 1850), 185–88.

21. H. W. Ravenel, "Contributions to the Cryptogamic Botany of South Carolina," *Charleston Medical Journal and Review* IV (July 1849), 428–33, V (May 1850), 324–27, VI (March 1851), 190–99.

22. Ibid., VI (March 1851), 199.

23. H. W. Ravenel to E. Tuckerman, December 31, 1850, Octavo Volume 7, Tuckerman Correspondence, AAS.

24. Edward Tuckerman, *Lichenes Americae Septentrionalis Exsiccati* (6 vols. in 3; Cambridge: Metcalf & Co., 1st vol., Joh. Wilson & Son, 2nd and 3rd vols., 1847–54); John A. Stevenson, *An Account of Fungus Exsiccati Containing Material from the Americas* (Lehre: J. Cramer, 1971), 297.

25. M. A. Curtis to H. W. Ravenel, January 22, 1852, Ravenel Correspondence, Clemson; C. L. Shear and Neil E. Stevens, "Studies of the Schweinitz Collections of Fungi—I, Sketch of His Mycological Work," *Mycologia* IX (1917), 195.

26. C. L. Shear and Neil E. Stevens, "Studies of the Schweinitz Collections of Fungi—II, Distribution and Previous Studies of Authentic Specimens," *Mycologia* IX (1917) 335.

27. M. A. Curtis to H. W. Ravenel, February 9, 1852, Ravenel Correspondence, Clemson.

28. Ibid., February 9, [ca. March 1], March 11, 1852.

29. Ibid.

30. Ibid., [ca. March 1, 1852].

31. H. W. Ravenel to A. Gray, April 2, 1852, Historic Letters, H. W. Ravenel.

32. M. A. Curtis to H. W. Ravenel, July 16, 26, 1852, Ravenel Correspondence, Clemson.

33. Ibid., July 16, 1852.
34. Childs (ed.), *Private Journal of HWR*, 318–19; A. Gray to H. W. Ravenel, June 5, 1852, Folder 7, Box 1, Botany Department Historical Collection, UNC.
35. M. A. Curtis to H. W. Ravenel, August 2, 13 (quotation), 1852, Ravenel Correspondence, Clemson.
36. M. A. Curtis to A. Gray, December 13, 1853, Historic Letters, M. A. Curtis.
37. H. W. Ravenel to E. Tuckerman, October 24, 1851, Octavo Volume 4, Tuckerman Correspondence, AAS; H. W. Ravenel to M. J. Berkeley, November 21, 1851, Berkeley Correspondence.
38. M. A. Curtis to H. W. Ravenel, July 6, 1852, Ravenel Correspondence, Clemson.
39. Ibid., July 6, 16, 1852.
40. W. G. Simms to H. W. Ravenel, July 28, 1852, Folder 7, Box 1, Botany Department Historical Collection; W. G. Simms to H. W. Ravenel, July 31, 1852, Ravenel Correspondence, Clemson.
41. M. A. Curtis to H. W. Ravenel, July 26, 1852, Ravenel Correspondence, Clemson.
42. Childs (ed.), *The Private Journal of HWR*, xvi; M. A. Curtis to H. W. Ravenel, August 2, 1852, Ravenel Correspondence, Clemson. Lester D. Stephens, "Francis Simmons Holmes: First Curator of the Charleston Museum and Premier Paleontologist in the Old South," unpublished ms, cited by kind permission of Professor Stephens.
43. *Aiken, S.C., as a Winter Resort.* [Aiken: Highland Park Hotel, 1885?]
44. Stoney (ed.), "Memoirs of F. A. Porcher," XLVII (April 1946), 108.
45. H. W. Ravenel to E. Tuckerman, November 5, 1852, Octavo Volume 4, Tuckerman Correspondence, AAS; M. A. Curtis to H. W. Ravenel, [November 1852], Ravenel Correspondence, Clemson.
46. H. W. Ravenel to L. R. Gibbes, November 26, December 8, 1852, Gibbes Letters.
47. M. A. Curtis to H. W. Ravenel, November 18, 1852, Ravenel Correspondence, Clemson.
48. Ibid., December 16, 1852.
49. Bureau of the Census, Original Agriculture, Industry, Social Statistics, and Morality Schedules for South Carolina, 1850–1880; Peyre Plantation Journal, 268; T. P. Ravenel Diary, November 25, 1852.
50. These transactions apparently were in cash. Various bills of sale, notes, and other documents from other transactions are preserved in Folder 9, Box 11-331, Henry Ravenel Papers (SCHS); Childs (ed.), *Private Journal of HWR*, 65.
51. S. W. Ravenel, "Christmas at Pooshee," 4–14; Robert Wilson, *Half Forgotten Byways of the Old South* (Columbia: State Co., 1928), 175–77.
52. T. P. Ravenel Diary, December 25, 1852.
53. Ibid., January 17, 21, February 3, 12, 16, 1853; also note in H. W. Ravenel's hand setting out property received from his father, Folder 9, Box 11–331, Henry Ravenel Papers, SCHS.
54. H. W. Ravenel to L. R. Gibbes, February 25, 1853, Gibbes Letters; Childs (ed.), *Private Journal of HWR*, xvi.
55. W. Dehon to J. H. Cornish, February 12, 1853, Ravenel Correspondence, Clemson; Saint Thaddeus Parish Register, 4 (Saint Thaddeus Episcopal Church, Aiken, S.C.); MS Private Journal of HWR, March 10, 17, 1861.
56. H. W. Ravenel to E. Tuckerman, April 19, 1853, Octavo Volume 4, Tuckerman Correspondence, AAS.
57. Childs (ed.), *Private Journal of HWR*, xvi.

Chapter 5: International Mycology, 1853–1859

1. H. W. Ravenel to L. R. Gibbes, March 21, May 25, 1853, Gibbes Letters.
2. Ibid., March 21, 1863.
3. M. A. Curtis to H. W. Ravenel, February 19, 1853, Ravenel Correspondence, Clemson.
4. Ibid., September 13, October 4, 1852.
5. E. Boissier to H. W. Ravenel, August 6, 1853, Folder 8, Box 1, Botany Department Historical Collection, UNC; M. A. Curtis to H. W. Ravenel, October 4, 1852, Ravenel Correspondence, Clemson.
6. Review of *Fungi Caroliniani Exsiccatti. Fungi of Carolina, Illustrated by Natural Specimens of the Species,* in *Charleston Medical Journal and Review* VII (1852), 690–91; E. M. Fries to H. W. Ravenel, December 28, 1852, Ravenel Correspondence, Clemson; H. W. Ravenel to L. R. Gibbes, February 25, 1853, Gibbes Letters. I must express my thanks to my friend Mary Winkler for help in translation.
7. M. A. Curtis to A. Gray, April 1, 4, 1853, Historic Letters, M. A. Curtis.
8. A[sa] G[ray], "[Notice of] *Fungi Caroliniani Exsiccati. Fungi of Carolina, Illustrated by Natural Specimens of the Species,*" *American Journal of Science and Arts,* 2nd ser., XVI (July 1853), 129–30.
9. M. A. Curtis to A. Gray, May 31, 1853, Historic Letters, M. A. Curtis.
10. H. W. Ravenel to E. Tuckerman, April 19, July 7, 1853, Octavo Volume 4, Tuckerman Correspondence, AAS.
11. H. W. Ravenel to E. G. Ravenel and their children, 9 A.M., August 3, 1853, citation number 11-331-12, Henry Ravenel Papers, SCHS.
12. Most of the letters home have survived. Citation number 11-331-12, Henry Ravenel Papers, SCHS.
13. H. W. Ravenel to E. G. Ravenel and their children, July 15, 1853, citation number 11-331-12, Henry Ravenel Papers, SCHS.
14. Ibid., July 26, 1853 (quotation); H. W. Ravenel to E. Tuckerman, August 22, 1853, Octavo Volume 4, Tuckerman Correspondence, AAS; E. Tuckerman to H. W. Ravenel, September 20, 1853, Folder 8, Box 1, Botany Department Historical Collection, UNC. Tuckerman married in May 1854. William L. Culberson (ed.), *The Collected Lichenological Papers of Edward Tuckerman* (2 vols.; Weinheim: J. Cramer, 1964), I, ix.
15. H. W. Ravenel to E. G. Ravenel and their children, July 26, 1853, citation number 11-331-12, Henry Ravenel Papers, SCHS.
16. Ibid., August 2, 1853; H. W. Ravenel to M. J. Berkeley, August 31, 1853, Berkeley Correspondence.
17. T. P. Ravenel Diary, August 24, September 7, 28, 1853.
18. F. S. Holmes to H. W. Ravenel, September 26, 1853, Ravenel Correspondence, Clemson.
19. F. S. Holmes, L. A. Frampton, and F. T. Miles to H. W. Ravenel, October 5, 1853, Folder 8, Box 1, Botany Department Historical Collection, UNC; Elliott Society of Natural History of Charleston, South-Carolina, *Proceedings* I (November 1853—December 1858) (Charleston, 1859), 1.
20. Elliott Society, *Proceedings* I, 1–3, 14; E. Boissier to H. W. Ravenel, February [?] 15, 1854, Ravenel Correspondence, Clemson; Sanders, "Charleston Museum and the Promotion of Science," 10–11, cited by kind permission of the author.
21. M. A. Curtis to A. Gray, December 13, 1853 (quotation), January 30, 1854,

Historic Letters, M. A. Curtis; M. A. C[urtis], "[Notice of] *Fungi Caroliniani Exsiccati. Fungi of Carolina, Illustrated by Natural Specimens of the Species,*" *American Journal of Science and Arts,* 2nd ser., XVII (March 1854), 285.

22. M. A. Curtis to H. W. Ravenel, August 13, October 4, [November], 1852, February 19, 1853, Ravenel Correspondence, Clemson.

23. E. Michener to H. W. Ravenel, July 1, 1854, ibid.

24. Thomas Minott Peters, "Sketch of John F. Beaumont," *Journal of Mycology* II (1886), 82.

25. J. F. Beaumont to H. W. Ravenel, August 5, September 8, 1854, Ravenel Correspondence, Clemson.

26. H. W. Ravenel to M. A. Curtis, November 12, 1854, Folder 38, Box 2, Curtis Papers, UNC.

27. H. W. Ravenel to L. R. Gibbes, December 9, 1854, Gibbes Letters; T. P. Ravenel Diary, August 28, September 13, October 5, 6, 14, 18, November 29, 1854.

28. T. P. Ravenel Diary, January 4, 9, 28, February 5, 1855.

29. Ibid., January 28, February 5, 1855.

30. H. W. Ravenel to E. W. "Liz" Ravenel, March 17, 1855, citation number 12-315-15, T. P. Ravenel Collection.

31. Ibid.

32. A. Gray to H. W. Ravenel, July 5, 1855, Ravenel Correspondence, Clemson.

33. H. W. Ravenel to A. Gray, July 17, 1855, Historic Letters, H. W. Ravenel.

34. H. W. Ravenel to J. B. Ellis, March 12, 1855, Ellis Collection, NYBG Library.

35. F. W. Anderson, "A Biographical Sketch of J. B. Ellis," *Botanical Gazette* XV (November 1890), 299–304; John William Harshberger, *The Botanists of Philadelphia and Their Work* (Philadelphia: [Press of T. C. Davis & Son], 1899), 259–69.

36. H. W. Ravenel to J. B. Ellis, March 22, 1855, Ellis Collection, NYBG Library.

37. Ibid., March 30, May 2, 1855.

38. Ibid., March 30, April 12, May 27, 1855.

39. M. A. C[urtis], "Ravenel; *Fungi Caroliniani Exsiccati.* Fasciculus III. John Russell, Charleston, S.C., 1855," *American Journal of Science and Arts,* 2nd ser., XX (September 1855), 284–85; Stevenson, *Account of Fungus Exsiccati,* 301.

40. H. W. Ravenel to L. R. Gibbes, August 4, 1855, Gibbes Letters.

41. H. W. Ravenel to J. B. Ellis, August 21, 1855, Ellis Collection, NYBG Library.

42. C. Montagne to H. W. Ravenel, October 22, 1854, Botany Department Historical Collection, UNC; H. W. Ravenel to C. Montagne, May 15, 1855, Folder 1, H. W. Ravenel Papers, SCL; C. Montagne to H. W. Ravenel, September 3, 1855, Ravenel Correspondence, Clemson.

43. C. Montagne to H. W. Ravenel, May 1, 1856, Ravenel Correspondence, Clemson.

44. Stevenson, *Account of Fungus Exsiccati,* 298–99.

45. H. W. Ravenel to J. B. Ellis, August 21, September 19, 24, October 26, November 14, 1855, Ellis Collection, NYBG Library.

46. Ibid., September 13, October 10, 26, 1855.

47. M. J. Berkeley and M. A. Curtis, "Centuries of North American Fungi," *Annals and Magazine of Natural History,* 2nd ser., XII (December 1853), 417–35, 417 (quotation).

48. H. W. Ravenel to J. B. Ellis, November 14, 1855, Ellis Collection, NYBG Library.

49. J. M. Deby to H. W. Ravenel, July 16, 1855, Ravenel Correspondence, Clemson.

50. J. X. R. Caspary to H. W. Ravenel, August 10, 1855, Folder 9, Box 1, Botany

Department Historical Collection, UNC; H. W. Ravenel to J. B. Ellis, September 6, 24, 1855, Ellis Collection, NYBG Library.

51. H. W. Ravenel, "Description of a New Baptisia Found near Aiken, S.C.," Elliott Society, *Proceedings* I, 38–39, and see 28; William M. Canby, "Notes on Baptisia," *Botanical Gazette* IV (March 1879), 129.

52. H. W. Ravenel to L. R. Gibbes, April 10, 1856, Gibbes Letters; L. Lesquereux to H. W. Ravenel, August 30, 1856, Folder 10, Box 1, Botany Department Historical Collection, UNC.

53. H. W. Ravenel to E. Tuckerman, March 28, July 22, August 5, 1856, Octavo Volume 4, Tuckerman Correspondence, AAS.

54. Ibid., August 5, 1856, February 28, March 23, 1857, all in Octavo Volume 4, October 29, 1859, Octavo Volume 8, Tuckerman correspondence. All letters dating from this period are interesting illustrations.

55. I am indebted to Nancy Reid of the Farlow Herbarium for this information.

56. H. W. Ravenel to E. Tuckerman, June 20, 1858, Octavo Volume 4, Tuckerman Correspondence, AAS.

57. Charles C. Dawson, *A Collection of Family Records, with Biographical Sketches and Other Memoranda of Various Families and Individuals Bearing the Name Dawson, or Allied to Families of That Name* (Charleston: Garnier & Co., 1969), 351; R. Conover Bartram, "Biography of a Church, Prelude to the Future: The History of the Church of St. Thaddeus, Aiken, South Carolina," 14, 16, 19–20, typescript, 1966.

58. Saint Thaddeus Parish Register, 129–30, 133–34, 139–40; MS Private Journal of HWR, May 8, 1870.

59. Childs (ed.), *Private Journal of HWR*, 197; H. W. Ravenel to F. P. Porcher, December 4, 1866, H. W. Ravenel Papers, SCL.

60. H. W. Ravenel to M A. Curtis, October 24, 1856, Folder 42, Box 3, Curtis Papers, UNC.

61. Ibid.

62. Bradbury, *Evolution of the Microscope*, 100–102, 200–201; Clay and Court, *History of the Microscope*, 75.

63. M. J. Berkeley to H. W. Ravenel, May 26, 1854, Ravenel Correspondence, Clemson.

64. H. W. Ravenel to J. B. Ellis, April 18, August 19, 1857, Ellis Collection, NYBG Library.

65. H. W. Ravenel to L. R. Gibbes, March 31, June 3, October 15, 1857, Gibbes Letters.

66. M. A. Curtis to H. W. Ravenel, June 11, 1857, H. W. Ravenel Correspondence, Clemson.

67. T. M. Peters to H. W. Ravenel, June 25, 1857, ibid.

68. A. Poe to H. W. Ravenel, June 22, 1859, ibid.

69. H. W. Ravenel to J. B. Ellis, September 16, 1859, Ellis Collection, NYBG Library.

70. Ibid.

71. H. W. Ravenel, "History of the Catawba Grape," (1851, manuscript in Ravenel's handwriting), Folder 9, Box 11-331, Henry Ravenel Papers, SCHS.

72. L. C. Gray, *History of Agriculture*, II, 825; James C. Bonner, "Advancing Trends in Southern Agriculture, 1840–1860," *Agricultural History* XXII (October 1948), 252–53; U. P. Hedrick, *A History of Horticulture in America to 1860* (New York: Oxford University Press, 1950), 283–86; Gary S. Dunbar, "Silas McDowell and

the Early Botanical Exploration of Western North Carolina," *North Carolina Historical Review* XLI (October 1964), 425–35.

73. H. W. Ravenel to E. G. Ravenel and their children, 9 P.M., August 2, 1853, citation number 11-331-12, Henry Ravenel Papers, SCHS.
74. Childs (ed.), *Private Journal of HWR*, 142, 154.
75. H. W. Ravenel to A. Gray, July 17, 1855, Historic Letters, H. W. Ravenel.
76. M. J. Berkeley to H. W. Ravenel, May 26, 1854, Ravenel Correspondence, Clemson.
77. H. W. Ravenel, *Address Delivered before the Aiken Fruit-Growing and Horticultural Association, July 21st, 1859* (Columbia: Robert M. Stokes, 1859).
78. H. W. Ravenel, "Paper on Grapes Read before the 'Aiken Vine-Growing and Horticultural Association,' September 15, 1859," U.S. Patent Office, *Report, Agriculture 1859* (Washington, 1860), 537–40, and also printed under the heading "Native Grapes Classified," *Southern Cultivator* XVIII (January 1860), 32–33.
79. H. W. Ravenel, "Premium Essay on the C[l]assification and Nomenclature of Fruits. Published by Order of the South Carolina State Agricultural Society," *Farmer and Planter* III (January 1861), 27–31; Childs (ed.), *Private Journal of HWR*, 39.
80. H. W. Ravenel to [M. J. Berkeley?], January 19, 1860, author's copy in Folder 12, Box 1, Botany Department Historical Collection, UNC.
81. Ravenel, *Address Delivered before the Aiken Fruit-Growing and Horticultural Association*, 16–22.
82. Asa Gray, "Review of Darwin's Theory on the Origin of Species by Means of Natural Selection," *American Journal of Science and Arts* XXIX (1860), 53–84, reprinted in Asa Gray, *Darwiniana: Essays and Reviews Pertaining to Darwinism*, ed. A. Hunter Dupree (Cambridge: Belknap Press of Harvard University Press, 1963), 7–50; Ravenel, "Premium Essay," 27–28.
83. Ravenel, "Premium Essay," 27.
84. Undated scrap of writing on evolution in Ravenel's handwriting in Folder 4, H. W. Ravenel Papers, SCL.
85. H. W. Ravenel to T. Meehan, December 1879, Folder 2, ibid.
86. Ibid.
87. Ibid.

Chapter 6: The Disruption of War, 1860–1865

1. Paul Fussell, *The Great War and Modern Memory* (New York: Oxford University Press, 1975).
2. Childs (ed.), *Private Journal of HWR*, 49, 54.
3. Ibid., 49, 60, and *passim.*
4. Ibid., 54, 61 (quotation).
5. John McCardell, *The Idea of a Southern Nation: Southern Nationalists and Southern Nationalism, 1830–1860* (New York: W. W. Norton & Co., 1979), 41–48.
6. Ravenel, *Memoir from the BOAS*, 19–23; Wm. H. [*sic*] Ravenel, "Agricultural Memoir," 131–47.
7. T. P. Ravenel Diary, November 2, 1850. Thomas actually says they were addressed by James B. Rhett. I have taken this as a mistake. See also Folder 6, "Receipts for Contributions to the Southern Rights Association of St. John's, Berkeley, and St. Stephen's," Box 3, T. P. Ravenel Collection.

8. Company Book of Middle St. John's Company, Folder 12, Box 4, T. P. Ravenel Collection.
9. H. W. Ravenel, *Anniversary Address, Delivered before the Black Oak Agricultural Society, April 1852.* (Charleston: Walker & James, 1852).
10. Ibid., 4–9.
11. Ibid., 11–14.
12. Ibid., 14–20, 14 (quotation). On Ravenel's use of progress as a justification for the collection of scientific data, see Ravenel, "Paper on the Subject of Meteorology," 19–20.
13. Ravenel, *Anniversary Address,* 4 (quotation), 10 (quotation). Seward is quoted in Samuel Eliot Morison, Henry Steele Commager, and William E. Leuchtenburg, *The Growth of the American Republic* (2 vols.; New York: Oxford University Press, 1969), I, 566.
14. H. W. Ravenel to E. Tuckerman, December 31, 1850, Octavo Volume 7, Tuckerman Correspondence, AAS.
15. Ibid., February 24, 1852.
16. Ibid., March 23, 1857 (quotation), and see December 7, 1860; McCardell, *Idea of a Southern Nation,* 5–6.
17. Childs (ed.), *Private Journal of HWR,* 20, 10, 17 (quotation).
18. Ibid., 4–5, 10–11, 20, 32–33, 40, 42.
19. A. Gray to H. W. Ravenel, November 30, 1860, Folder 12, Box 1, Botany Department Historical Collection, UNC; H. W. Ravenel to A. Gray, December 11, 1860, Historic Letters, H. W. Ravenel; H. W. Ravenel to E. Tuckerman, December 7, 1860, Octavo Volume 8, Tuckerman Correspondence, AAS.
20. H. W. Ravenel to A. Gray, March 21, 1861, Historic Letters, H. W. Ravenel; MS Private Journal of HWR, March 21, 1861.
21. John Ulric Nef, *War and Human Progress: An Essay on the Rise of Industrial Civilization* (Cambridge: Harvard University Press, 1950).
22. MS Private Journal of HWR, January 4, March 2, June 16, 1860, and *passim*; H. W. Ravenel to E. Tuckerman, December 7, 1860, Octavo Volume 8, Tuckerman Correspondence, AAS; H. W. Ravenel to L. R. Gibbes, April 16, 1860, Gibbes Letters.
23. MS Private Journal of HWR, April 3, 14, 21, 1860, October 16, 1864.
24. Ibid., December 9, 1860, March 10, 17 (quotation), June 25, 27, 28, 30, July 3, 7, 11, 25, 1861.
25. Childs (ed.), *Private Journal of HWR,* 20; L. R. Gibbes to H. W. Ravenel, May 28, 1860, Ravenel Correspondence, Clemson; H. W. Ravenel to L. R. Gibbes, June 4, 1860, Gibbes Letters.
26. Childs (ed.), *Private Journal of HWR,* 19–21.
27. M. A. Curtis to A. Gray, July 11, 1860, Historic Letters, M. A. Curtis; A[sa] G[ray], "[Notice of] *Fungi Caroliniani Exsiccati: Fungi of Carolina, Illustrated by Natural Specimens of the Species . . .* Fasc. I–V," *American Journal of Science and Arts,* 3rd ser, XXXI (January 1861), 130–31; L. R. Gibbes, "Ravenel's Fungi of Carolina," Charleston *Daily Courier,* October 12, 1860.
28. A. W. Chapman to H. W. Ravenel, January 21, June 6, 1860, Ravenel Correspondence, Clemson; H. W. R[avenel], "A New Work," Charleston *Daily Courier,* June 11, 1860.
29. MS Private Journal of HWR, March 25, May 20, 1861.
30. Childs (ed.), *Private Journal of HWR,* 82, 144, 414; H. W. R[avenel], untitled

article, Charleston *Daily Courier,* July 8, 1861; [H. W.] R[avenel], "Cotton Seed Coffee," Charleston *Daily Courier,* April 8, 1862; Justice [H. W. Ravenel], "A Plea for Justice to the Manufacturers," Charleston *Daily Courier,* May 29, 1862.

31. MS Private Journal of HWR, June 5, 19, August 7, 1862; H. W. Ravenel to M. A. Curtis, September 13, 1847, Folder 22, Box 2, Curtis Papers, UNC.
32. MS Private Journal of HWR, September 1, 4, 1862.
33. Ibid., October 22, 1863, October 3, 1864; [H. W.] R[avenel], "Cryptogamous Origin of Fevers," *Southern Quarterly Review,* n.s., I (April 1850), 154; H. W. Ravenel to M. A. Curtis, October 14, 1864, Folder 50, Box 3, Curtis Papers, UNC.
34. Childs (ed.), *Private Journal of HWR,* 150–51.
35. Ibid., 169–71.
36. MS Private Journal of HWR, April 13, 16, 27, 1864.
37. Ibid., June 22, 27, 1861, September 3, 1863, June 14, 1864.
38. Childs (ed.), *Private Journal of HWR,* 135; F. L. Childs to H. W. Ravenel, April 23, 1862, Ravenel Correspondence, Clemson; Bartram, "Biography of a Church," 23.
39. MS Private Journal of HWR, April 18, 1861, January 28, February 15, May 8, July 2, 1862, February 16, March 3, July 4, 1863, March 14, 15, 22, 1864.
40. Childs (ed.), *Private Journal of HWR,* 200–204.
41. MS Private Journal of HWR, December 25, 1864.
42. Childs (ed.), *Private Journal of HWR,* 205–6.
43. Ibid., 211–28; Susan B. Jervey and Charlotte St. J. Ravenel, *Two Diaries From Middle St. John's, Berkeley, South Carolina, February–May, 1865: Journals Kept by Miss Susan R. Jervey and Miss Charlotte St. J. Ravenel, at Northampton and Pooshee Plantations* (n.p.: St. John's Hunting Club, 1921).
44. Jervey and Ravenel, *Two Diaries,* 14.
45. Physical description of Ravenel from a pass issued to Ravenel for travel between Charleston and Aiken and pasted into MS Private Journal of HWR under date of January 8, 1863.

Chapter 7: Getting By, 1865–1869

1. John Samuel Ezell, *The South Since 1865* (New York: Macmillan Co., 1963), 25–31; Thomas D. Clark and Albert D. Kirwan, *The South Since Appomattox: A Century of Regional Change* (New York: Oxford University Press, 1967), 20–24.
2. Childs (ed.), *Private Journal of HWR,* 224, 247–48.
3. Ibid., 237–38.
4. Ibid., 238.
5. Ibid., 238, 259, 265.
6. Ibid., 240.
7. Ibid., 239–40.
8. Ibid., 247, 269.
9. Ibid., 242, 246, 249, 276.
10. Ibid., 247, 248.
11. MS Private Journal of HWR, April 17, 1866, March 30, 1867.
12. Childs (ed.), *Private Journal of HWR,* 325, 327–28.
13. MS Private Journal of HWR, December 3, 1867.

14. Childs (ed.), *Private Journal of HWR,* 274.
15. MS Private Journal of HWR, February 9, 1871, January 14, 1873.
16. Childs (ed.), *Private Journal of HWR,* 245, 250.
17. Series of nine letters between Brevet Major General R. K. Scott, Captain F. W. Leidtke, and Richard Y. Dwight, June 15, 1866–October 14, 1866, Richard Y. Dwight Papers (South Caroliniana Library).
18. Childs (ed.), *Private Journal of HWR,* 85, 197.
19. Ibid., 242.
20. Ibid., 258, 259, 260.
21. H. W. Ravenel to E. Tuckerman, August 25, 1865, Octavo Volume 9, Tuckerman Correspondence, AAS.
22. Ibid., November 8, 1865; Childs (ed.), *Private Journal of HWR,* 257, 260, 261.
23. H. W. Ravenel to G. Engelmann, July 26, 1866, George Engelmann Papers (Missouri Botanical Garden, St. Louis); MS Private Journal of HWR, November 25, 1865, June 19, 1868; H. W. Ravenel to J. B. Ellis, April 29, 1873, Ellis Collection, NYBG Library; H. W. Ravenel to E. Tuckerman, March 22, 1870, Octavo Volume 10, Tuckerman Correspondence, AAS.
24. H. W. Ravenel to G. Engelmann, March 23, June 6, July 2, 20, 1866, Engelmann Papers; H. W. Ravenel to E. Tuckerman, July 12, 1866, Octavo Volume 9, Tuckerman Correspondence, AAS; H. W. Ravenel to A. Gray, July 19, 1866, Historic Letters, H. W. Ravenel; H. W Ravenel to M. J. Berkeley, July 17, 1866, Berkeley Correspondence; Childs (ed.), *Private Journal of HWR,* 293–94.
25. A. Gray to H. W. Ravenel, July 30, 1866, Folder 13, Box 1, Botany Department Historical Collection, UNC; H. W. Ravenel to F. P. Porcher, August 16, 1866, Francis Peyre Porcher Papers (South Caroliniana Library). Ravenel did provide seeds to Kew. H. W. Ravenel to J. D. Hooker, September 9, 1868, J. D. Hooker Correspondence (Kew Gardens). This information was kindly provided by David Rembert, F.L.S., of the University of South Carolina.
26. H. W. Ravenel to F. P. Porcher, August 16, 1866, F. P. Porcher Papers; Childs (ed.), *Private Journal of HWR,* 293–94; J. W. Blankinship, "Lindheimer, the Botanist-Editor," *Missouri Botanical Garden Eighteenth Annual Report* (St. Louis, 1907), 131–32; Samuel Wood Geiser, *Naturalists of the Frontier* (2nd ed.; Dallas: Southern Methodist University, 1948), 137–47.
27. Ray Desmond, *Dictionary of British and Irish Botanists and Horticulturists Including Plant Collectors and Botanical Artists* (London: Taylor & Francis, 1977), 146; M. C. Cooke to H. W. Ravenel, August 25, 1866, Folder 13, Box 1, Botany Department Historical Collection, UNC.
28. H. W. Ravenel to G. Engelmann, June 6, July 2, September 21, November 19, 1866, Engelmann Papers.
29. M. C. Cooke to H. W. Ravenel, December 6, 1867, Ravenel Correspondence, Clemson; Childs (ed.), *Private Journal of HWR,* 311.
30. Childs (ed.), *Private Journal of HWR,* 312; M. C. Cooke to H. W. Ravenel, December 6, 1867, Ravenel Correspondence, Clemson.
31. M. C. Cooke to H. W. Ravenel, December 6, 1867, Ravenel Correspondence, Clemson.
32. M. C. Cooke to H. W. Ravenel, December 6, 1867, E. C. Bolles to H. W. Ravenel, March 23, 1868, both in Ravenel Correspondence, Clemson; Childs (ed.), *Private Journal of HWR,* 319.

33. H. W. Ravenel to M. A. Curtis, May 28, 1868, Item R253, Farlow Reference Library (Harvard University); MS Private Journal of HWR, March 30, May 8, 14, June 3, 1868.
34. MS Private Journal of HWR, April 2, 1867, February 1, 27, March 14, May 7, June 3, 1868; H. Mann to H. W. Ravenel, February 22, 1868, Ravenel Correspondence, Clemson.
35. H. W. Ravenel to E. Tuckerman, January 12, February 21, 1868, Octavo Volume 10, Tuckerman Correspondence, AAS.
36. Childs (ed.), *Private Journal of HWR*, 289, 291; H. W. Ravenel to F. P. Porcher, August 16, 1866, F. P. Porcher Papers.
37. H. W. Ravenel to F. P. Porcher, August 16, 1866, F. P. Porcher Papers; Childs (ed.), *Private Journal of HWR*, 292, 293.
38. H. W. Ravenel to F. P. Porcher, August 16, 1866, F. P. Porcher Papers; Childs (ed.), *Private Journal of HWR*, 293–94, 296–300, 299 (quotation).
39. D. H. Hill to H. W. Ravenel, November 19, 1866, Ravenel Correspondence, Clemson.
40. Childs (ed.), *Private Journal of HWR*, 298–99, 321; H. W. Ravenel to F. P. Porcher, December 4, 1866, Folder 1, H. W. Ravenel Papers, SCL; Charleston *Daily Courier*, December 8, 1866, p. 2.
41. Hal Bridges, *Lee's Maverick General: Daniel Harvey Hill* (New York: McGraw-Hill Book Co., 1961), 273–85. Ravenel's articles in *The Land We Love* were: "The Leaves of Plants—Their Structure and Functions.—Nature's Provision against the Effect of Droughts," III (May 1867), 30–35; "On Pruning and Training of the Grape," III (June 1867), 167–73; "Peach Culture," III (July 1867), 257–64; "Grape Culture," IV (January 1868), 208–16; and "Lespedeza Striata, or Japan Clover, the New Forage Plant of the South," IV (March 1868), 405–9. A sixth article, "Orange Culture," V (June 1868), 166–70, might also be Ravenel's, though it did not carry his name, and its style was rather unlike his. Ravenel mentioned Hill's request for such an article April 14, 1868, MS Private Journal of HWR.
42. Bridges, *Daniel Harvey Hill*, 274.
43. Ravenel, "Lespedeza Striata," 405–9.
44. Childs (ed.), *Private Journal of HWR*, 314, 328, 329; H. W. Ravenel to M. A. Curtis, August 26, 1868, Item R253, Farlow Reference Library.
45. Childs (ed.), *Private Journal of HWR*, 318, 320, 331; F. W. Putnam to H. W. Ravenel, December 13, 1868, Ravenel Correspondence, Clemson.
46. I have found only one other mention of advertising in journal or letters. W. R. Gerard to H. W. Ravenel, June 9, 10, 1880, typescripts in box labeled "Letters of Henry W. Ravenel," Letters and Diaries, South Carolina Collection, Charleston Museum, hereinafter cited as H. W. Ravenel Letters, CM.
47. H. W. Ravenel to M. A. Curtis, August 26, 1868, Item R253, Farlow Reference Library; H. W. Ravenel to John Torrey, July 14, 1869, Torrey Correspondence, NYBG Library; Barnhart (comp.), *Biographical Notes upon Botanists*.
48. Obituary of Horace Mann, *American Naturalist* II (January, 1869), 609; Childs (ed.), *Private Journal of HWR*, 327, 330–31.
49. Childs (ed.), *Private Journal of HWR*, 327, 329.
50. H. W. Ravenel to M. A. Curtis, May 28, 1868, Item R253, Farlow Reference Library.
51. Ibid., June 11, 1868.

52. Childs (ed.), *Private Journal of HWR*, 312–13; H. W. Ravenel to M. A. Curtis, August 26, 1868, Item R253, Farlow Reference Library.
53. H. W. Ravenel to E. Tuckerman, August 25, 1865, Octavo Volume 9, Tuckerman Correspondence, AAS.
54. Childs (ed.), *Private Journal of HWR*, 251–52.
55. H. W. Ravenel to G. Engelmann, September 21, 1866, Engelmann Papers; H. W. Ravenel to M. A. Curtis, June 11, 1868, Item R253, Farlow Reference Library.
56. MS Private Journal of HWR, November 14, 24, December 30, 1868; J. S. Billings to H. W. Ravenel, January 6, 1869, Ravenel Correspondence, Clemson.
57. J. S. Billings to H. W. Ravenel, January 6, 1869, Ravenel Correspondence, Clemson.
58. Ibid.; MS Private Journal of HWR, February 20, 1869.
59. Childs (ed.), *Private Journal of HWR*, 332.
60. [H. W.] R[avenel], "Cryptogamous Origin of Fevers," 146–59; J. K. Mitchell, *On the Cryptogamous Origin of Malarious and Epidemic Fevers* (Philadelphia: Lea and Blanchard, 1848).
61. Childs (ed.), *Private Journal of HWR*, 332.
62. MS Private Journal of HWR, March 20, 1869–May 11, 1869; H. W. Ravenel to J. Torrey, June 16, 1869, Torrey Correspondence, NYBG Library.
63. MS Private Journal of HWR, April 21, 1869.
64. Ibid., May 8–12, 1869.
65. Ibid., May 12–30, June 9, 10, 1869; J. Torrey to H. W. Ravenel, June 29, 1869, Ravenel Correspondence, Clemson; H. W. Ravenel to G. Engelmann, November 21, 1870, Engelmann Papers.
66. H. W. Ravenel, "Letter of Mr. H. W. Ravenel, South Carolina, on the Fungi of Texas," in Department of Agriculture, *Reports on the Diseases of Cattle in the United States, Made to the Commissioner of Agriculture, with Accompanying Documents* (Washington: Government Printing Office, 1869), 169–73.
67. Theobald Smith and F. L. Kilborne, *Investigations into the Nature, Causation, and Prevention of Texas or Southern Cattle Fever* (Washington: Government Printing Office, 1893).
68. MS Private Journal of HWR, May 21, June 6, 1869.
69. Childs (ed.), *Private Journal of HWR*, 340, 341.
70. "Obituary—H. W. Ravenel," *Journal of Mycology* III (September 1887), 106–7; W. G. Farlow, "H. W. Ravenel," *Botanical Gazette* (August 1887), 195; L. M. B[ragg], "Contributions toward a History of Science in South Carolina, I—Henry W. Ravenel, LL.D.," Charleston Museum, *Bulletin* XVI (February 1920), 17; Leiding, *Historic Houses*, 145.
71. Gee, "South Carolina Botanists," 38; Teague, "Henry W. Ravenel," 7.
72. J. Torrey to H. W. Ravenel, June 29, 1869, Ravenel Correspondence, Clemson.
73. H. W. Ravenel to J. Torrey, July 14, 1869, Torrey Correspondence, NYBG Library. Author's copy of the first draft of this letter is preserved in Folder 2, H. W. Ravenel Papers, SCL.
74. MS Private Journal of HWR, November 10, 1869.
75. Childs (ed.), *Private Journal of HWR*, 319.
76. MS Private Journal of HWR, July 7, 1869.
77. Ibid., January 4, July 9, 1867, February 17, July 14, 1869, and passim.
78. Ibid., March 2, 1869, and passim.

Chapter 8: A Botanist Once More, 1869–1887

1. Edward Tuckerman, *Genera Lichenum: An Arrangement of the North American Lichens* (Amherst: Edwin Nelson, 1872), 277.
2. H. W. Ravenel to L. R. Gibbes, September 14, 1870, Gibbes Letters.
3. A. Gray to H. W. Ravenel, June 5, 28, 1870, both in Folder 16, June 27, September 20, 1871, both in Folder 17, all in Box 1, Botany Department Historical Collection, UNC.
4. H. W. Ravenel to J. B. Ellis, February 12, 20, 1872, April 29, 1873, Ellis Collection, NYBG Library.
5. Ravenel, "Contributions to the Cryptogamic Botany" (July 1849) 428–30; Harry Morton Fitzpatrick, "Historical Background of the Mycological Society of America," *Mycologia* XXIX (January–February 1937), 14–18. The growth of American mycology during this period is made plain in Donald P. Rogers, *A Brief History of Mycology in North America* (Amherst: Mycological Society of America, 1981), 12–18.
6. Petersen, *"B. & C.,"* 41, 67–68; A. Featherman to H. W. Ravenel, August 28, 1871, Folder 2, H. W. Ravenel Papers, SCL.
7. "Botanical Necrology, 1872–3," *American Journal of Science and Arts,* 3rd ser., V (May 1873), 391–93; MS Private Journal of HWR, April 25, 1872; H. W. Ravenel to Mrs. M. A. Curtis, n.d., September 25, December 19, 1872, Folder 57, Box 3, Curtis Papers, UNC.
8. Asa Gray, "Notes on a Botanical Excursion to the Mountains of North Carolina, &c.; with Some Remarks on the Botany of the Higher Allegheny Mountains," *London Journal of Botany* I (1842), 14; E. C. Howe to C. H. Peck, December 14, 1868, Charles Horton Peck Letters, Mycological Collections (New York State Museum, Albany), hereinafter cited as Peck Letters, quoted in Petersen, *"B. & C.,"* 68.
9. S. T. Olney to H. W. Ravenel, July 27, 1872, H. W. Ravenel Letters, CM.
10. M. J. Berkeley, "Notices of North American Fungi," *Grevillea* I (1872–73), 33–39, 49–55, 65–71, 97–102, 145–50, 161–66, 177–80; II (1873–74), 3–7, 17–20, 33–35, 49–53, 65–69, 81–84, 97–101, 153–57, 177–81; III (1874–75), 1–17, 49–64, 97–112, 145–60; IV (1875–76), 1–16, 45–52, 93–108, 141–61.
11. Frances Leigh Williams, *Matthew Fontaine Maury: Scientist of the Sea* (New Brunswick, N.J.: Rutgers University Press, 1963).
12. Lester D. Stephens, *Joseph LeConte: Gentle Prophet of Evolution* (Baton Rouge: Louisiana State University Press, 1982), 105–12.
13. E. J. Wickson, et al., "Addresses at Memorial Services in Honor of Dr. E. W. Hilgard, University of California, January 30, 1916," *University of California Chronicle* XVIII (April 1916), 161.
14. H. W. Ravenel to L. R. Gibbes, March 13, September 17, 1872, Gibbes Letters; H. W. Ravenel to G. Engelmann, March 16, 1871, July 22, 1872, Engelmann Papers; A. W. Chapman to S. T. Olney, July 20, 1872 (typescript), Folder 18, Box 1, Botany Department Historical Collection, UNC; MS Private Journal of HWR, June 30, July 4, 6, 17, 1872.
15. H. W. Ravenel to G. E. Davenport, November 24, 1873, Historic Letters, H. W. Ravenel. See also A. W. Chapman to S. T. Olney, July 20, 1872 (typescript), Folder 18, Box 1, Botany Department Historical Collection, UNC.

16. H. W. Ravenel to J. B. Ellis, January 19, 1872, Ellis Collection, NYBG Library.
17. H. W. Ravenel to G. E. Davenport, November 24, 1873, Historic Letters, H. W. Ravenel.
18. H. W. Ravenel to E. Tuckerman, October 9, December 16, 1869, March 22, 1870, Octavo Volume 10, Tuckerman Correspondence, AAS; MS Private Journal of HWR, August 25–September 18, 1871, June 20–July 19, 1872.
19. H. W. Ravenel to A. Gray, June 19, 1871, Historic Letters, H. W. Ravenel; A. Gray to H. W. Ravenel, September 1, 1871, Folder 17, Box 1, Botany Department Historical Collection, UNC. The papers were "On the Seemingly One-Ranked Leaves of Baptisia Perfoliata," AAAS, *Proceedings* XX (1871), 391–93; and "On the Relation of the Tendril to the Phyllotaxis in Certain Cucurbitaceous Plants," ibid., 393–97. The former was reprinted in the *Journal of Botany*, n.s., I, 84–85, the *American Journal of Science and Arts* (December 1871), and an abstract of it appeared in the *Annals and Magazine of Natural History* IX (February 1872), 174–75.
20. H. W. Ravenel, "Notes on our Native Flora—I" (September 1873), 652–54, "II" (October 1873), 27–29, "III" (December 1873), 144–45, "Our Native Flora—IV" (January 1874), 195–96, "V" (February 1874), 249–50, "VI" (May 1874), 419–21, "Our Native Flora" (July 1874), 538–39, "Our Native Flora—VIII" (August 1874), 584–85, "IX" (September 1874), 642–43, all in *Rural Carolinian*.
21. H. W. Ravenel to E. Tuckerman, July 23, 1877, Folder 40, Edward Tuckerman Botanical Papers (Amherst College, Amherst, Mass.).
22. Childs (ed.), *Private Journal of HWR*, 345, 365–67; H. W. Ravenel to J. B. Ellis, December 21, 1873 (quotation), Ellis Collection, NYBG Library.
23. Childs (ed.), *Private Journal of HWR*, 374–75.
24. Ibid., 376–77.
25. Ibid., 377, 378 (quotation).
26. F. von Thuemen to H. W. Ravenel, February 10, 1872, Ravenel Correspondence, Clemson.
27. Childs (ed.), *Private Journal of HWR*, 373; F. von Thuemen to H. W. Ravenel, March 15, 1876, Ravenel Correspondence, Clemson.
28. F. von Thuemen to H. W. Ravenel, March 15, 1876, Ravenel Correspondence, Clemson; Stevenson, *Account of Fungus Exsiccati*, 448–56, 461–62.
29. W. G. Farlow to H. W. Ravenel, December 7, [1875], Ravenel Correspondence, Clemson; Hilda F. Harris, "The Correspondence of William G. Farlow during His Student Days at Strasbourg," *Farlowia* II (January 1945), 11–12; A. Gray to H. W. Ravenel, June 26, 1873, Folder 18, Box 1, Botany Department Historical Collection, UNC; H. W. Ravenel to Mrs. M. A. Curtis, n.d., Folder 57, Box 3, Curtis Papers, UNC.
30. H. W. Ravenel to W. G. Farlow, December 14, 1875, W. G. Farlow Letter Books, vol. III (Farlow Reference Library).
31. W. G. Farlow to H. W. Ravenel, September 5, 1878, October 28, [1878], H. W. Ravenel Letters, CM; H. W. Ravenel to W. G. Farlow, September 10, 1878, Farlow Letter Books.
32. W. G. Farlow to H. W. Ravenel, July 18, [1878], Ravenel Correspondence, Clemson.
33. W. G. Farlow to H. W. Ravenel, December 25, [1878], H. W. Ravenel Letters, CM; H. W. Ravenel to W. G. Farlow, September 10, November 4, 1878, Farlow Letter Books.

34. C. H. Peck to H. W. Ravenel, December 12, 19, 1878; W. M. Canby to H. W. Ravenel, May 25, 30, July 26, 1878, H. W. Ravenel Letters, CM.

35. F. Wolle's first letter to Ravenel was dated April 24, 1876, Ravenel Correspondence, Clemson; H. W. Ravenel to W. G. Farlow, December 23, 1881, Farlow Letter Books.

36. W. G. Farlow to H. W. Ravenel, January 1, [1882], H. W. Ravenel Letters, CM.

37. H. W. Ravenel to W. G. Farlow, January 3 (quotation), 5 (quotation), 1882, Farlow Letter Books.

38. An afternoon's inspection of only 20 to 25 percent of Ravenel's phanerogamous herbarium from this period preserved at the biology department of Converse College in Spartanburg, South Carolina, revealed plants collected by twelve other botanists and sent to Ravenel.

39. M. C. Cooke to H. W. Ravenel, July 27, 1877, Ravenel Correspondence, Clemson.

40. Childs (ed.), *Private Journal of HWR*, 389; H. W. Ravenel to E. Tuckerman, January 8, 30, 1878, Tuckerman Papers, Amherst.

41. [M. C. Cooke,], "Fungi of Florida," *Grevillea* VI (1878), 78; M. C. Cooke, "Note on Fungi Exsiccati," *Grevillea* X (1882), 154–55 (quotation). See also Stevenson, *Account of Fungus Exsiccati,* 6–7, 307–9.

42. H. W. Ravenel to J. B. Ellis, June 3, 1880, Ellis Collection, NYBG Library; H. W. Ravenel to W. G. Farlow, August 10, 1878, March 15, 24 (quotation), 1884, Farlow Letter Books.

43. M. C. Cooke, "New American Fungi," *Grevillea* XII (1883), 22–33; "North American Fungi," *Grevillea* V (1877), 150–55, and XI (1883), 106–11; "North American Fungi," *Hedwigia* XVII (1878), 37–40; "Ravenel's American Fungi," *Grevillea* VI (1878), 129–46, VII 32–35, 43–54; H. W. Ravenel to W. G. Farlow, August 10, 1878, March 24, 1884, Farlow Letter Books; H. W. Ravenel to L. R. Gibbes, July 21, 1879, Gibbes Letters.

44. Stevenson, *Account of Fungus Exsiccati,* 106, and passim, 310–13.

45. H. W. Ravenel to E. Tuckerman, February 26, 1882, December 26, 1884, Tuckerman Papers, Amherst.

46. H. W. Ravenel to W. G. Farlow, July 19, 1882 [or 1883?], Farlow Letter Books; H. W. Ravenel to J. B. Ellis, April 24, 1884, Ellis Collection, NYBG Library; H. W. Ravenel to E. Tuckerman, July 8, August 2, 7, 1883, Folder 40, Tuckerman Papers, Amherst.

47. Childs (ed.), *Private Journal of HWR*, 260, 399–400, 405–7, 410.

48. W. G. Farlow to H. W. Ravenel, May 28, [1879], H. W. Ravenel Letters, CM; H. W. Ravenel to L. R. Gibbes, July 28, 1880, Gibbes Letters; L. R. Gibbes to H. W. Ravenel, August 30, 1880, J. M. McBryd to H. W. Ravenel, April 20, 1882, H. W. Ravenel Letters, CM.

49. Inventory is in Nathaniel Henry Rhodes Dawson Papers (Southern Historical Collection).

50. Childs (ed.), *Private Journal of HWR,* 368–69, 380, 390, 402; H. E. Ravenel, *Ravenel Records,* 167–68.

51. H. W. Ravenel to J. B. Ellis, September 6, 1886, Ellis Collection, NYBG Library.

52. Ibid., September 12, 25, 1886.

53. Childs (ed.), *Private Journal of HWR,* 401, 409–10; F. P. Venable to H. W. Ravenel, May 15, 1886, Ravenel Correspondence, Clemson; Faculty Minutes, May 7, June 2, 3, 1886, Trustee Minutes, June 2, 1886 (University Archives, University of

North Carolina, Chapel Hill); K. P. Battle to H. W. Ravenel, July 1, 1886, J. A. Holmes to H. W. Ravenel, July 2, 1886, Ravenel Correspondence, Clemson.
54. Childs (ed.), *Private Journal of HWR,* 411.
55. Thomas F. Wood, "A Sketch of the Botanical Work of the Rev. Moses Ashley Curtis, D.D.," Elisha Mitchell Scientific Society, *Journal* II (1884–85), 19.

Epilogue

1. Childs (ed.), *Private Journal of HWR,* 412; Saint Thaddeus Parish Register, 299. I have visited the grave.
2. H. W. Ravenel Will, Package 11, Box 10, Estate Papers, Aiken County Probate Records (South Carolina Archives, Columbia).
3. Memorandum dated February 4, 1878, Folder 12, Box 11–133, Henry Ravenel Papers, SCHS.
4. M. H. Ravenel to W. G. Farlow, September 9, 10, 25, October 27, 1888, October 2, 1893, Farlow Letter Books. M. H. Ravenel to N. H. R. Dawson, June 4, October 27, and n.d. (letter of June 4 does not include year, letter of October 27 bears the year 1887 but was almost surely written in 1888), Dawson Papers.
5. Elizabeth A. Williams, "Henry W. Ravenel, Distinguished Carolina Botanist," Garden Club of South Carolina, *Bulletin,* No. 21 (n.d.), 2; Lillian Adele Kibler, *The History of Converse College,* 1889–1971 (Spartanburg: Converse College, 1973), 29–30; interview with Robert Powell at Converse College, January 1982.

Conclusion

1. E. Tuckerman to H. W. Ravenel, July 12, 1877, Ravenel Correspondence, Clemson.
2. E. C. Howe to C. H. Peck, October 29, 1868, Peck Letters, quoted in Petersen, "*B. & C.*," 68.
3. W. G. Farlow to H. W. Ravenel, December 25, [1878], H. W. Ravenel Letters, CM.

Bibliography

Unpublished Sources

American Antiquarian Society, Worcester, Mass.
    Tuckerman, Edward. Correspondence.
Amherst College Library, Amherst, Mass.
    Tuckerman, Edward. Botanical Papers.
British Museum (Natural History), the Botany Library, Department of Library
    Services, London.
    Berkeley, M. J. Correspondence.
Charleston Museum, South Carolina Collection (Letters and Diaries), Charleston,
    S.C.
    Curtis, Dr. Moses A., Dr. J. H. Mellichamp, Gilbert Rossignol. Letters.
        Typescripts.
    Ravenel, Dr. Henry W. Letters. Typescripts of letters to Ravenel and letters from
        Ravenel to the Reverend M. J. Berkeley, Dr. Richard Yeadon Dwight, Dr.
        Henry Ravenel, and Dr. Edward Tuckerman.
Clemson University, Robert Muldrow Cooper Library, Special Collections, Clemson,
    S.C.
    Ravenel, Henry William. Correspondence, 1841–86.
Converse College, Biology Department, Herbarium, Spartanburg, S.C.
    Ravenel, H. W. Collection.
Farlow Reference Library, Harvard University, Cambridge, Mass.
    Farlow, W. G. Letter Books, vol. III.
    Item R253.
Gray Herbarium, Harvard University, Cambridge, Mass.
    Historic Letters, M. A. Curtis.
    Historic Letters, H. W. Ravenel.
Kew Gardens, London.

Hooker, J. D. Correspondence.
Hooker, W. J. Correspondence.
Missouri Botanical Garden, St. Louis.
    Englemann, George. Papers.
New York Botanical Garden Library, New York City.
    Torrey, John. Correspondence.
    Ellis, Job B. Collection.
New York State Museum, Mycological Collections, Albany.
    Peck, Charles Horton. Letters.
Saint Thaddeus Episcopal Church, Aiken, S.C.
    Parish Register.
South Carolina Archives, Columbia.
    Ravenel, H. W. Will. Package 11, Box 10, Estate Papers, Aiken County Probate
        Records.
South Carolina Historical Society, Charleston.
    Peyre, Thomas Walter (1812–51). Plantation Journal. Microfiche no. 50-7.
    Pineville Police Association. Minutes. Collection 34-301.
    Porcher Family. Papers.
    Ravenel, Henry. Papers. Box 11-331.
    Ravenel, Thomas Porcher. Collection.
    Saint Stephen's Jockey Club—the Santee Jockey Club. Rules and Minutes. Col-
        lection 34-111.
South Caroliniana Library, University of South Carolina, Columbia.
    Dwight, Richard Y. Papers.
    Gibbes, Professor Lewis R. Letters to Gibbes from Dr. Henry W. Ravenel, 1850–
        84, from transcriptions of the originals in possession of the Charleston Mu-
        seum. 2 vols.: vol. I—1850–57, vol. II—1857–84.
    Kirkland-Withers-Snowden-Trotter Families. Papers.
    Porcher, Francis Peyre. Biography. Typescript, ca. 1935.
    Porcher, Francis Peyre. Papers.
    Ravenel, Henry William (1814–1887). Papers, April 1844–July 25, 1887, and
        n.d.
    Ravenel, Henry William. Private Journal.
    Stevens, Neil T. "Henry W. Ravenel." Includes research notes and a short sketch.
Southern Historical Collection, University of North Carolina Library, Chapel Hill.
    Botany Department of the University of North Carolina. Historical Collection.
    Curtis, Moses Ashley. Papers.
    Dawson, Nathaniel Henry Rhodes. Papers.
University of North Carolina, University Archives, Chapel Hill.
    Faculty Minutes.
    Trustee Minutes.
University of South Carolina, University Archives, Columbia.
    Clariosophic Society. Membership List, 1806–92 (Accession no. 171). Minutes,
        1826–31 (Accession no. 167). Record Group 13 SL, Vice-President, Student
        Affairs—Student Activities and Organizations.
    Faculty of the South Carolina College. Minutes, Commencing on the Thirtieth
        Day of May, 1814.
    Board of Trustees. Proceedings, November 24, 1813–November 27, 1837.

Published Works of Ravenel

Ordinarily Ravenel published under the name "H. W. Ravenel," but he sometimes used initials, published anonymously, or used a pseudonymn. Only these alternative names are listed below. Not included in this list are a number of short agricultural articles appearing under his name in the *Rural Carolinian*, the Charleston *Weekly News*, and the Aiken *Press*, though those cited in the text are listed. The works are listed chronologically.

Ravenel, Wm. H. [*sic*]. "Agricultural Memoir." *Southern Agriculturist, Horticulturist, & Register of Rural Affairs* (April 1843), 131–47.

A Memoir from the Black Oak Agricultural Society, Read Before The State Agricultural Society, at its Meeting in December, 1842, at Columbia. Charleston: Miller & Browne, 1843.

"Mr. Ravenel's Letter on Marlling." In *Proceedings of the Agricultural Convention and of the State Agricultural Society of South Carolina, from 1839 to 1845—Inclusive . . .* Columbia: Summer & Carroll, 1846.

"Polygonum Punctatum." *Southern Journal of Medicine & Pharmacy* I (1846), 629–30.

"An Enumeration of Some Few Phanegamous Plants, Not Heretofore Published as Inhabiting This State, Found in the Vicinity of the Santee Canal." *Charleston Medical Journal and Review* IV (1849), 32–38.

"Contributions to the Cryptogamic Botany of South Carolina." *Charleston Medical Journal and Review* IV (July 1849), 428–33.

A Meteorological Journal for the Year 1848. Kept in St. John's, Berkley, So. Ca., for the Black Oak Agricultural Society. Charleston: Miller & Browne, 1849.

"A Paper on the Subject of Meteorology in Its Connection with Agriculture &c." In *The Constitution and Proceedings of the Black Oak Agricultural Society, for 1848 & 1849.* Charleston: Miller & Browne, 1849.

R. "Cryptogamous Origin of Fevers." *Southern Quarterly Review*, n.s., I (April 1850), 146–59.

"Contributions to the Cryptogamic Botany of South Carolina." *Charleston Medical Journal and Review* V (May 1850), 324–27.

"A Catalogue of the Natural Orders of Plants, Inhabiting the Vicinity of the Santee Canal, S.C., as Represented by Genera and Species; with Observations on the Meteorological and Topographical Conditions of that Section of Country." American Association for the Advancement of Science, *Proceedings* III (1850), 2–17.

A Meteorological Journal for the Year 1849, Kept in St. John's, Berkley, So. Ca., for the Black Oak Agricultural Society. Charleston: Miller & Browne, 1850.

"Contributions to the Cryptogamic Botany of South Carolina." *Charleston Medical Journal and Review* VI (March 1851), 190–99.

[Ravenel, H. W.?]. "Physical Science, in Its Relation to Natural and Revealed Religion." *Southern Quarterly Review*, n.s., III (April 1851), 420–55.

A Meteorological Journal for the Year 1850, Kept in St. John's, Berkley, So. Ca., for the Black Oak Agricultural Society. Charleston: A. E. Miller, 1851.

Anniversary Address, Delivered before the Black Oak Agricultural Society, April 1852. Charleston: Walker & James, 1852.

Fungi Caroliniani Exsiccati: Fungi of Carolina, Illustrated by Natural Specimens of the Species. 5 Fasc. Charleston: John Russell (Russell & Jones, 5th Fasc.), 1852–60.

A Meteorological Journal for the Year 1851, Kept in St. John's Berkley, Parish, So. Ca., for the Black Oak Agricultural Society. Charleston: A. E. Miller, 1852.

"Meteorological Observations Made at Aiken, in South-Carolina, for the Month of May 1854." *Charleston Medical Journal and Review* IX (1854), 575.

"Meteorological Observations Made at Aiken, in South-Carolina, for the Month of August 1854." *Charleston Medical Journal and Review* IX (1854), 860.

"Meteorological Observations Made at Aiken, in South-Carolina, for the Month of September 1854." *Charleston Medical Journal and Review* IX (1854).

"Description of a New Baptisia Found near Aiken, S.C.," Elliott Society of Natural History of Charleston, South-Carolina, *Proceedings* I (November 1853–December 1858) (Charleston, 1859), 38–39, but located in portion of the *Proceedings* dedicated to June and July 1856.

"The Amelanchier, or 'Currant Tree,'—A New Southern Fruit." *Southern Cultivator* XIV (September 1856), 285.

"Notice of Some New and Rare Phaenogamous Plants Found in this State." Elliott Society of Natural History of Charleston, South-Carolina, *Proceedings* I (November 1853–December 1858) (Charleston, 1859), 50–54, but located in portion of the *Proceedings* dedicated to November 1856.

Address Delivered before the Aiken Fruit-Growing and Horticultural Association, July 21st, 1859. Columbia: Robert M. Stokes, 1859.

"Native Grapes Classified." *Southern Cultivator* XVIII (January 1860), 32–33.

"Report on Grapes." *Southern Cultivator* XVIII (April 1860), 128.

R., H. W. "A New Work," Charleston *Daily Courier,* June 11, 1860.

"Paper on Grapes. Read before the 'Aiken Vine-Growing and Horticultural Association,' September 15, 1859." U.S. Patent Office, *Report.* Agriculture 1859. Washington, 1860, 536–40.

"Premium Essay on the C[l]assification and Nomenclature of Fruits. Published by Order of the South Carolina State Agricultural Society." *Farmer and Planter* III (January 1861), 27–31.

R., H. W. Untitled article. Charleston *Daily Courier,* July 8, 1861.

R. "Cotton Seed Coffee." Charleston *Daily Courier,* April 8, 1862.

Justice, "A Plea for Justice to the Manufacturers." Charleston *Daily Courier,* May 29, 1862.

"The Leaves of Plants—Their Structure and Functions—Nature's Provision against the Effect of Droughts." *Land We Love* III (May 1867), 30–35.

"On Pruning and Training of the Grape." *Land We Love* III (June 1867), 167–73.

"Peach Culture." *Land We Love* III (July 1867), 257–64.

"Grape Culture." *Land We Love* IV (January 1868), 208–16.

"Lespedeza Striata, or Japan Clover, the New Forage Plant of the South." *Land We Love* V (March 1868), 405–9.

"Vegetables All the Year Round." In Francis Simmons Holmes, *The Southern Farmer and Market Gardener.* [3rd ed.] Charleston: n.p., [1868].

"Letter of Mr. H. W. Ravenel, South Carolina, on the Fungi of Texas." In Department of Agriculture, *Reports on the Diseases of Cattle in the United States, Made to the Commissioner of Agriculture, with Accompanying Documents.* Washington: Government Printing Office, 1869, 169–73.

R. "Enlightened Agriculture." *Rural Carolinian* II (August 1870), 467–69.

"On the Relation of the Tendril to the Phyllotaxis in Certain Cucurbitaceous Plants." American Association for the Advancement of Science, *Proceedings* XX (1871), 393–97.

"On the Seemingly One-Ranked Leaves of Baptisia Perfoliata." American Association for the Advancement of Science, *Proceedings* XX (1871), 391–93.

"Pinus Elliottii, Engelm." Torrey Botanical Club, *Bulletin* III (July 1872), 35–36. This is actually a report by the editor upon a letter sent by Ravenel.

"Notes on Our Native Flora—I," *Rural Carolinian* (September 1873), 652–54, "II" (October 1873), 27–29, "III" (December 1873), 144–45, "Our Native Flora—IV" (January 1874), 195–96, "V" (February 1874), 249–50, "VI" (May 1874), 419–21, "Our Native Flora" (July 1874), 538–39, "Our Native Flora—VIII" (August 1874), 584–85, "IX" (September 1874), 642–43.

"Some Rare Southern Plants." Torrey Botanical Club, *Bulletin* VI (March 1876), 81–82.

R., H. W. "Acanthospermum Xanthoides, DC." Torrey Botanical Club, *Bulletin* VI (1876), 88.

"Some More Rare Southern Plants." Torrey Botanical Club, *Bulletin* VI (June 1876), 93–94.

Ravenel, H. W. (collector), and M. C. Cooke. *Fungi Americani Exsiccati.* 8 cents., London, 1878–82.

"Abnormal Habit of Asclepias Amplexicaulis." Torrey Botanical Club, *Bulletin* VIII (August 1881), 87–88.

"Gordonia Pubescens L'Her (Franklinia Altamaha Marshall)." *American Naturalist* XVI (March 1882), 235–38.

"The Migration of Weeds." Torrey Botanical Club, *Bulletin,* IX (September 1882), 112–14.

"Large Grape-Vines." Torrey Botanical Club, *Bulletin* XVIII (1882), 23.

"Note on the Tuckahoe." Torrey Botanical Club, *Bulletin* XVIII (1882), 140.

"Query." Torrey Botanical Club, *Bulletin* XVIII (1882), 128.

"Morphology in the Tuber of Jerusalem Artichoke." Torrey Botanical Club, *Bulletin* X (May 1883), 54–55.

"Some North American Botanists; VII. Stephen Elliott," *Botanical Gazette* VIII (July 1883), 249–53.

"A List of the More Common Native and Naturalized Plants of South Carolina." In State Board of Agriculture of South Carolina, *South Carolina: Resources and Population, Institutions and Industries.* Charleston: Walker, Evans, and Cogswell, 1883.

"Big Grape-Vines." Torrey Botanical Club, *Bulletin* XI (1884), 132–33.

"Report of the Botanist." In *Seventh Annual Report of the Commissioner of Agriculture of South Carolina, for the Fiscal Year Ending October 31, 1885,* pp. 91–93.

"[Notes on the Collection of Fleshy Fungi]." *Botanical Gazette* III (June 1886), 145.

"Agricultural Grasses of South Carolina: Prepared for the Annual Report of the South Carolina Department of Agriculture, 1885." In *Sixth Annual Report of the Commissioner of Agriculture of South Carolina, for the Fiscal Year Ending October 31, 1885,* in Reports and Resolutions of the General Assembly of the State of South Carolina at the Regular Session Commencing November 24, 1885. Columbia: Charles A. Calvo, Jr., 1886, II, 110–53.

Ravenel, Henry William. "Recollections of Southern Plantation Life," *Yale Review* XXV (Summer 1936), 748–77.

The Southern Gardener; or, Short and Simple Directions for the Culture of Vegetables and Fruits at the South. Charleston: Walker, Evans, & Cogswell, n.d.

Contemporary Botanical Works (Prior to 1887)

Berkeley, M. J. "Notices of North American Fungi." *Grevillea* I (1872–73), 33–39, 49–55, 65–71, 97–102, 145–50, 161–66, 177–80, II (1873–74), 3–7, 17–20, 33–

35, 49–53, 65–69, 81–84, 97–101, 153–57, 177–81, III (1874–75), 1–17, 49–64, 97–112, 145–60, IV (1875–76), 1–16, 45–52, 93–108, 141–61.

———. "On Some Entomogenous *Sphaeriae*." Linnaean Society, *Journal* I (1857), 157–59.

———. "On the Fructification of the Pileate and Clavate Tribes of Hymenomycetous Fungi." *Annals and Magazine of Natural History* I (April 1838), 80–101.

Berkeley, M. J., and M. A. Curtis. "Centuries of North American Fungi." *Annals and Magazine of Natural History,* 2nd ser., XII (December 1853), 417–35, 3rd ser., IV (October 1859), 284–96.

———. "Contributions to the Mycology of North America," *American Journal of Science and Arts,* 2nd ser., VIII (November 1849), 401–3, IX (March 1850), 171–75, X (September 1850), 185–88.

"Botanical Necrology, 1872–3." *American Journal of Science and Arts,* 3rd ser., V (May 1873), 391–93.

Canby, William M. "Notes on Baptisia." *Botanical Gazette* IV (March 1879), 129–32.

[Cooke, M. C.]. "Fungi of Florida." *Grevillea* VI (1878), 78.

Cooke, M. C. "New American Fungi." *Grevillea* XII (1883), 22–33.

———. "North American Fungi." *Grevillea* V (1877), 150–55.

———. "North American Fungi." *Grevillea* XI (1883), 106–11.

———. "North American Fungi." *Hedwigia* XVII (1878), 37–40.

———. "Note on Fungi Exsiccati." *Grevillea* X (1882), 154–55.

———. "Ravenel's American Fungi." *Grevillea* VI (1878), 129–46, VII, 32–35, 43–54.

Curtis, M. A. "An Account of Some New and Rare Plants of North Carolina." *American Journal of Science and Arts* XLIV (January 1843), 80–84.

———. "Contributions to the Mycology of North America." *American Journal of Science and Arts,* 2nd ser., VI (November 1848), 349–53.

———. "Enumeration of Plants Growing Spontaneously around Wilmington, North Carolina, with Remarks on Some New and Obscure Species." Boston Society of Natural History, *Journal* I (May 1835), 82–141.

———. "New and Rare Plants, Chiefly of the Carolinas." *American Journal of Science and Arts,* 2nd ser., VII (May 1849), 406–11.

C[urtis], M. A. "[Notice of] *Fungi Caroliniani Exsiccati. Fungi of Carolina, Illustrated by Natural Specimens of the Species.*" *American Journal of Science and Arts,* 2nd ser., XVII (March 1854), 285.

———. "Ravenel, *Fungi Caroliniani Exsiccati.* Fasciculus III. John Russell, Charleston, S.C. 1855." *American Journal of Science and Arts,* 2nd ser., XX (September 1855), 284–85.

Engelmann, George. "Revision of the Genus Pinus, and Description of Pinus Elliottii," St. Louis Academy of Science, *Transactions* IV (1880). Reprinted in William Trelease and Asa Gray, eds., *The Botanical Works of the Late George Engelmann Collected for Henry Shaw, Esq.* Cambridge: John Wilson and Son, 1887.

Gibbes, Lewis R. *A Catalogue of the Phoenagamous [sic] Plants of Columbia, S.C., and Its Vicinity.* Columbia: Printed at the Telescope Office, 1835. Copy in Box 10, Natural History Pamphlet Collection, Charleston Museum.

———. "Ravenel's Fungi of Carolina." Charleston *Daily Courier,* October 12, 1860.

"Fungi Caroliniani Exsiccati. Fungi of Carolina, Illustrated by Natural Specimens of the Species." *Charleston Medical Journal and Review* VII (1852), 690–91.

Gray, Asa. *Darwiniana: Essays and Reviews Pertaining to Darwinism,* edited by A. Hunter Dupree. Cambridge: Belknap Press of Harvard University Press, 1963.

———. "A Monograph of the North American Species of Rhynchospora." Lyceum of Natural History of New-York, *Annals* III (1828–36), 191–219.

———. "Notes on a Botanical Excursion to the Mountains of North Carolina, &c.; with Some Remarks on the Botany of the Higher Alleghany Mountains." *London Journal of Botany* I (1842), 1–14, 217–37, II (1843), 113–25, III (1844), 230–42.

———. "[Notice of] *Musci Alleghanienses, sive Spicilegia Muscorum atque Hepaticarum quos in Itinere a Marylandia usque ad Georgiam per tractus montium . . .*" *American Journal of Science and Arts,* 2nd ser., I (January 1846), 70–81.

———. "Review of Darwin's Theory on the Origin of Species by Means of Natural Selection." *American Journal of Science and Arts* XXIX (1860), 153–84.

G[ray], A[sa]. "[Notice of] *Fungi Caroliniani Exsiccati. Fungi of Carolina, Illustrated by Natural Specimens of the Species.*" *American Journal of Science and Arts,* 2nd ser., XVI (July 1853), 129–30.

———. "[Notice of] *Fungi Caroliniani Exsiccati: Fungi of Carolina, Illustrated by Natural Specimens of the Species . . .* Fasc. I–V." *American Journal of Science and Arts,* 3rd ser., XXXI (January 1861), 130–31.

Greville, Robert Kaye. *Scottish Cryptogamic Flora; or, Coloured Figures and Descriptions of Cryptogamic Plants, Belonging Chiefly to the Order Fungi; and Intended to Serve as a Continuation of English Botany.* 6 vols. Edinburgh: Maclaclan & Stewart, 1823–28.

Porcher, F. P. "A Medico-Botanical Catalogue of the Plants and Ferns of St. John's, Berkley, South-Carolina." *Charleston Medical Journal and Review* II (May 1847), 255–86 (July 1847), 397–417.

Sargent, Charles Sprague. *The Silva of North America: A Description of the Trees Which Grow Naturally in North America Exclusive of Mexico.* 14 vols. in 7. New York: Peter Smith, 1947.

Tuckerman, Edward. "An Enumeration of Some Lichenes of New England, with Remarks." *Boston Journal of Natural History* II (February 1839), 245–62.

———. "A Further Enumeration of Some New England Lichenes." *Boston Journal of Natural History* III (July 1840), 281–306.

———. "Further Notices of Some New England Lichenes." *Boston Journal of Natural History* III (November 1840), 438–64.

———. *Genera Lichenum: An Arrangement of the North American Lichens.* Amherst: Edwin Nelson, 1872.

———. *Lichenes Americae Septentrionalis Exsiccati.* 6 vols. in 3. Cambridge: Metcalf & Co., 1st vol., Joh. Wilson & Son, 2nd and 3rd vols., 1847–54.

———. "A Synopsis of the Lichenes of the Northern United States and British America." American Academy of Arts and Sciences, *Proceedings* I (1846–48), 195–285.

Secondary Literature (Including Pre-1887 Nonbotanical and Post-1887 Botanical Publications)

Aiken, S.C., as a Winter Resort. [Aiken: Highland Park Hotel, 1885?].

Anderson, F. W. "A Biographical Sketch of J. B. Ellis." *Botanical Gazette* XV (November 1890), 299–304.

Barnhart, John Hendley, comp. *The New York Botanical Garden Biographical Notes upon Botanists.* 3 vols. Boston: G. K. Hall & Co., 1965.

Berkeley, Edmund, and Dorothy Smith Berkeley. *Dr. Alexander Garden of Charles Town.* Chapel Hill: University of North Carolina Press, 1969.

Blankinship, J. W. "Lindheimer, the Botanist-Editor." *Missouri Botanical Garden Eighteenth Annual Report*. St. Louis, 1907, 127–41.

Bonner, James C. "Advancing Trends in Southern Agriculture, 1840–1860." *Agricultural History* XXII (October 1948), 248–59.

Bradbury, S. *The Evolution of the Microscope*. Oxford: Pergamon Press, 1967.

B[ragg], L[aura] M. "Contributions toward a History of Science in South Carolina, I— Henry W. Ravenel, LL.D." Charleston Museum, *Bulletin* XVI (February 1920), 17–23.

Bragg, Laura M. "The Museum Herbaria," Charleston Museum, *Bulletin* VIII (May 1912), 43–49.

Bridges, Hal. *Lee's Maverick General: Daniel Harvey Hill*. New York: McGraw-Hill Book Co., 1961.

Bronson, Walter C. *The History of Brown University, 1764–1914*. Providence: Published by the University, 1914.

Bruce, Robert V. "A Statistical Profile of American Scientists, 1846–1876." In George H. Daniels, ed., *Nineteenth-Century American Science: A Reappraisal*. Evanston: Northwestern University Press, 1972, 63–94,

Bryan, John Morrill. *An Architectural History of the South Carolina College, 1801–1855*. Columbia: University of South Carolina Press, 1976.

Cabaniss, James Allen. *A History of the University of Mississippi*. University, Miss.: University of Mississippi, 1949.

Carson, Joseph. *A History of the Medical Department of the University of Pennsylvania from Its Foundation in 1765. With Sketches of the Lives of Deceased Professors*. Philadelphia: Lindsay and Blakiston, 1869.

Channing, Steven A. *Crisis of Fear: Secession in South Carolina*. New York: W. W. Norton & Co., 1970.

Childs, Arney Robinson, ed. *The Private Journal of Henry William Ravenel, 1859–1887*. Columbia: University of South Carolina Press, 1947.

Clark, Thomas D., and Albert D. Kirwan. *The South Since Appomattox: A Century of Regional Change*. New York: Oxford University Press, 1967.

Clay, Reginald S., and Thomas H. Court. *The History of the Microscope: Compiled from Original Instruments and Documents, up to the Introduction of the Achromatic Microscope*. Boston: Longwood Press, 1978.

Clemens, William Montgomery. *North and South Carolina Marriage Records from the Earliest Colonial Days to the Civil War*. New York: E. P. Dutton & Co., 1927.

The Constitution, Acts, and Proceedings of the Black Oak Agricultural Society, during the Past Year, Published by Order of the Society. Charleston: Walker & Browne, 1843.

Constitution and Proceedings of the Black Oak Agricultural Society, for 1844 & 1845. Charleston: Miller & Browne, 1845.

The Constitution and Proceedings of the Black Oak Agricultural Society, for 1846 & 1847. Charleston: Miller & Browne, 1847.

The Constitution and Proceedings of the Black Oak Agricultural Society, for 1848 & 1849. Charleston: Miller & Browne, 1849.

Corgan, James X. "Some Firsts? In the Colleges of Tennessee." Tennessee Academy of Science, *Journal* LV (July 1980), 86–91.

Craven, Avery. *Edmund Ruffin, Southerner: A Study in Secession*. Baton Rouge: Louisiana State University Press, 1966.

Culberson, William L., ed. *The Collected Lichenological Papers of Edward Tuckerman*. 2 Vols. Weinheim: J. Cramer, 1964.

Dalcho, Frederick. *An Historical Account of the Protestant Episcopal Church, in South-Carolina, from the First Settlement of the Province, to the War of the Revolution; . . .* New York: Arno Press, 1970, reprint of Charleston, 1820 edition.

Dawson, Charles C. *A Collection of Family Records, with Biographical Sketches and Other Memoranda of Various Families and Individuals Bearing the Name Dawson, or Allied to Families of That Name.* Charleston: Garnier & Co., 1969.

Desmond, Ray. *Dictionary of British and Irish Botanists and Horticulturists Including Plant Collectors and Botanical Artists.* London: Taylor & Francis, 1977.

Dunbar, Gary S. "Silas McDowell and the Early Botanical Exploration of Western North Carolina." *North Carolina Historical Review* XLI (October 1964), 425–35.

Dupree, A. Hunter. *Asa Gray, 1810–1888.* Cambridge: Belknap Press of Harvard University Press, 1959.

———. "The Measuring Behavior of Americans." In George H. Daniels, ed., *Nineteenth-Century American Science.* Evanston: Northwestern University Press, 1972, 22–37.

———. "The National Pattern of American Learned Societies, 1769–1863." In Alexandra Oleson and Sanborn C. Brown, eds., *The Pursuit of Knowledge in the Early American Republic: American Scientific and Learned Societies from Colonial Times to the Civil War.* Baltimore: Johns Hopkins University Press, 1976.

Easterby, J. H. *A History of the College of Charleston, Founded 1770.* Charleston: Trustees of the College of Charleston, 1935.

Eaton, Clement. *Freedom of Thought in the Old South.* New York: Peter Smith, 1951, reprint of 1940 edition.

———. *A History of the Old South: The Emergence of a Reluctant Nation.* 3rd ed. New York: Macmillan Publishing Co., 1975.

———. *The Mind of the Old South.* Revised ed. Baton Rouge: Louisiana State University Press, 1967.

Ewan, Joseph. "The Growth of Learned and Scientific Societies in the Southeastern United States to 1860." In Alexandra Oleson and Sanborn C. Brown, eds., *The Pursuit of Knowledge in the Early American Republic: American Scientific and Learned Societies from Colonial Times to the Civil War.* Baltimore: Johns Hopkins University Press, 1976, 208–18.

Ezell, John Samuel. *The South Since 1865.* New York: Macmillan Co., 1963.

Farlow, W. G. "H. W. Ravenel." *Botanical Gazette* (August, 1887), 194–97.

Fitzpatrick, Harry Morton. "Historical Background of the Mycological Society of America." *Mycologia* XXIX (January–February 1937), 1–25.

Fitzpatrick, T. J. *Rafinesque: A Sketch of His Life with Bibliography.* Des Moines: Historical Department of Iowa, 1911.

Fussell, Paul. *The Great War and Modern Memory.* New York: Oxford University Press, 1975.

Gee, Wilson. "South Carolina Botanists: Biography and Bibliography." University of South Carolina, *Bulletin,* no. 72 (September 1918), 5–52.

Geiser, Samuel Wood. *Naturalists of the Frontier.* Dallas: Southern Methodist University, 1948.

Gray, Lewis Cecil. *History of Agriculture in the Southern United States to 1860.* 2 vols. New York: Peter Smith, 1941.

Guralnick, Stanley M. *Science and the Ante-Bellum American College.* Philadelphia: American Philosophical Society, 1975.

Harris, Hilda F. "The Correspondence of William G. Farlow During His Student Days at Strasbourg." *Farlowia* II (January 1945), 9–38.

Harris, Seymour E. *Economics of Harvard.* New York: McGraw-Hill Book Co., 1970.

Harshberger, John William. *The Botanists of Philadelphia and Their Work.* Philadelphia: [Press of T. C. Davis & Son], 1899.

Heck, W. H. *Mental Discipline & Educational Values.* New York: John Lane Co., 1909.

Hedrick, U. P. *A History of Horticulture in America to 1860.* New York: Oxford University Press, 1950.

Hesseltine, William B. *The South in American History.* 2nd ed. New York: Prentice-Hall, 1943.

Hindle, Brooke. *The Pursuit of Science in Revolutionary America, 1735–1789.* Chapel Hill: For the Institute of Early American History and Culture, Williamsburg, Virginia, by the University of North Carolina Press, 1956.

Hirsch, Arthur Henry. *The Huguenots of Colonial South Carolina.* Hamden: Archon Books, 1962.

Holcomb, Brent H. *Marriage and Death Notices from the (Charleston) "Times," 1800–1821.* Baltimore: Genealogical Publishing Co., 1979.

Hollis, Daniel Walker. *University of South Carolina.* 2 vols. Columbia: University of South Carolina Press, 1951 and 1956.

Hunt, Kenneth W. "The Charleston Woody Flora." *American Midland Naturalist* XXXVII (May 1947), 670–750.

Jellison, Richard M., and Phillip S. Swartz. "The Scientific Interests of Robert W. Gibbes." *South Carolina Historical Magazine* LXVI (April 1965), 77–97.

Jervey, Susan B., and Charlotte St. J. Ravenel. *Two Diaries from Middle St. John's, Berkeley, South Carolina, February-May, 1865: Journals Kept by Miss Susan R. Jervey and Miss Charlotte St. J. Ravenel, at Northampton and Pooshee Plantations.* n.p.: St. John's Hunting Club, 1921.

Johnson, Thomas Cary, Jr. *Scientific Interests in the Old South.* New York: D. Appleton-Century Co., 1936.

Jordan, David Starr. *Science Sketches.* Chicago: A. C. McClurg and Co., 1896.

Kelley, Brooks Mather. *Yale: A History.* New Haven: Yale University Press, 1974.

Kelly, Howard A. *Some American Medical Botanists Commemorated in Our Botanical Nomenclature.* Boston: Longwood Press, 1977, reprint of Troy, N.Y., 1914 edition.

Kibler, Lillian Adele. *The History of Converse College, 1889–1971.* Spartanburg: Converse College, 1973.

Kirk, Francis Marion. *A History of the St. John's Hunting Club. An Address Delivered by Francis Marion Kirk at the Sesqui-centennial Celebration Held April 29, 1950, at the Club House, Pooshee Plantation, St. John's, Berkeley.* n.p.: St. John's Hunting Club, 1950.

Knight, Edgar W. *A Documentary History of Education in the South before 1860.* 5 vols. Chapel Hill: University of North Carolina Press, 1949–53.

Kolesnik, Walter B. *Mental Discipline in Modern Education.* Madison: University of Wisconsin Press, 1958.

LaBorde, M. *History of the South Carolina College, from Its Incorporation, Dec. 19, 1801, to Dec. 19, 1865, Including Sketches of Its Presidents and Professors.* Charleston: Walker, Evans, & Cogswell, 1874.

Leiding, Harriette Kershaw. *Historic Houses of South Carolina.* Philadelphia: J. B. Lippincott Co., 1921.

McCardell, John. *The Idea of a Southern Nation: Southern Nationalists and Southern Nationalism, 1830–1860.* New York: W. W. Norton & Co., 1979.

McNeill, John T. *The History and Character of Calvinism.* London: Oxford University Press, 1954.

Malone, Dumas. *The Public Life of Thomas Cooper, 1783–1839.* Columbia: University of South Carolina Press, 1961, reprint of Hartford, 1923 edition.

Meisel, Max. *Bibliography of American Natural History: Pioneer Century, 1789–1865.* 3 vols. New York: Hafner, 1967, reprint of New York, 1924–29 edition.

Meriwether, Colyer. *History of Higher Education in South Carolina with a Sketch of the Free School System.* Washington: Government Printing Office, 1889.

Miller, Howard. *The Revolutionary College: American Presbyterian Higher Education, 1707–1837.* New York: New York University Press, 1976.

Misenhelter, Jane Searles. *St. Stephen's Episcopal Church, St. Stephen, S.C., Including Church of the Epiphany, Upper St. John's, Berkeley, and Chapel of Ease, Pineville, S.C. . . .* Columbia: State Printing Co., 1977.

Mitchell, Betty L. *Edmund Ruffin: A Biography.* Bloomington: Indiana University Press, 1981.

Mitchell, J. K. *On the Cryptogamous Origin of Malarious and Epidemic Fevers.* Philadelphia: Lea and Blanchard, 1848.

Morison, Samuel Eliot, Henry Steele Commager, and William E. Leuchtenburg. *The Growth of the American Republic.* 2 vols. New York: Oxford University Press, 1969.

Nef, John Ulric. *War and Human Progress: An Essay on the Rise of Industrial Civilization.* Cambridge: Harvard University Press, 1950.

Newby, I. A. *The South, A History.* New York: Holt, Rinehart, and Winston, 1978.

Numbers, Ronald L., and Janet S. Numbers. "Science in the Old South: A Reappraisal," *Journal of Southern History* XLVIII (May 1982), 163–84.

"Obituary—H. W. Ravenel." *Journal of Mycology* III (September 1887), 106–7.

Obituary of Horace Mann. *American Naturalist* II (January 1869), 609.

"Orange Culture." *Land We Love* V (June 1868), 166–70.

Peters, Thomas Minott. "Sketch of John F. Beaumont." *Journal of Mycology* II (1886), 81–83.

Petersen, Ronald H. *"B. & C.": The Mycological Association of M. J. Berkeley and M. A. Curtis.* Vaduz: J. Cramer, 1980.

Porcher, F. A. *Report on Manures, Read before the Black Oak Agricultural Society, by F. A. Porcher, Chairman of the Committee on Manures.* Charleston: Miller & Browne, 1844.

———. "Upper Beat of St. John's, Berkeley." Huguenot Society of South Carolina, *Transactions* XIII (1906), 31–78.

Praeger, R. Lloyd. "William Henry Harvey 1811–1866." In F. W. Oliver, ed., *Makers of British Botany: A Collection of Biographies by Living Botanists.* Cambridge: Cambridge University Press, 1913, 204–24.

Ramage, B. James. "Local Government and Free Schools in South Carolina." In Herbert B. Adams, ed., *Johns Hopkins University Studies in Historical and Political Science* I, no. 12 (October 1883).

Ravenel, Edmund. *Echinidae, Recent and Fossil, of South Carolina, January 1848.* Charleston: Burges & James, 1848.

———. "On the Medical Topography of St. John's, Berkeley, S.C., and Its Relations to Geology." *Charleston Medical Journal and Review* IV (November 1849), 697–704.

Ravenel, Henry Edmund. *Ravenel Records: A History and Genealogy of the Huguenot Family of Ravenel, of South Carolina; with Some Incidental Account of the Parish of St. John's, Berkeley, Which Was Their Principal Location.* Atlanta: Franklin Printing and Publishing Co., 1898.

Rembert, David H. *Thomas Walter, Carolina Botanist.* Columbia: South Carolina Museum Commission, 1980.

Rice, James Henry, Jr. *The Aftermath of Glory*. Charleston: Walker, Evans & Cogswell, 1934.

Rogers, Donald P. *A Brief History of Mycology in North America*. Amherst: Mycological Society of America, 1981.

Rooker, Henry Grady. "A Sketch of the Life and Work of Dr. Gerard Troost." *Tennessee Historical Magazine*, 2nd ser., III (October 1932), 3–19.

Rossiter, Margaret W. *The Emergence of Agricultural Science: Justus Liebig and the Americans, 1840–1880*. New Haven: Yale University Press, 1975.

Rothrock, G. A. *The Huguenots: A Biography of a Minority*. Chicago: Nelson-Hall, 1979.

Rudolph, Frederick. *The American College and University: A History*. New York: Alfred A. Knopf, 1962.

Ruffin, Edmund. *Report of the Commencement and Progress of the Agricultural Survey of South Carolina for 1843*. Columbia: A. H. Pemberton, State Printer, 1843.

Sass, Herbert Ravenel. *The Story of the South Carolina Lowcountry*. 3 vols. West Columbia, S.C.: J. F. Hyer Publishing Co., n.d..

Savage, Henry, Jr. *River of the Carolinas: The Santee*. Chapel Hill: University of North Carolina Press, 1968.

Savitt, Todd L. *Medicine and Slavery: The Diseases and Health Care of Blacks in Antebellum Virginia*. Urbana: University of Illinois Press, 1978.

———. "The Use of Blacks for Medical Experimentation and Demonstration in the Old South." *Journal of Southern History* XLVIII (August 1982), 331–48.

Seabrook, Whitemarsh B. *A Memoir on the Origin, Cultivation, and Uses of Cotton, from the Earliest Ages to the Present Time, with Especial Reference to the Sea-Island Cotton Plant,* . . . Charleston: Miller & Browne, 1844.

Shear, C. L., and Neil E. Stevens. "Studies of the Schweinitz Collections of Fungi—I, Sketch of his Mycological Work." *Mycologia* IX (1917), 191–204.

———. "Studies of the Schweinitz Collections of Fungi—II, Distribution and Previous Studies of Authentic Specimens." *Mycologia* IX (1917), 333–44.

Shepard, C. U. *Report of an Analysis of Cotton-Wool, Cotton-Seed, Indian Corn, and the Yam Potato, Made for the Black Oak Agricultural Society*. Charleston: Miller & Browne, 1846.

Simkins, Francis Butler. *A History of the South*. 2nd ed. New York: Alfred A. Knopf, 1953.

Sims, J. Marion. *The Story of My Life*. New York: D. Appleton & Co., 1884.

Smallwood, William Martin. *Natural History and the American Mind*. New York: Columbia University Press, 1941.

Smith, D. E. Huger. *A Charlestonian's Recollections, 1846–1913*. Charleston: Carolina Art Association, 1950.

Smith, Theobald, and F. L. Kilborne. *Investigations into the Nature, Causation, and Prevention of Texas or Southern Cattle Fever*. Washington: Government Printing Office, 1893.

Stampp, Kenneth M. *The Era of Reconstruction, 1865–1877*. New York: Alfred A. Knopf, 1975.

Stephens, Lester D. *Joseph LeConte: Gentle Prophet of Evolution*. Baton Rouge: Louisiana State University Press, 1982.

Stevens, Neil E. "The Mycological Work of Henry W. Ravenel." *Isis* XVIII (1932), 133–49.

———. "Two Southern Botanists and the Civil War." *Scientific Monthly* IX (August 1919), 157–66.

Stevenson, John A. *An Account of Fungus Exsiccati Containing Material from the Americas*. Lehre: J. Cramer, 1971.

Stoney, Samuel Gaillard. *Plantations of the Carolina Low Country.* 3rd ed. Charleston: Carolina Art Association, 1945.

———, ed. "The Memoirs of Frederick Adolphus Porcher," *South Carolina Historical Magazine* XLIV (1943), 65–80, 135–47, 212–19, XLV (1944), 30–40, 80–98, 146–56, 200–16, XLVI (1945), 25–39, 78–92, 140–58, 198–208, XLVII (1946), 32–52, 83–108, 150–62, 214–27, XLVIII (1947), 20–25.

Sutherland, N. M. *The Huguenot Struggle for Recognition.* New Haven: Yale University Press, 1980.

Terry, George D. "Eighteenth Century Plantation Names in Upper St. John's, Berkeley." *Names in South Carolina* XXVI (Winter 1979), 15–19.

Thomas, Albert Sidney. *A Historical Account of the Protestant Episcopal Church in South Carolina, 1820–1957; Being a Continuation of Dalcho's Account, 1670–1820.* Columbia: R. L. Bryan Co., 1957.

[Thomas, Theodore Gaillard, ed.]. *"Liste des Francois et Suisses" from an Old Manuscript List of French and Swiss Protestants Settled in Charleston, on the Santee, and at the Orange Quarter in Carolina Who Desired Naturalization Prepared Probably About 1695–6.* Baltimore: Genealogical Publishing Co., 1968, reprint of Charleston, 1868 edition.

Trescott, William H. "The States Duties in Regard to Popular Education." *De Bow's Review,* n.s., X (February 1856), 145–56.

Tuomey, Michael. *Report on the Geology of South Carolina.* Columbia: A. S. Johnston, 1848.

Waring, Joseph Ioor. *A History of Medicine in South Carolina, 1670–1825.* Columbia: South Carolina Medical Association, 1964.

———. *A History of Medicine in South Carolina, 1825–1900.* Columbia: South Carolina Medical Association, 1967.

Wickson, E. J., et al. "Addresses at Memorial Services in Honor of Dr. E. W. Hilgard, University of California, January 30, 1916." *University of California Chronicle* XVIII (April 1916), 159–90.

Williams, Elizabeth A. "Henry W. Ravenel, Distinguished Carolina Botanist," Garden Club of South Carolina, *Bulletin,* no. 21, n.d.

Williams, Frances Leigh. *Matthew Fontaine Maury: Scientist of the Sea.* New Brunswick, N.J.: Rutgers University Press, 1963.

Wilson, Robert. *An Address Delivered before the St. John's Hunting Club, at Indianfield Plantation, St. John's, Berkeley, July 4, 1907, Together with an Historical Sketch of the Club, Rules, and List of Members.* Charleston: Walker, Evans & Cogswell, 1907.

———. *Half Forgotten By-Ways of the Old South.* Columbia: State Co., 1928.

Wood, Thomas F. "A Sketch of the Botanical Work of the Rev. Moses Ashley Curtis, D.D." Elisha Mitchell Scientific Society, *Journal* II (1884–85), 9–31.

Miscellaneous Sources

U.S. Bureau of the Census. *Population Schedules of the United States, 1850.* Microcopy 432, Roll 850, South Carolina, Charleston County. Washington: National Archives Microfilm Publications, 1964.

U.S. Bureau of the Census. Original Agriculture, Industry, Social Statistics, and Mortality Schedules for South Carolina, 1850–80, Agriculture, Seventh Census, 1850. South Carolina Archives Microcopy 2, Roll 1, Abbeville—Lancaster.

Bartram, R. Conover. "Biography of a Church, Prelude to the Future: The History of the Church of St. Thaddeus, Aiken, South Carolina." Typescript, 1966.

Flint, Wanda Leeper, Cleo Corley Flint, and Linda Flint Powell. "Readings from the Stones . . . Inscriptions from St. Stephen's Protestant Episcopal Church Cemetery." Typescript, St. Stephen's, S.C., February, 1970, photocopy in Clayton Library, Houston, Tex.

Sanders, Albert E. "The Charleston Museum and the Promotion of Science in Antebellum South Carolina." Paper presented at the third Citadel Conference on the South, April 25, 1981.

Teague, Elizabeth. "Henry W. Ravenel." Typescript memoir, private collection of Harry Shealy, University of South Carolina at Aiken.

Index

ABOUT THE AUTHOR

Tamara Miner Haygood is a medical student at the University of Texas at Houston. She received her M.A. and Ph.D. degrees in history from Rice University.